TRANSACTIONS
AND ENCOUNTERS

Science and culture in the
nineteenth century

∽

EDITED BY ROGER LUCKHURST
AND JOSEPHINE MCDONAGH

Manchester University Press
Manchester and New York

distributed exclusively in the USA by Palgrave

Published by Manchester University Press
Oxford Road, Manchester M13 9NR, UK
and Room 400, 175 Fifth Avenue, New York, NY 10010, USA
http://www.manchesteruniversitypress.co.uk

Distributed exclusively in the USA by
Palgrave, 175 Fifth Avenue, New York, NY 10010, USA

Distributed exclusively in Canada by
UBC Press, University of British Columbia, 2029 West Mall, Vancouver, BC, Canada V6T 1Z2

British Library Cataloguing-in-Publication Data
A catalogue record for this book is available from the British Library

Library of Congress Cataloging-in-Publication Data applied for

ISBN   0 7190 5910 0   *hardback*
          0 7190 5911 9   *paperback*

First published 2002

10 09 08 07 06 05 04 03 02   10 9 8 7 6 5 4 3 2 1

Typeset by
D R Bungay Associates, Burghfield, Berks

Printed in Great Britain by
Bell & Bain Ltd, Glasgow

Contents

ᔐ

List of figures

⌐

List of contributors

David Amigoni is senior lecturer in English, Keele University. He is the author of *Victorian Biography: Intellectuals and the Ordering of Discourse* and the co-editor of *Charles Darwin's* Origin of Species: *New Interdisciplinary Essays*. He is working on a book to be entitled *Colonies, Cults and Evolution: The Spread of the Culture Concept in Nineteenth-Century Writing*.

Isobel Armstrong is professor of English at Birkbeck College, University of London. She is the author of *Victorian Poetry* and, most recently, *The Radical Aesthetic*. She is currently completing her study of glass and Victorian culture.

Carolyn Burdett is principal lecturer at the University of North London. She is the author of *Olive Schreiner and the Progress of Feminism* and co-editor of *The Victorian Supernatural*.

Steven Connor is professor of modern literature and theory at Birkbeck College, University of London. He is the author of numerous books, including *Dumb-Struck: A Cultural History of Ventriloquism*.

Roger Luckhurst lectures in nineteenth- and twentieth-century literature at Birkbeck College, University of London. He has co-edited *The Fin de Siècle: A Reader in Cultural History c.1880–1900* and is the author of *The Invention of Telepathy 1870–1901*.

Josephine McDonagh is reader in romantic and Victorian culture at Birkbeck College, University of London. She is the author of *De Quincey's Disciplines* (1994) and *George Eliot* (1997) and is currently completing a study of child murder in eighteenth- and nineteenth-century British culture.

Lindsay Smith is professor of English at the University of Sussex. She specialises in Victorian photography and is the author of *Victorian Photography, Painting and Poetry* (1995) and *The Politics of Focus* (1998)

Rebecca Stott is head of English at Anglia Polytechnic University. She is the author of *The Fabrication of the Late Victorian Femme Fatale* and editor of the Longman *Tennyson*. She is currently completing a book on Victorian marine zoology, *Darwin and the Barnacle*, and a co-authored book on Elizabeth Barrett Browning.

Lynnette Turner lectures in English studies at Oxford Brookes University. She has published articles on Victorian anthropology, ethnography and gender, colonial travel, and Mary Kingsley. She is currently researching empathy in cross-cultural writing of the romantic period.

Paul S. White is research fellow on the Darwin Project at Cambridge University. He is the author of *Thomas Huxley: Making the Man of Science* (2002).

Acknowledgements

The seeds for this book were sown at the conference 'Science and Culture 1780–1900', held at Birkbeck College in September 1997. We thank both speakers and audience for making the event so stimulating, and especially Anne Hartman, who collaborated in shaping and organising it. Since then the project has grown with the addition of essays from other contributors.

The editors would like to thank Matthew Frost at Manchester University Press for being patient with a project so buffeted by various unforeseeable Acts of God.

A grant from the Faculty of Arts, Birkbeck College, assisted Roger Luckhurst in completing work on part of the manuscript.

Introduction: 'encountering science'

~

ROGER LUCKHURST AND JOSEPHINE MCDONAGH

Alone in the laboratory at night, the scientist glances through the window and catches sight of the hideous face of his labour: 'I trembled, and my heart failed within me; when, on looking up, I saw, by the light of the moon, the daemon at the casement. A ghastly grin wrinkled his lips as he gazed on me, where I sat fulfilling the task which he had allotted to me.' 'With a sensation of madness', the scientist reconsiders his promise to carry out the 'allotted' task, to create a mate for the monster. '[T]rembling with passion', he confesses, '"[I] tore to pieces the thing on which I was engaged"'. Outside the window, the monster retreats 'with a howl of devilish despair and revenge'.[1]

This brief encounter, one of many that are staged in *Frankenstein* (1818), stands as an allegory for the perils of scientific endeavour. In this case the encounter takes the form of a haunting: the solitary, obsessive scientist, plagued by the fruits of his labour, his 'hideous progeny'. The monster's ghastly form is an embodiment of the moral perversion of the scientist, but his howl of despair, a mournful reproach addressed to his creator, expresses the pathos of his existence. Often regarded as the inaugural text of science fiction, the plot and characters of which have been replicated endlessly in print and on celluloid, *Frankenstein* has framed the popular relationship between science and culture for generations of readers and film-goers. This is a conflictual and critical relationship that turns on the dehumanising effects of science. In his misplaced endeavour to create human life, the scientist's work is shown to be, paradoxically, dehumanising – as witnessed by the monstrous form of his creation. But the monster's feelings, his sentient body, and his capacity for pain, give him a humanity that in fact turns back on his

creator. In the Frankenstein story, it is the scientist who is de-human-
ised and the monster who is made human. Frankenstein's overwrought
body, his constant 'trembling', his 'heart failing', his acting on nervous
impulse, transform the man into an unreflective automaton, while the
monster's unjust abandonment makes him human – Christ-like, even –
through suffering and loss. As the novel interrogates the boundaries of
the human, it is science that marks its exterior limits, while literature,
indeed the novel, comes to be an embodiment of the human. This nexus
of literature, art, culture, human and the humanities stands over against
science, constructing the opposition that has shaped many aspects of
modern society, from the organisation of the university to the development of the humanities as a 'civilising' force, the state's funding of the
arts and the emergence of popular ecology movements.

Frankenstein presents a prevailing trope of the scientist in modern
society. We continue to be surrounded by images of inhuman scientists
like Frankenstein, isolated and withdrawn, nowadays often pictured in
outlandish space-age protective garb, the new signature of dangerous science. We have witnessed the agents from the Ministry of Agriculture hurl-
ing lambs on funeral pyres during the 2001 foot and mouth epidemic; and
we are aware that secretive scientists are working in genetic research, cut
off from humanity in high-security laboratories, patenting 'our' genes
while under threat from direct action groups; and that the developers of
'Frankenstein foods' are apparently deforming the population through
the selfish pursuit of profit. In all such images, the isolation of the scientist, his (such specialists are invariably male) detachment from the mass
of throbbing humanity, is emphasised. Likewise, science fictions, in novels
and films, repeatedly evoke the vulnerability of fragile human culture to
attacks from cyborgs, clones, terminators, eugenically re-programmable
populations and cunning new weapons of mass-destruction. In all these
cases, humanity itself is under fire from the blind ambitions of science.

From the perspective of science, however, the encounter between science and culture is differently conceived, although it is no less conflictual.
If culture criticises science for its failure of feeling, science criticises culture for its inability to understand and the intellectual poverty of its
modes of critique. Along these lines, popular science writing reflects on

the subtle and malign influence of banal anti-scientific thinking in the broad cultures of the West. In Carl Sagan's *Demon-Haunted World* (1997), for instance, science sheds only feeble light, as 'pseudoscience and superstition' become more tempting: 'The candle flame gutters. Its pool of light trembles. Darkness gathers. The demons begin to stir.'[2] Less prophetically, Daniel Dennett suggests that the 'universal acid' of Darwin's evolutionary theory renders culture (and its resistances to science) secondary and epiphenomenal. For Richard Dawkins, culture always tends to fall for the easy superstition, the magical thought, and requires re-education by professors in the relatively recent discipline of the public understanding of science.[3] In the academic world, too, the 'science and culture wars' have developed an extensive literature, and several *causes célèbres*. These usually criticise the humanities for their meagre grasp of the scientific, a special target being the field of cultural studies, awash with the 'antiscientific, pseudo-sociological fads' of Leftist cultural theory.[4] Interestingly, it is when the study of culture has diverted from its traditional humanistic project that scientists are most critical of its endeavours. Alan Sokal's 1996 hoax essay 'Transgressing the Boundaries: Towards a Transformative Hermeneutics of Quantum Gravity', published in the cultural studies' journal *Social Text*, exemplifies this point. Once the essay was published, Sokal revealed that the journal editors had been duped by meaningless jargon and ideological correctness. His was nothing more than a parody of the discourse of cultural theory, and he followed it with a book that lambasted cultural theory for its woeful ignorance of science.[5]

These points of misrecognition, or 'radical misunderstanding',[6] are deeply rooted within our culture. The idea that science and the humanities belong to mutually exclusive worlds – 'two cultures' – was endorsed by C. P. Snow's 1959 Rede Lecture, in which he warned that scientists and, in particular, literary intellectuals 'had almost ceased to communicate at all'. As Stefan Collini has observed, the phrase has outlived the very specific 1950s' English context in which it was first uttered.[7] A product of the postwar industrialisation of science (1959 was the year in which Eisenhower worried about the emergence of an immensely powerful formation he termed the 'military–industrial complex'), Snow was also responding to English class and educational rigidities and to the hegemony in the 'corridors of power' – another Snow coinage – of a cultural elite with a contempt for scientific knowledge. The 'two cultures' tag continues to imply a monolithic opposition between modes of knowledge, and the contrary encounters of the last decade or so reinforce a sense of tectonic plates drifting apart, leaving tremors and quakes in their wake as they judder further away from each other.

The repeated invocation of 'two cultures', however, might be read in a different way: as a defensive reaction formation to proximity, not distance, to the collapsing *inwards* of the lineaments of the post-war settlement of science and culture addressed by Snow. Rosanne Stone, for instance, has recently suggested that quotidian cultural life in the West has become saturated by portable technologies, so that the 'technosocial milieu' has turned technology into nature for many social beings.[8] Cultural spaces that remain untouched by science are increasingly difficult to imagine. Apocalyptic narratives of technological penetration and de-humanisation thus attempt to reconstitute the limits of human culture. Meanwhile, a number of science theorists have argued for a transition from 'Science', as an autonomous and clearly demarcated mode of knowledge production, to a more diffuse and uncertainly bordered mode of 'Research'. In *Re-Thinking Science*, Helga Nowotny, Peter Scott and Michael Gibbons propose that in the late twentieth and early twenty-first centuries the categories of society, culture and the market have 'become so "internally" heterogeneous and "externally" interdependent, even transgressive, that they had ceased to be distinctive and distinguishable'.[9] Many aspects of scientific research are increasingly market-led and take place in privately funded multinational corporations; marketability takes science and its applications into the heteroglossic public world, where findings are suspected of being dictated by financial interest groups, where the economics of investment in 'profitable' diseases is condemned and the environmentally catastrophic impact of rapacious development is subject to violent contest. Closed systems of expertise have now become opened up to 'heterogeneity, pluralism and fuzziness', with these new contexts breaching 'the channelled and predictable interactions which take place under a socio-scientific regime that still practices (and believes in) some form of separation or segregation'.[10]

For Nowotny, Scott and Gibbons it is a post-modern world that explodes a previously stable, coherent and separable science. But to historians of science and, latterly, cultural historians, the idea that science and culture are distinct spheres is a relatively recent and temporary structuration. Much has been written about the class-inflected 'gentlemanly' conceptions of scientific authority characteristic of the English Scientific Revolution in the seventeenth century, where science was enacted in spaces largely co-extensive with other forms of activity.[11] The nineteenth century has also become an important locus for histories attentive both to the emergence of a recognisably modern institutional formation of professional and separable science and to the complex and messy interactions between cultural, religious and scientific claims. In 1979, James Moore noted that conceptions of a Victorian battle between evolutionary biology and Christian theology mistook the *rhetoric* internal to the debate for the actual pragmatic processes of negotiation, accommodation, assimilation and creative misprision between scientists, theologians and a reading general public.[12] Similarly, Gillian Beer has produced inter-disciplinary work that aims to recover diverse instances of interconnectedness between literary and scientific discourses throughout the Victorian era. Her metaphor of *open fields*, dynamic spaces in which lines of influence and interaction are multi-directional and non-hierarchical, organises a sequence of encounters which 'mean that relations never form a single system: what may be perceived as outcrops or loose ends may prove to be part of the tracery of other connections'. 'More is to be gained', Beer suggests for studies of Victorian and early twentieth-century culture, 'from analysing transformations that occur when ideas change creative context and encounter fresh readers' than it is in containing ourselves within subsequent disciplinary structures.[13]

Transactions and Encounters aims to enrich understanding of the negotiations that were undertaken across these open fields in the mid- and late nineteenth century and at the beginning of the twentieth century. Rather than see culture as separate from, or hostile to, science – as in *Frankenstein* – the chapters of this book are concerned with aspects of nineteenth-century culture in which scientific knowledge is produced and disseminated alongside the work of art or literature, mutually entwined in networks of overlapping interest and concern. Our sense of encounter here thus has less to do with conflict than it does with surprise: as for the surrealists, the *rencontre* evoked chance, desire, the unforeseen yet meaningful connection.[14] Similarly, we have chosen to investigate *transactions* between the cultural and the scientific in order to emphasise what is carried over, conducted between, passed on. 'Transaction' evokes the cognitive behaviour of formal transfer and fair exchange, but also the less rational passages of transgression or transference, in which precisely what material gets passed over, and how, are much more uncertain.

It is worth pausing on some of the general resources we might call upon to conceptualise this more open sense of encounter. English historians of science have saturated Victorian scientific practice with its social contexts, from the strongly embedded socio-political biographies of leading savants, to the examination of the new, socially constructed, topographies that were carved out with the result that science was carried out increasingly in isolation from other social practices.[15] To these valuable studies, we might add the less empirical accounts generated by continental theorists. It was Michel Foucault who proposed that an examination beginning with the discursive 'statement' rather than with any extant or subsequently imposed disciplinary boundary might open a network of relations previously obscured by conventional historiography. Foucault's *Archaeology of Knowledge* (1974) built up from statements of the distinctive rules of specific discursive formations to a sense of the 'constellation' of discourses at work in any particular epoch. He was also careful to recognise that apparently abstract knowledge could be imbued with the traceries of desire, becoming 'the place for a phantasmatic representation, an element of symbolisation, a form of the forbidden'.[16] It has been the combination of the transdisciplinary comparative focus and the invested desires of knowledge that has helped develop, for instance, a large body of work on how concepts of 'evolution' in the Victorian period stretched by powerful analogy from biology, to psychiatry, social policy, urban theory and literary exemplifications of hereditary monstrosity. Foucault's 'field of vectors' and 'interplay of exchanges' have done much to generate interest in the cultural history of Victorian science.[17]

More recently, the German theorist Friedrich Kittler has set his aim at 'explod[ing] the two-cultures schema of our academic departments' by exploring what he terms 'discourse networks'.[18] Kittler analyses 'the network of technologies and institutions that allow a given culture to select, store and process relevant data', his complaint being that traditional cultural and literary criticism have ignored the material channels of transmission and the successive technological revolutions (industrial, electronic and digital) that have transformed those channels since 1800.[19] Through his eccentric prose, sometimes pithily epigrammatic, sometimes impenetrably gnomic, Kittler juxtaposes analyses of Goethe and Rilke with circuit diagrams, networking together 'pedagogy, Poetry, and philosophy' with 'media technology, psychophysics, and literature'.[20] Kittler is but one of the critics who have helped foster diverse and productive encounters between literary and cultural criticism and histories of Victorian technology. Studies of the imbrication of telegraphs, typewriters and gramophones with re-configurations of modern subjectivities have stretched from ventriloquy, via spiritualism and automatic writing, to the emergence of the serial killer as an exemplary subject-position of a newly saturated machine culture in the late nineteenth century.[21]

The French sociologist of science Bruno Latour has also situated himself in the interstices *between* the two cultures, dissatisfied with both 'internalist' (science only) and 'externalist' (context only) narratives of the history of science. From his early encounters with scientists in the laboratory, through his work on the scientific paper and the mathematical equation as apparently *pure* scientific forms which in fact bind together a huge array of intrinsically *social* resources, to his recent essays which attempt to displace the realist–relativist disputes at the core of many battles in the 'science and culture wars', Latour has consistently used the imagery of matrices, networks and loops which interlink and knot together intra- and extra-scientific resources.[22] His view that a concept becomes successfully scientific 'because it is *more* intensely connected to a much larger repetoire of resources', comes about by his rejection of the usual view of the separation of science from culture.[23] Instead, the

truth of what scientists say no longer comes from their breaking away from society, convention, mediations, connections, but from the safety provided by the circulating references that cascade through a great number of transformations and translations, modifying and constraining speech acts of many humans over which no one has any durable control ... The quality of a science's reference ... depends rather on the extent of its transformations, the safety of its connections, the progressive accumulation of its mediations, the number of interlocutors it engages ... its capacity to convince others, and its routine institutionalisation of these flows.[24]

Latour's version of 'science studies' is one that 'follows leads, nodes, and pathways no matter how crooked and unpredictable they may look'.[25] His analyses criss-cross between fieldwork, the mobilisation of 'Nature', and modes of disciplinary autonomisation and discursive exclusion, but do not privilege these over the 'loops' of political, financial and ideological alliances and the channels of cultural communication and representation. In his studies of Louis Pasteur's attempts in the 1850s and 1860s to convince his fellow-scientists and the French public that microscopic life-forms are responsible for fermentation and the spreading of disease, Latour has examined how the 'Pasteurisation of France' was effected by combining highly regulated and controlled laboratory practice with a vast network of social alliances to farmers, financiers, politicians, scientific bodies and popular newspapers.[26] This lattice of multi-directional transactions helpfully problematises any idea of strictly separable spheres of science and culture. It also once again emphasises that it was the communicational infrastructures and expanded participatory public spheres of the nineteenth century that generated the conditions in which the authority of scientific explanations could enter the arena of debate.

A final type of encounter informs this volume: the *colonial* encounter. Since the great scientific expeditions of the Enlightenment – the voyages to the South Pacific of Cook and Banks, for instance – the work of science has been punctuated by encounters with exotic peoples and cultures. Despite the development of laboratory science in the nineteenth century, the scientific expedition to foreign places was no less prominent a site for the production of scientific knowledge: witness, for instance, the importance of Darwin's voyages on HMS *Beagle* in the development of evolutionary science. The colonial encounter, particularly during this period of Britain's expansion of its foreign interests, underpinned the development in the latter part of the century of the new sciences of ethnology and anthropology. But as a structure of dominance and control, it also leant a framework to all kinds of scientific endeavour. Mary Shelley's *Frankenstein* provides a telling commentary on the politics of scientific discovery through the vexed relationship between the scientist and his subject, master and slave; and the racialising of the monster in later nineteenth-century adaptations and illustrations of the novel underlines an increasing tendency to identify racial difference within the objects of scientific knowledge.[27]

In recent studies, models of primary encounter, rather like the 'two cultures' divide, have moved away from binary structures of (Occidental) dominance and (Oriental) submissiveness to examine the more dynamic and less foreseeable transactions that take place at the frontier. Mary Louise Pratt has coined 'contact zone' for these encounters, a term which aims

> to foreground the interactive, improvisational dimensions of colonial encounters so easily ignored or suppressed by diffusionist accounts of conquest and domination. A 'contact' perspective emphasizes how subjects are constituted in and by their relations to each other. It treats the relations among colonizers and colonized ... in terms of copresence, interaction, interlocking understandings and practices, often within radically asymmetrical relations of power.[28]

Pratt's emphasis on *transculturation* does not deny imposition and domination, but it does allow for subaltern appropriation, the re-routing of meanings and creative misprision, such as the marvellous hybrid document she discusses (in her Introduction) which fuses Spanish Catholicism and Andean mythology in a way that left it ignored as uncategorisable, rejected knowledge for centuries. The model of the contact zone is a useful one for analysing the encounters that frame scientific work in our period, not merely because it alerts us to the relationships of power that are involved, but also because it highlights the embeddedness of science in cultures that are similarly constituted of diverse and uneven strands.

The nine chapters of this volume are attempts to unravel those strands and to show how scientific thinking participates in the construction of the complex cultures of nineteenth-century Britain. They investigate the transactions between different bodies of knowledge, the formation of new fields or disciplines, the dissemination of scientific ideas in print and through the spread of new technologies of sound and vision, and, especially, in the ways in which science shaped people's relationships with their environment, fundamentally changing the order of nature, culture and society. The picture that emerges is one in which the boundaries between disciplines are blurred and frequently contested, and in which experts in particular fields often sought to assert their authority by looking across the disciplines, finding allegiances and models elsewhere. Thus Paul White shows how Dickens, in response to the controversy provoked by his spontaneous-combustion scene in *Bleak House*, turned to science, rather than literary precedents, to validate his work; how George Henry Lewes, wounded by Huxley's criticism of his work as that of an 'amateur' scientist, acquired a microscope and set about transforming himself into a 'man of science'; while George Eliot, as editor of *Westminster Review*, criticised the narrow perspective of its new science reviewer, Huxley. By 1874, however, when Lewes was called as expert witness to the Royal Commission on vivisection, he made an arresting comparison between vivisection and literary criticism – both were required, according to Lewes, for the advance of knowledge and the progress of society. As White points out, the Royal Commission marks an interesting and complex stage in the formation of literary criticism as an academic discipline, in which it gained the privileged status and authority already ascribed to the sciences. At the same moment, however, scientists such as Huxley recognised the benefits of a 'liberal education' in which the effects of science would be moderated by the sympathy to be gained from reading literature and the Bible.

David Amigoni picks up the story some twelve years later, in 1884, and shows how discussions about the role of literature continued to be inflected by the claims of science. He focuses on Huxley's Arnoldian emphasis on *imitation* as the primary pedagogic tool in literary education, a ploy, according to Amigoni, by which to defend English culture from foreign 'contagion'. The term *imitation*, however, is a complex one, drawing its meanings both from literary culture and from evolutionary science, where it indicates an instinctual, or unconscious, process which theorists such as Gabriel Tarde used to contest the power of inheritance, especially racial inheritance, in contemporary social scientific thought. Amigoni's deft reading ranges across popular science, psychology, literary criticism, etymology and biology, revealing the complex interrelatedness of these diverse fields and illuminating an important episode in the history of English studies.

The complex negotiations between disciplines uncovered by White and Amigoni are typical of the scenarios analysed in this volume. Some of the chapters are concerned specifically with the formation of disciplines. Lynnette Turner's study of Otis Tufton Mason's *Woman's Share in Primitive Culture* (1895) focuses on developments in anthropology during the 1890s, a crucial moment in the history of that discipline; while Carolyn Burdett is concerned with the Karl Pearson's widely influential biometrics, his mathematical statistics that were to transform social science methodologies in the twentieth century, and which lay behind the development of eugenics. Burdett points out the importance of Pearson's cultural enthusiasms for German literature and philosophy – witnessed in particular in his literary works, including his novel *The New Werther* – and the ways in which they shaped his scientific thinking. His science, she shows, was deeply embedded in a social and political vision, which led him in 1934 to praise Hitler: his was, as Burdett notes, 'a fully ideological commitment to number'.

Other chapters are concerned with new technologies that became available in the nineteenth century, the new sites of scientific enquiry thereby opened, and the new forms of knowledge they facilitated. Isobel Armstrong examines the impact of the microscope, which was cheaply available in mid-century. This revealed an extraordinary 'sub-visible' world, which made a significant contribution to the forging of evolutionary theory in biology. Armstrong also examines the microscope's 'intense phenomenological disturbance of the visual field', which had profound implications for epistemology in this period, and the regimes of knowledge that shaped social and cultural life. Armstrong emphasises the diversity of responses to the microscope – from Lewes's and Gosse's fascination with the minutiae of marine life to Ruskin's defence of the 'innocent eye', and his antipathy to the false objectivity and authority conferred on the instrument of magnified seeing. Rebecca Stott's chapter is similarly concerned with the impact of the microscope and the revelation of the subvisible world. Her discussion focuses on marine invertebrates, which, according to evolutionary scientists, were a 'parent' life-form for the human species. Stott demonstrates the way in which this strange species operates in the cultural imaginary, as an object through which anxieties about the place of men in bourgeois domesticity were expressed.

Lindsay Smith also broaches the impact of new technologies of seeing. In this case it is not the microscope that is the focus of attention but the camera and its strange effect of removing colour from the world. Steven Connor investigates auditory technologies, in particular the forms of communicative technologies over distance – instruments that enabled the reproduction, amplification and telephonic displacement of the human voice. These, according to Connor, reconfigured 'the sensorium in terms of the ear rather than the eye'. Connor's essay explores the curious interface between the world of technological innovation and that of the séance, the Victorian venture into the ghost world of the dead. Roger Luckhurst also is concerned with this eccentric social and intellectual space, poised between science, supernatural belief and popular entertainment. His attention is focused on a mind-reading act staged at the offices of the new journal the *Pall Mall Gazette*, in 1884, in order for an assembled group of luminaries – including prominent doctors, scientists, businessmen and writers – to examine the alleged powers of the popular mind-reader Stuart Cumberland. For Luckhurst the event serves to demonstrate both the ways in which competing interests in psychical phenomena converged at this moment and the existence of diverse conceptions of mind which provided the confusing context in which a recognisably modern subjectivity began to be articulated.

All the contributors to this volume relate episodes from the boundaries of science and culture in the nineteenth century, and tell stories that necessarily overlap with each other. We have organised their accounts around three themes. Connor, Armstrong and Smith consider the impact of technology on nineteenth-century culture. White, Amigoni, and Luckhurst deal with sites of scientific knowledge, and their limits. All in this second group are particularly concerned with the periodical as, in

White's words, a 'highly important, but volatile, medium for the negotiation of scientific authority', necessarily in conflict with the more closed spheres of the learned societies, the laboratories and the specialised journals. The significance of the periodical in the production of knowledge, its organisation and impact in shaping intellectuals, in this period cannot be underestimated.[29] The final chapters, by Stott, Turner and Burdett, deal with evolutionary science and its impact on notions of 'progress'.

At the end of *Frankenstein*, the monster is 'borne away by the waves and lost in darkness and distance',[30] absorbed into nature, to which his very being was an affront. But there is no real resolution for the scientist, who is locked in everlasting struggle with his invention. Although the idea of Frankenstein was an important fantasy of science throughout the century, the scientists discussed in this book are not Frankensteins, but have varied and complex relationship with their work, and with the culture of their work. The aim of this book is to reassess those relationships, aside from the everlasting agon between Frankenstein and his monster.

Notes

1 Mary Shelley, *Frankenstein, or the Modern Prometheus. The 1818 Text*, ed. Marilyn Butler (Oxford: Oxford University Press, 1993), p. 138.

2 Carl Sagan, *The Demon-Haunted World: Science as a Candle in the Dark* (London: Headline, 1997), p. 29.

3 Daniel Dennett, *Darwin's Dangerous Idea: Evolution and the Meanings of Life* (NY: Simon & Schuster, 1995); and Richard Dawkins, *Unweaving the Rainbow: Science, Delusion and the Appetite for Wonder* (Harmondsworth: Allen Lane, 1998).

4 Paul R. Gross and Norman Levitt, *Higher Superstition: The Academic Left and its Quarrels with Science*, 2nd edn (Baltimore, MD: Johns Hopkins University Press, 1998), p. x.

5 Sokal's essay first appeared in *Social Text*, 14, 46/47 (1996). Alan Sokal and Jean Bricmont, *Intellectual Impostures: Postmodern Philosophers' Abuse of Science* (London: Profile, 1999).

6 Wendy Wheeler, *A New Modernity? Change in Science, Literature and Politics* (London: Lawrence & Wishart, 1999), p. 135, discussing the Sokal case.

7 C. P. Snow, *The Two Cultures*, with an Introduction by Stefan Collini (Cambridge: Canto, 1998). Citation, p. 2. On the Victorian roots of the 'two cultures', see Paul White, below (pp. 75–95).

8   Alluquère Rosanne Stone, *The War of Desire and Technology at the Close of the Mechanical Age* (Cambridge, MA: MIT Press), p. 39.

9   Helga Nowotny, Peter Scott and Michael Gibbons, *Re-Thinking Science: Knowledge and the Public in an Age of Uncertainty* (Cambridge: Polity, 2001), p. 1.

10 Nowotny *et al.*, *Re-Thinking Science*, p. 19.

11 See in particular Steven Shapin, *A Social History of Truth: Civility and Science in the Seventeenth Century* (Chicago, IL: University of Chicago Press, 1994).

12 James R. Moore, *The Post-Darwinian Controversies: A Study of the Protestant Struggle to Come to Terms with Darwin in Great Britain and America, 1870–1900* (Cambridge: Cambridge University Press, 1979).

13 Gillian Beer, *Open Fields: Science in Cultural Encounter* (Oxford: Clarendon Press, 1996), pp. 1 and 173.

14 See particularly André Breton, *Mad Love* [1937], trans. Mary Ann Caws (Lincoln: University of Nebraska Press, 1987). For commentary on the surrealist encounter, see Margaret Cohen, *Profane Illumination: Walter Benjamin and the Paris of the Surrealist Revolution* (Berkeley: University of California Press, 1995).

15 For representative biographies, see Adrian Desmond, *Huxley: From Devil's Disciple to Evolution's High Priest* (Harmondsworth: Penguin, 1997), and Crosbie Smith and M. Norton Wise, *Energy and Empire: A Biographical Study of Lord Kelvin* (Cambridge: Cambridge University Press, 1989). For work on the spatial topographies of science, see Adi Ophir and Steven Shapin, 'The Place of Knowledge: A Methodological Survey', *Science in Context*, 4, 1 (1991), and Crosbie Smith and John Agar (eds), *Making Space for Science: Territorial Themes in the Shaping of Knowledge* (Basingstoke: Macmillan, 1998). This last collection contains Sophie Forgan's useful conceptual analysis of the move of Victorian science from 'juxtaposition' in mid-century to 'separation' by the end of the nineteenth century. See '"But indifferently lodged … "': Perception and Place in Building for Science in Victorian London'.

16 Michel Foucault, *The Archaeology of Knowledge*, trans. Alan Sheridan (London: Tavistock, 1974), p. 68.

17 *Ibid.*, p. 161.

18 Friedrich A Kittler, *Discourse Networks, 1800–1900*, trans. Michael Metteer, with Chris Cullens (Stanford, CA: Stanford University Press, 1990), p. 371.

19 *Ibid.*, p. 369.

20 *Ibid.*, p. 371.

21 See Steven Connor, *Dumb-Struck: A Cultural History of Ventriloquism* (Oxford: Oxford University Press, 2000); Tim Armstrong, *Modernism, Technology and the Body* (Cambridge: Cambridge University Press, 1999); and Mark Seltzer, *Serial Killers* (London: Routledge, 1998). The latter two

are particularly indebted to Kittler. For some reservations, see Lisa Gitelman, *Scripts, Grooves and Writing Machines: Representing Technology in the Edison Era* (Stanford, CA: Stanford University Press, 1999).

22 Bruno Latour and Steve Woolgar, *Laboratory Life: The Construction of Scientific Facts*, 2nd edn (Princeton, NJ: Princeton University Press, 1986); Bruno Latour, *Science in Action* (Cambridge, MA: Harvard University Press, 1987); Bruno Latour, *Pandora's Hope: Essays on the Reality of Science Studies* (Cambridge, MA: Harvard University Press, 1999).

23 Latour, *Pandora's Hope*, p. 108.

24 *Ibid.*, p. 92.

25 *Ibid.*, p. 99.

26 Bruno Latour, *The Pasteurisation of France*, trans. Alan Sheridan and John Law (Cambridge, MA: Harvard University Press, 1988).

27 Chris Baldick, *In Frankenstein's Shadow: Myth, Monstrosity and Nineteenth-Century Writing* (Oxford: Oxford University Press, 1987).

28 Mary Louise Pratt, *Imperial Eyes: Travel Writing and Transculturation* (London: Routlege, 1992), p. 7.

29 The historical understanding of this channel in the periodical will no doubt be transformed by the SciPer project, being undertaken at Leeds and Sheffield Universities, which is mapping the place of science in the Victorian era.

30 Shelley, *Frankenstein*, p. 191.

1

Voice, technology and the Victorian ear

⌒

STEVEN CONNOR

Jonathan Crary has described the 'autonomization of sight' brought about during the nineteenth century as a dissociation of sight from touch, which is itself part of a separation and re-mapping of the senses. The loss of touch in particular meant 'the unloosening of the eye from the network of referentiality incarnated in tactility and its subsequent relation to perceived space'. The isolation of vision, and its promotion as a unifying sense or a meta-sense 'enabled the new objects of vision (whether commodities, photographs, or the act of perception itself) to assume a mystified and abstract identity, sundered from any relation to the observer's position within a cognitively unified field'.[1] The sense of sight became separated from the body; it became the means whereby the other senses were to be ordered and distinguished. We have become accustomed to identify the rise of scientific rationality with this cognitive promotion of seeing, and the demotion of the other senses, especially hearing and touch. The rational remodelling of the world in the nineteenth century can be seen in terms of the bringing of light, but also in terms of the massive production of objects for sight. To take only one example: the efforts to modernise cities like Paris and London meant converting the archaic urban experience, composed of smells, sounds and uncomfortable concussions – the world of miry indistinctness conjured up in the opening pages of *Bleak House* – into a rational structure available for actual or ideal sight. The development of gas and, subsequently, electric lighting in the second half of the century would emphasise this conversion.

In this chapter I enquire about the other side of seeing, or about what in the sensorium was subdued by seeing, and in particular the cultural and scientific–technological transformations of sound and hearing. My suggestion is this: an observational, calculative, scientific culture organised around the sequestering powers of the eye began in the last quarter of the nineteenth century to produce new forms of technology, especially communicative technology, which themselves promoted a reconfiguring of the sensorium in terms of the ear rather than the eye. Far from signifying simple resistance to or reversion from scientific rationality, cultural experiences of hearing as newly mediated by technologies such as the telephone, the phonograph, the loudspeaker, the microphone and the radio anticipated the new scientific understandings of the nature of materiality that we think of as characteristic of twentieth-century science, understandings in which the simple powers and privileges of optical rationality come to seem crude and limiting. Such an account runs the risk of what Raymond Williams once called 'technological determinism' – the view that technological changes themselves simply form and change consciousness. My view is that, rather than bearing the impress of technology and the forms of scientific understanding that it encoded, cultural experiences of hearing acted as a kind of laboratory for new understandings of the nature of scientific work: they constituted a relay in which science came to hear itself differently. Here I am in only partial agreement with Carolyn Marvin, who suggests, in her study of the social and cultural effects of the new electrical technologies of the late nineteenth century, that the body may itself be seen as 'a communications medium, that is, as a mode for conveying information about electricity'. I think that Marvin overstates the distinction between the experts and technically informed who communicated in textual form about the new technologies, and those 'groups without recourse to special textual expertise [who] approached the electrical unknown directly, learning with their bodies what it was, and what their relationship to it should be'.[2] Science attempted through the nineteenth century to put the senses to work: at the end of the century, the senses began to perform interesting kinds of work upon the self-understanding of science, as the newly mobile relations between sight and hearing (along with the increasing incorporation of the other senses) formed a correlative to emerging scientific conceptions of the complexity of matter and our relations to it. The distinction between the uninformed body and the informed expert is thus far from absolute.

What in hearing does the promotion of sight attempt to subdue and sequester? Hearing has traditionally been seen as the medium of experience, intuition, intensity and immediacy. As such, the difference between hearing and sight is approximated in the difference between oral and literate epochs, between unhistorical and historical cultures. Walter Ong suggests that the difference between a visual–typographic perspective and an oral–aural perspective is the difference between being in front of as opposed to being in the midst of a world: '*Sound situates man in the middle of actuality and in simultaneity, whereas vision situates man in front of things and in sequentiality.*'[3]

In hearing, one is open to the world in which one is placed. Seeing becomes associated with interiority – or with the defining gap between interiority and exteriority. In allowing, even requiring, the reflective distancing of human beings from the world they inhabit, seeing, so to speak, scoops out from the plenitude of shared social existence, out in the open, that invisible and imaginary concavity which will come to be occupied by the subject. Subsequently, hearing will come to be associated with everything that predates and even threatens the rational reflective subject: the oral, the infantile, the archaic, the instinctive, the irrational.

Sound appeared to nineteenth-century physicists to be more obviously and measurably material than light. Sound has measurable velocity and recordable dynamic effects. The apprehension of the dynamic materiality of sound, which goes back at least as far as Aristotle's *De Anima*, may register a physiological and cultural fact about human beings which is simple in its nature but profound in its effects. Human beings respond to light, but do not produce it. Human beings produce sound as well as apprehending it. If the eye corresponds to the ear, in apprehending light in the same way as the ear apprehends sound, there is no specifically visual correlative to the voice. The production of sound is tied intimately to its unbound transience: sound arises as an action or occasion.

Vision embodies or guarantees knowability, because seeing makes available the idea of persistence, or duration over time. Sound always involves the sense of something *happening*, here and now; but the very intensity of that here and now happening derives from the fact that it is volatile, always passing away. To see the world, or to see it as an object presented to sight, is to believe that it has a form; to hear the world, or to experience it as something heard (importantly, we can no longer speak of an 'object for hearing' with the same assurance) is to encounter materiality without continuity of form. What you see is there, and then is still there. What you hear is here, and then at that same instant is no longer here. Surprisingly, cinema, as the art of images in movement, may be seen as an approximation, within sight, to the conditions of hearing.

The dynamic nature of hearing allowed it to be conceived in terms of the dominant nineteenth-century scientific paradigm of the mechanical production, exchange and transmissibility of forces. During the mid-nineteenth century, the period that Lewis Mumford has characterised as that of palaeotechnics, this world of relations and transformations (actualisable as opposed to merely symbolic analogies between different forces and states of matter) was dominated by the thermodynamic correlation of heat and energy. Mid-nineteenth-century technologies had led to a massive augmentation of the motor or kinetic powers of the human body – its powers of extension, movement. Thus the machines for replicating, accelerating and multiplying the capacities of the human hand - from the spinning jenny onwards – were matched by the development of machines for replicating, and then accelerating, the powers of movement – in the railway, in the development of aeronautics and the internal combustion engine. Not only were such technologies allied to the world of work: they summoned up a 'world of work', of striving, resistance, production, idleness and decay. They involved the organisation and subordination of space: the conquest of distance, weight and inertia. They produced and expressed a *moralisation of matter* that saw processes of conversion in terms of the minimisation of waste or idleness and the maximisation of profitable work.

Though it had been known about at least since Faraday's demonstrations of electromagnetic induction, it was not until the last quarter of the century that electrodynamic convertibility – the conversion of heat into light, of sound into variable electric current – began to have important cultural effects. The mechanisation of sound was part of the

process of putting the senses to work, in line with the project of exploit-
ing the kinetic powers of the body. Telephonic and phonographic investigations began with the idea of reducing or translating hearing into
sight. Both Alexander Graham Bell and Thomas Edison were driven to
their experiments with the transmission and reproduction of sound by
experiences of deafness – Bell with the deafness of his wife and Edison
with his own deafness. Both worked with the idea of relaying sound
through sight. Bell was, perhaps, inspired by the example of his father
who invented a highly influential system of phonetic notation, or visible speech (the word 'phonography', which came to be applied to the
early techniques of sound recording, originally denoted systems of phonetic shorthand). Bell worked for some considerable time with appara-
tuses which rendered sound waves in visible terms. He hoped, for
example, that deaf people could learn to reproduce pitch and timbre by
reproducing the voice-prints obtained by the influence of particular
sounds on flames, or the characteristic signatures produced by a device
called the phonautograph, which traced vibrations caused in a
diaphragm. Both were working, that is to say, with a conversion principle, in which sounds were first translated to a visual–linguistic form, and
then translated back to sound, rather than with a photographic principle, in which sounds would inscribe themselves directly without the
mediation of the interpreting human eye and mind.

'For some time', declared an article in *The Times* in 1877 celebrating the coming of the telephone, 'there has been a prophetic idea that a
speech ought to be able to report itself'.[4] The telephone amazed and dis-
quieted early users, because it seemed to have achieved this condition
of autonomised hearing. The autonomisation of sight evoked by
Jonathan Crary separated sight from the other senses and led to the cen-
tring and consolidation of a subject. The autonomisation of hearing separated the act of hearing from the individual subject and opened on to
a world in which human sensory operations appeared to take place not
merely *through* but *in* machines. The telephone appeared to effect a
specifically ventriloquial illusion in that the voice transmitted through
the apparatus appeared to speak from it. Time and again, early commentators on the telephone expressed their amazement that Bell had

succeeded in making the mute material world speak. Thermodynamic technology made iron move: electrodynamic technology, as the *Manchester Guardian* put it, had succeeded 'in making iron talk'.[5]

This autonomisation of speech and hearing brought about a curious revival of a very ancient conception of the expressiveness of the material world, a sense that the world could speak, and a vitalist sense that the life of the world consisted in its auditory powers. But it did more than this. Telephony and phonography also seemed to demonstrate that the world could listen to itself, without the agency of the human ear. Bell, it is well known, employed a real dead human ear in his experiments, and actually incorporated its tympanum in one of his early telephones; though he noted that the ear was poorer as an instrument than the diaphragm he constructed of boiler-plate iron, three feet across and one inch thick. Bell's achievement was, in the end, not to make it possible for the deaf to hear by means of sight (a telegraphic ambition), but to take an inert and deaf medium, and give it ears with which to hear. Listening to the telephone or to that other version of the 'talking machine', the phonograph, one appeared to be listening in to, or overhearing, an act of hearing. Later in his life, Edison wrote in his journal that he regarded his deafness as a positive advantage when it came to perfecting the sound produced by the phonograph, and that modern urban life was characterised by a kind of phonographic hearing. 'I haven't heard a bird sing since I was twelve years old. But I can hear anything upon the phonograph ... We are building a world in which the person who is deaf will have a definite advantage.'[6]

The romantic image for this autonomous hearing–speaking of the inhuman world was the Aeolian harp. A poem written in the 1890s by John Payne presented an interesting post-telephonic update of this image. *The Telephone Harp* asks us to imagine the inhuman and, literally, unearthly voices that might be rendered audible by the telephone wires that were becoming a common sight in city and country:

The hand of the storm-wind sweeps the harp of the telephone-wires.

One hears in the storm of sound the plaint of the unknown powers
The concert of wail that comes from other worlds than ours,
The inarticulate cry of things that till now were mute

And speak out their need through the strings of this monstrous
man-made lute.

Nay, cruel it is to hear the cry of the lives unknown,
That voice their ineffable woes in a speech that is not their own,
A speech that is neither theirs nor ours, that can but wail,
Nor give us to understand a word of their mournful tale.[7]

The inarticulate cry of things is here both actualised and suppressed –
expressed only as needy ineffability – by the telephone. The cry of things
becomes noise or interference, not exactly on the line, but between the
lines.

This separation of hearing from the ears of individual subjects confirmed a cultural fantasy that was widely diffused through the nineteenth
century, the fantasy of the mobility of the senses. Early in the nineteenth
century, the tendency to identify Mesmer's 'magnetic force' with electricity had already led to the enactment of forms of imaginary electrical telephony in mesmeric experiments in the early nineteenth century.
The electrical researcher J. H. D. Pétetin thought that he had proof of
the dependence on electricity of hysterical insensibility, reporting that,
although a female patient would show no signs of response to questions
directed to her ears, she would respond if the mesmeriser placed the fingertips of one hand on her abdomen and whispered his remarks to the
fingertips of the other hand.[8] It became widely believed among mesmerists that the senses of hearing and sight could migrate in an
entranced subject from the head to the abdomen. There are a number
of reports in *The Zoist*, the journal of phreno-mesmerism published
during the 1840s, of women suffering from deafness and dumbness, who
could hear perfectly well when someone would whisper close to their
stomachs.[9] Frank Podmore's account of a further elaboration of this
experiment in his *Modern Spiritualism* of 1902 makes clear its anticipation of the telephonic process: 'the same results would follow', writes
Podmore, 'if the operator stood at the remote end of a chain of persons
holding each other's hands, of whom the last only touched the patient.
But if a stick of wax were placed in the circuit, communication at once
ceased.'[10] In Podmore's account, it is the word 'operator' (a word in
use from the 1840s to designate the telegraphist which transferred

readily to the men and later women who performed the same function in the new telephone switchboards) that establishes the circuit between mesmerism, telegraphy and telephony.

Indeed, spiritualist practice provides the most striking and sustained example of this kind of phantasmal experiment with bodily matter. It is routinely claimed that Victorian spiritualism is the expression of a widespread dissatisfaction with the materialism of nineteenth-century science, industry and social and political thought, an assertion of the transcendence of spirit, as a principle of moral, religious and even political renewal, in an objectified world of inert things and blindly mechanistic processes. This ignores the fact that spiritualists shared with their opponents the language of investigation, evidence, exhibition and exposure, and the séance was seen by spiritualists themselves as a kind of laboratory for the investigation of the spirit world, a stage on which to unveil or bring to light hitherto concealed mysteries. Indeed, spiritualism also shared with its materialist adversaries an impatience with supernatural explanations of its phenomena. Annie Besant defended her surprising embrace of theosophy after a lifetime of secularism with the claim that 'the repudiation of the supernatural lies at the very threshold of Theosophy', a sentiment with which Charles Maurice Davies concurred in 1874 in declaring that 'Spiritualism has no such word as Supernatural' and which Florence Marryat echoed even more emphatically in 1894 in asserting: 'There is no such thing as super-nature.'[11]

Spiritualist practice is much more accurately thought of as a kind of phantasmal commentary upon the work of science; a sort of cultural dreamwork, or series of embodied reflections upon the reconfigurations of the body induced and potentiated by new communicational technologies. One of the less often remarked ways in which the 'other world' of spiritualism became entangled with the 'real world' of science and progress was in its mirroring of the communicational technologies of the second half of the nineteenth century. For some years after spiritualism began its career in 1848, with the 'Rochester Rappings' experienced in a house in Hydesville, New York, it was believed that the principal means of communication with the dead was the system of, usually, alphabetic knocks, which had to be decoded, knock by knock, by the sitters. No more literal parallel to the digital system of the electric telegraph could be imagined. In 1858, Charles Partridge had already published his account of spiritualist experiences under the imprint of the 'Spiritual Telegraph Office'; and, as one might expect, the spirits soon began themselves to communicate in morse code.[12] When, in 1871, members of a spirit circle in Cincinatti working with the mediumship of a Mrs Hollis received messages in morse, they were prompted to incorporate a telegraphic instrument into their séances. The spirits claimed to have invented telegraphy in advance of its invention in the human world (one wonders just what *for*?), and indeed to have given unseen encouragement to its inventor and developers. Although this encouraged hopes that 'the time is not very distant when telegraphic communication between the two worlds will be as much established as it now is between Louisville and Cincinatti', spiritual telegraphy made considerable demands on the spirits' powers of organisation and engineering. It was necessary, for example, to find and retrain a deceased telegraph operator in the spirit world, whose efforts would need to be supported, as on earth, by a 'band of electricians to sustain the community spirit, while he handles the key of the instrument'.[13] Nor was it possible for the spirits simply to commandeer the telegraph instrument placed in the centre of the circle: first of all, it was necessary to materialise a 'battery' to power it.

During the 1860s and 1870s, the systems of 'visible speech', which enabled the direct transformation of acoustic signals into verbal or visual form, find parallels in the automatic writing and 'direct writing' practised by mediums during this period, neither of which dispensed with the requirement for the members of the séance to decode the spirit messages. Then came the near-simultaneous invention of the telephone (in 1876) and the phonograph (1877). Both of these technologies, especially the former, quickly entered the language of spiritualism. The effect was both further to 'materialise' spiritualism itself and to highlight the ghostliness of the new technological power to separate the voice from its source, either in space, as with the telephone, or in time, as with the gramophone. Spiritualism moved from the high-definition visibility of the full-figure materialisation which thrilled participants in séances during the 1870s, towards more indeterminate experiences in which invocation predominated over materialisation, and the ear over the eye. The twentieth century was the period of what one spiritualist memoir called 'the voice triumphant'.[14]

There is a deeper relation between the evolution of ghost phenomena and the developing logic of technological communications. For both involved the move from somatic to telematic processes of relay, as effects and manifestations that took place in or through the physical person of the medium – the easiest of these to achieve being the production of the voices of the spirits by the medium's own vocal organs – were replaced by manifestations taking place at a distance from the medium's body. The two forms of climax were, firstly, the 'full materialisation' brought about most spectacularly by mediums like Florence Cook, who, in the person of 'Katie King', moved around the room, conversed with sitters, sat on their knees to be tickled, and so on, and, secondly, and less often discussed, the phenomenon of the 'direct voice', which is to say, a voice that speaks independently of the medium's vocal organs.[15] In the direct voice, the phenomenon must be thought of as being *facilitated* rather than produced by the medium, who acts as a telephonist rather than as a telegraphist, making the connection rather than herself relaying, embodying and interpreting the signal.

Often, in 'direct voice' manifestations, the spirits would employ a trumpet (resembling a speaking trumpet or megaphone rather than the musical instrument), or even a series of trumpets, which might be placed in the room at a distance from the medium. The trumpet served both to amplify the voice, and to change its position: trumpets would be moved telekinetically through the air and around the room. Mediums who specialised in this mode of manifestation became known as 'trumpet mediums'. The spiritualist use of the trumpet was probably first suggested by the use of hearing trumpets for the deaf, as well as biblical uses of the instrument as a sign of spiritual warning and revelation, rather than by the characteristic amplifying horn of the phonograph and later the gramophone. But the technique of making spiritual voices audible came increasingly to cohere with the technological means of amplification. I think we might interpret this use of the apparatus of reproduction and amplification in terms of an anthropomorphising of

the telephonic and phonographic apparatus that has been described by
Kenneth Haltman.[16]

The flourishing of the 'direct voice' during the twentieth century was
undoubtedly encouraged by the development of acoustic technologies –
the telephone, the phonograph, the gramophone, the microphone, the
megaphone, the radio and the tape recorder. One of the most successful
and widely-known of direct-voice mediums, Leslie Flint, first manifested
his power to conjure voices in the darkness of the cinema during the early
1920s: his psychic gifts were a technological supplement to the silent film,
providing a kind of soundtrack.[17]

The séance occupies a central position in the Victorian exploration of
the possibilities of a world governed by the principles of sound, and a form
of human embodiment governed by hearing, and the proximity senses
with which it is associated. The suffusive body of the séance is a body characterised by the mobility of sound, in its influx to the interior of the body,
and its passage outwards again into the world. (Later, in the twentieth-century, ectoplasmic materialisation itself would be explained by reference to
a theory of matter vibrating at different rates.) Where the optical body is an
anatomy unfolded to the eye, which allows it to be clearly differentiated
from its outside and from other bodies, the phantasmal body of the spiritualists is a transmissive or connective medium: it is experienced in terms
not of the relationship between interiority and exteriority but in terms of
passage between them. Hearing the voice from beyond issuing from the
mouth of the medium, and, in later years, hearing the 'direct voice' of the
spirit, separated from the medium's body, bring about a temporary ascen-
dancy of acoustic over visual space. For all its startling visual apparitions,
the séance's tendency is to replace a visual body with the fundamentally
auditory-acoustic phenomenology of the sonorous body.

Telephones and phonographs were initially enjoyed and sometimes
even dismissed as mere tricks and gadgets. From the telescope onwards,
inventions which began life as toys and gimmicks have developed 'serious'
scientific or social uses. Such serious purposes were quickly invented for
the telephone. It was employed in coalmines and in hospitals; there was
very considerable interest in the medical and the military applications of
the telephone; and the powers of the telephone to assist in the maintenance

of public order quickly became apparent – the Boston police force had already installed a telephone network by 1878. Early representations of the telephone stressed its involvement with the worlds of commerce and work (women, for example, are not presented as users of the telephone until relatively late in its development, when, in the 1920s and 1930s, it began to be marketed as a leisure device; until then, by contrast, women were addressed via the telephone, and so formed part of the circuit or exchange of voices). The telephone came rapidly to be seen as a way of making businesses and other kinds of serious social processes more efficient. The telephone as a rationalising device channelled speech into calculable purposes. It reconfigured discursive relations into the form of networks and mapped the vectors of speech. The development of the telephone belongs to that generalised rationalisation of communication and sensation which characterised the twentieth century.

Seen in this way, there is an unbroken continuity between the sciences and technological enhancements of the senses and the cruder forms of technology characteristic of the earlier nineteenth century: a putting of the senses to work in the same way as steam engines derived work from the principle of thermodynamic equivalence. But, alongside these developments, the telephone and the phonograph, along with ancillary inventions like the microphone and the loudspeaker, also represent something new. They retained their early associations with fantasy, pleasure and secret excitement. The telephone and the phonograph would develop as part of the commodification of information and communications. But, in entering and transforming intimate everyday life, this technology itself also began, and continued, to *play*. In these inventions, science would begin its long and still-uncompleted sojourn with pleasure, style and the techniques of the self. Like the camera and the cinema, the telephone began to provide forms for self-imaging and self-transformation. It is surely no accident that the cases of divided and multiple personality encountered and analysed by Pierre Janet and Morton Prince at the end of the nineteenth century and beginning of the twentieth century took the forms not of the multiplication of appearance, or the presentation of visual symptoms, but the production from a single human body of multiple centres of personality identifiable by their different voices.[18] In these examples, as in the paranoia of a Schreber, pathology lies close to the mainstream of techno-cultural transformation.[19] If the telephone plays a part in the reduction of 'culture' to rationality, the putting of the senses to work, it also installs culture and sensation at the heart of rational structures and cognitive operations, and begins to transform them from the inside outwards. The technologies of the voice and the ear inaugurate the process whereby the subordination of culture by science was inverted – in which science became 'culturised'. At the very inauguration of that fierce antagonism between professional scientific expertise and the realms of culture, whether in the commodified forms of the culture industry or the idealised forms of anti-scientific avant-garde art and culture, an antagonism that has often been said to characterise the modern world, we can see the beginnings of that commingling of scientific ideas and cultural practices which has become characteristic of our contemporary world.

Notes

1 Jonathan Crary, *Techniques of the Observer: On Vision and Modernity in the Nineteenth Century* (Cambridge, MA, and London: MIT Press, 1990), p. 19.

2 Carolyn Marvin, *When Old Technologies Were New: Thinking about Electric Communication in the Late Nineteenth Century* (New York and Oxford: Oxford University Press, 1988), pp. 110, 117.

3 Walter J. Ong, *The Presence of the Word: Some Prolegomena for Religious and Cultural History* (Minneapolis: University of Minnesota Press, 1981), p. 128.

4 'A Great Invention', *The Times*, 19 November 1877, p. 9.

5 'A New Voice', *Manchester Guardian*, 3 December 1877, quoted in Kate Field, *The History of Bell's Telephone* (London: Bradbury, Agnew & Co., 1878), p. 56.

6 Thomas A. Edison, *The Diary and Sundry Observations of Thomas Alva Edison* (New York: Philosophical Library, 1948), pp. 50, 52.

7 John Payne, *The Telephone Harp, in Carol and Cadence: New Poems 1902–1907* (London: Villon Society, 1908), pp. 96–7.

8 J. H. D. Pétetin, *Théorie du galvanisme: ses rapports avec le nouveau mécanisme de l'électricité* (Paris: Chez Brunot and Lyon: Chez Reymann, 1803), p. 22.

9 See, for instance, the case of Elizabeth Halliday, described in 'Cases of Mesmerism, by Mr. Chandler', *The Zoist*, 3 (1845–46): 190.

10 Frank Podmore, *Modern Spiritualism* [1902], repr. as *Mediums of the Nineteenth Century*, 2 vols (New Hyde Park, NY: University Books, 1963), vol. 1: 63–4.

11 Charles Maurice Davies, *Heterodox London: Or, Phases of Free Thought in the Metropolis*, 2 vols. (London: Tinsley Brothers, 1874), vol. 2: 41; Florence Marryat, *The Spirit World* (London: F. W. White, 1894), p. 34.

12 Charles Partridge, *Spiritualism: Its Phenomena and Significance, Spiritual Telegraph Tract no. 1* (New York: Spiritual Telegraph Office, 1858).

13 N. B. Wolfe, *Startling Facts in Modern Spiritualism* (Cincinatti, OH: no publisher, 1874), p. 250.

14 Ellen A. Pennau Cook, *The Voice Triumphant: The Revelations of a Medium* (New York and London: A. A. Knopf, 1931).

15 Steven Connor, 'The Machine in the Ghost: Spiritualism, Technology and the "Direct Voice"', in Peter Buse and Andrew Stott (eds), *Ghosts: Deconstruction, Psychoanalysis, History* (Basingstoke: Macmillan, 1999), pp. 203–25.

16 Kenneth Haltman, 'Reaching Out to Touch Someone? Reflections on a 1923 Candlestick Telephone', *Technology in Society*, 12 (1990): 333–54.

17 *Behold I Live, Compiled by Lucy Chauncy Bridges, from Tape-Recordings* (London: Regency Press, 1966).

18 Steven Connor, 'Satan and Sybil: Talk, Possession and Dissociation', in S. I. Salemensky (ed.), *Talk Talk Talk: The Cultural Life of Everyday Conversation* (New York and London: Routledge, 2001), pp. 163–80.

19 Mark S. Roberts, 'Wired: Schreber as Machine, Technophobe, and Virtualist', *TDR: The Drama Review*, 40 (1996): 31–46.

2

The microscope: mediations of the sub-visible world

~~

ISOBEL ARMSTRONG

In 1846, beginning his career as a naval scientist, T. H. Huxley bought a microscope. It cost £13, more than a third of his quarterly salary of £37, and twice as much as his £6.10s dress suit.[1] In 1851, microscopes were shown at the Great Exhibition. They cost about £5, and the jury praised their low cost.[2] Thus they were within reach of the middle-class purchaser. In the nineteenth century – it is a commonplace of the history of science – the microscope replaced the camera obscura, which had been the dominant visual device of the eighteenth century, as the most fetishised optical instrument of the time.[3] Its prosthetic technology was one of the foundational elements both of high science and of popular instruction in empirical research into the world's infinitely small things. At the same time, ludic-lens and mirror-based devices intended for play – the stereoscope, the kaleidoscope, the magic lantern – existed side by side with serious, utilitarian, 'philosophical', instruments, as they were termed – the microscope, the telescope, the lighthouse – in mimicry of their transformation of vision.[4] Thus the lens was a dominant element of nineteenth-century culture, the more so as the distinction between 'amateur' and 'professional' had not hardened in the field of microbiology. The distinction between T. H. Huxley, for instance, who saw himself as a career scientist, and professionalised the discipline of biology towards the end of the century, and G. H. Lewes, an independent intellectual without institutional affiliation, was subtle.[5] Frequently at the margins, on the seashores of the west country, at Ilfracombe or Teignmouth, free of urban phantasmagoria and replacing these with alternative imagery, microbiologists explored a new world of the infinitesimal object. Their discoveries were rapidly popularised. G. H. Lewes, for example, began to publish his 'Sea-Side Studies' in *Blackwood's Edinburgh Magazine* in 1856. Philip Gosse's *Evenings at the Microscope* (1859), sub-titled *Researches Among the Minuter Organs and Forms of Animal Life*, and published by the Society for Promoting Christian Knowledge, was followed by his *A Year at the Shore* in 1865.[6]

Small things existing in the sub-visible world opened up unknown regions to sight. These were invisible but for the mediating art of the optical instrument maker. Their existence also created a strange double vision, as the peering microscopist adjusted to one set of proportions under the microscope and to another outside it. The disproportion of two worlds, concurrently existing in seething activity but oddly independent of one another, is nothing like so evident in the telescope, which brings distant things close but makes them commensurate with objects seen by the naked eye. Pullulating and diaphanous, the world of the microscope seemed to offer up the secret of the origin of life in a way that the telescope did not.

How the pursuit of the miniscule was conceptualised in popularising projects, generating rival epistemologies of the microscope, is my concern. The almost obsessive fascination of Lewes and Gosse with microscopy, and John Ruskin's hostility to its intense phenomenological disturbance of the visual field, produce a series of case studies for me. Another is Henry James's late short story *Glasses* (1916).[7]

The scopic experience of the microscope at this stage can be demarcated from earlier accounts by the intensified diction of the microscopist's descriptive prose, with its thesaurus of transparency, from the 'semi-pellucid' to the 'crystal'. 'There I have just detected an ascidian, standing up like an amphora of crystal, containing strange wine of yellow and scarlet', Lewes wrote in *Blackwood's* of August 1856. 'The *Noctilucae* are pin-heads of crystal, which in the dark are brilliantly phosphorescent', he wrote later, in September, 1857.[8] In his *Evenings at the Microscope*, Gosse remarked the 'pale red glass' comprising the disks of a frog's blood: one of his own hairs became a 'perfectly translucent cylinder, having a light brown tinge'. The scales of a goldfish took on the nacre of mother of pearl, a perch's scales were 'fine crystalline points', the cuttlefish's shell was like an iceberg 'rendered porous and laminated', rising in floors supported by an 'infinite number' of 'thin pillars of crystal'. The transparent webbing of a fly's wing, its crystal viscera and respiratory organs, and the 'glass-like' tongue of the slug, presented the world as diaphane, calling out a poetics of limpidity that aimed at a lyrical accuracy[9] (though it must be remembered that none of the objects described *was* transparent to the naked eye). Often using resources of language associated with quartz and semi-precious stones – chrysophrase, lustre, iridescence – this fascination with the transparent amounted to what we might call crystalophilia. The microbiologist also took sensuous pleasure in the vitreous, glassy apparatus of the profession, transparent glass containers, the slides that trap specimens.

'Besides, the transparency of most Objects renders them much more difficult than if they were opacous', Robert Hooke wrote in *Micrographia* (1665).[10] Seventeenth-century microscopists found the transparency created by the microscope a problem rather than a pleasure for the eye. For the microscope endowed beings with an artificial translucency that betrayed what could be seen by the eye. On the contrary, the nineteenth-century microscopic gaze seemed to want to see through creation rather than to look upon it. The pleasure of looking through a hair to its other side or of viewing both surfaces of a polyzoa's cells simultaneously is a cognitive as well as an aesthetic triumph. '[I]f you will imagine 20,000 wicker cradles stuck together … 20,000 more glued on to these, bottom to bottom'[11] Gosse wrote of such cells. He was discovering a descriptive language for the interstice, rather than the solid, that is paradoxically living matter itself. Indeed, the act of penetrating the mesh of veins and arteries in an organism was like seeing through to the other side of life itself.

This stress on transparency elided the properties of the transparent lens of the microscope with the object or specimen it enlarged and with the transparency of the eye. Observer, specimen and optical instrument occupied the same field, becoming indistinguishable and interchangeable. Thus the microscope's mediation could be repressed. Margaret Cavendish, contributing another seventeenth-century critique of the microscope, recognised that the virtual image it created is seen in dissassociation from its object, and is not coincident with it. The mediation of the virtual image troubled her. The image created an enlargement that could be deceptive, exaggerating convexity and offering visual ambiguity.[12] This was the consequence of the atopic image, severed from space, and thus without grounds for comparison and relationship. By the nineteenth century it was perhaps easier to ignore the microscope's virtual image and the uncomfortable evidence of mediation. Joseph Lister's work had corrected achromatic and spherical aberration. British technologies of the microscope had improved. James Glaisher, commenting on the microscopes exhibited at the Crystal Palace in 1851, remarked that 'the British microscopes were distinguished by the great amount of light obtained, the large angle of the aperture, and consequent fine definition; also by the large, flat, and perfectly defined field'.[13]

The clarity afforded by the contemporary microscope could sustain the illusion of the unmediated gaze. Thus the microscopist hastened to sketch, simultaneously with the act of looking, the pullulating embryo or surging disks of blood, as if the immediacy of an organism's living being could be represented. Although the very act of drawing belied the seemingly unmediated work of the microscope, the microbiologist was forced to draw in order to publicise his research and to engage with the experimental comparative process that was the essence of the discipline of natural science. The micrometer was available for measurement by the 1850s, but photomicrography was not available until the 1870s. In his first article in *Blackwood's*, Lewes described a lady sketching the land and seascape, as if a sketch of the macro-world of landscape had become obsolete in comparison with the hidden world of the sub-visible. But in reality both were submitting to the mediating process of pictorial representation. Mediation was either ignored or uneasily repressed. But the less directly it was confronted, the more the status of observation became problematical.

George Eliot recognised the third term of optical technology when, reviewing Charles Kingsley's *Westward Ho!* in the *Westminster Review* in 1855, she wrote of the 'medium' of the artist's sensibility, like a 'delicate acoustic or optical instrument, bringing home to our coarser senses what would otherwise be unperceived by us'.[14] For her both the mind and the instrument are mediating agents. (Did this recognition determine her presentations of the remembered landscape that begin and end *The Mill on the Floss* (1860)? Memory as painting, flushed with the colour and the hues of a 'realist' art, opens the novel. But this is superseded by memory as colourless image seen through a lens, which implicitly criticises the earlier model. Maggie negotiates exactly the same landscape in the flood as that of the opening scene, by deducing hidden connections and detail that have become sub-visible, now under the surface of water.)

At issue in discourses of the microscope is the amnesia that neglects mediation, and thus fails to problematise seeing both in itself and as a function of prosthetic agents. And here I differ somewhat from Jonathan Crary's virtuosic discussion of nineteenth-century scopic regimes in his *Techniques of the Observer* (1990).[15] He remarks on the phenomenon of the coalescence of observer and specimen, with the mediating instrument seen as a mere optical conduit from the one to the other. He argues that an epistemic break more or less at the end of the eighteenth century initiated a new disciplinary regime in which the observer was redefined. By the 1830s and 1840s the dualism that established a connection between veridical correspondence and viewing subject as a privileged form of knowing had collapsed. It was replaced by techniques for considering observing as itself an object of observation. Autonomous perception severed from a referent (anticipating changes usually associated with modernism) led the way for him to a Foucauldian understanding of regulation that is ignored when the merely aesthetic implications of this phenomenon are addressed. A new physiology and psychology that insisted on the eye as neural object and the body as a site of physiological perception created a reorganisation of its object. (Goethe's experiment with the changing auras of colour independent of an image in a darkened room signalled this change, and with it the end of the dualism implied by the camera obscura.) While this appears to guarantee an isolated individuality, in actuality it does nothing of the sort. What in fact occurred was the formation of a consumer-observer, whose body became codified and fragmented into multiple areas of sensory experience as a consequence of the arbitrary relation between stimulus and sensation. First, the exchangeability and equivalence required by consumerism and an exchange economy can be achieved when the body as an independent somatic entity is divorced from mind. Second, a new spectacular or scopic subject is born, as the modern dissassociated body becomes open to a play of varied visual phantasmagoria, and as different arenas of perception inscribe a promiscuous range of effects. (The stereoscope, which deranges sight by a discrete assembly of elements of binocular vision organised as disjunct experiences, is one of the technologies for organising this new subjectivity.) Third, since the body becomes the site of repetition, it is made available for mechanised labour. Above all, it is available for the control of observation, so that a surveillance that manipulates the normalisation and management of attention – whether of the student, the patient, the worker, consumer, soldier, or criminal – can be achieved.

Crary has recast the history of the nineteenth-century gaze in some extraordinary ways, not least through an immense range of scholarship. Only a thoroughgoing critique beyond the scope of this essay would do justice to his work. Nevertheless, while recognising his achievement, I want to make two observations on his use of Foucault's panoptical grand narrative. First, his model produces a monolithic account of technologies of vision in the nineteenth century that ignores the degree of conflict and ideological challenge created by rival epistemologies of seeing. Foucault thought of himself as a Nietszchean genealogical critic, mapping the sequence of disjunctions and misprisions that constitute cultural and political meanings at any one time.[16] Yet such an analysis can easily become the detection of a permanent immanence in which a discourse or form of enquiry never does what it experiences itself as doing but always something else. The logic of genealogical readings, though, argues for keeping in play the meanings that have been elided rather than organising cultural meaning in terms of monologic discourse.

My second point follows from this. The monologic discourse of technologies of the observer accepts the complete untethering of seeing from the object. Thus it accepts the unmediated power, though now unlinked from the veridical, almost as unequivocally as some microbiologist crystalophiles of the nineteenth century, and leaves out of account the uncomfortable interventions of mediation. Nor is mediation itself a unitary matter. Multiple forms exist in proportion to the complexity of a society. In the nineteenth century the mediation of labour, of money, and of scopic implements themselves – what we might describe as the implements of a tertiary technology, those instruments that were the prosthesis for vision –

created different orders of the third term. The mechanisation of sight became a crucial issue, calling out for ideological readings of knowledge.

Epistemologies of the microscope

For Gosse an invisible God sanctioned the pursuit of the invisible world revealed by the microscope, guaranteeing the accuracy of the monocular gaze and excluding the third term of mediation. Implicitly the believing scientist is God's representative, who can directly 'trace the handiwork of the God of glory' in the sub-visible world.[17]

> Thus the praise of the all-glorious God lies latent in all his creatures, whether man educe it or not. Too often, when we observe the wondrous variety, the incomparable delicacy, elegance, beauty, the transcendent fitness and perfection of every organ and structure, we are most occupied with our own pleasure or our own glory than with the praise of God.[18]

Modern science, of course, is associated with the 'infidelity' that proposes evolutionary ideas. The non-sceptical scientist, on the other hand, can deputise as a privileged agent of revelation:

> Here, bathed in its native sea-water, as clear as crystal, you shall see it [the Corkscrew Coralline] … You gaze; but you know not what you see. The presence of many lines representing transparent vessels of strange and dissimilar shapes, overlying each other … are quite bewildering I must act the showman, and tell you what you see.[19]

The scientist's mastery here takes control of the expositional process, as Gosse plays with the idea of the 'stage' of the microscope and theatrical performance, assuming biblical language – 'you know not what you see' – as a mode of authority.

Why should the microscope be the crucial agent of God, and his works 'never more great than when minutely great'?[20] Gosse does not work with a taxonomical scheme, or structure of categories or classification such as Huxley was evolving.[21] Indeed, his work eschews classification and offers instead the blind teleology of the infinite regression of detail. God is detail without end, generating ever smaller and infinitesimal minutiae. Gosse's exposition is governed by a progressive movement through degrees of minuteness. It aims for an accurate inventory of myriad, teeming, miniscule life, finding a descriptive language to match the data of the invisible world that is determined to be ever more specific and precise for ever smaller phenomena. For a feather he invents a language in descending order of minuteness – 'barbs', 'barbules', 'barbulets'. 'The magnifying power shows us that these barbs are not simple filaments, but are themselves double bearded in the same fashion; and further, that these barbules of the second series are furnished with a third series'.[22] The grosser the visual experience the more illusory it becomes. In fact, we do not *see* with the naked eye, which is effectively blind. Gosse works through a series of corrective descriptions of each organism, or rather, of each part of an organism he chooses to examine, recalibrating the visual meaning of an object by discovering further detail and complexity every time he moves a stage further into its previously invisible being. The canals on a goldfish scale are 'illusory', for instance, for when more closely studied they yield interrelated multiple layers rather than a single corrugated plate.[23] In such demonstrations both the connectedness of particles of phenomena and the will to control become apparent. But this apparentness also becomes an observer's delirium. An infinite regression of detail sanctioned by an invisible God, luring the observer on to ever more invisible phenomena produces a world of proliferating parts that contradicts the interdependence Gosse perceives. It is a world, strangely, without repression, where no detail can be subordinated and nothing can be left undescribed. At the same time, it is impossible to get to the end of seeing, impossible to see everything.

Thrown back upon himself and nature because he could verify the work of others in only that way, compelled to observe *de novo*, and trusting to his own eye,[24] Gosse offers meticulous observation, with a certain hubris, as truth. But his readers learn to recognise a familiar expositional move. He tells us that we see one level of complexity through the microscope's magnifying power; but what we see is not *in fact* the case; there is a further revelation still that reorganises the prior knowledge. The result is an authoritarian stance – 'I must … tell you what you see' – combined with a kind of manic scepticism. For instance, the cuttlefish shell that appeared as a glittering, laminated iceberg constructed of floors supported by pillars, or 'thin perpendicular plates', is, when seen as a horizontal, and not a perpendicular section, something different. The pillars disappear, to be

replaced by one continuous corrugated substance constructed of 'dou-
blings' and 'infoldings'. The 'brilliant sparkling substance' now apparent is
'in fact the basal portions of what we saw in the other section as thin perpendicular plates'.[25] Who is to know that further magnification and new
perspectives will not reveal further transformations? Gosse's extraordinary account of the saw fly's progressively complex weapons of aggression
is worth quoting at length.

> The first portion of the apparatus that protrudes on pressure, was this
> pair of saws of a f-like figure. These agree is general with those described
> [by other microbiologists]; here is, in each, the doubly-curved blade, the
> strengthened back, the rasp-like jagging of the lateral surfaces, the teeth
> along the edge, and the secondary toothlets of the latter ... Each main
> tooth of the saw in this case is the central point in the edge of a square
> plate, which appears to be slightly concave in its two surfaces, being thick-
> ened at its two sides, at each of which, where it is united to the following
> plate, it rises and forms with it a prominent ridge running transverse to
> the course of the saw. Each of these ridges then forms a second tooth, as
> stout as the main edge-tooth, which, with the rest of the same series, form
> a row of teeth on the oblique side of the saw, in a very peculiar manner
> difficult to express by words.

After describing sets of 'incongruous' hairs and bristles that seem to
interfere with the action of the saw and remain inexplicable to him,
Gosse goes on:

> There is, however, in this species of mind, a second set of implements
> [not so far discovered] ... This pair of saws that we have been looking
> at is but the sheath of a still finer pair of lancets or saws which you may
> see here ... Their extreme tip only bears saw-teeth, and these are directed
> backwards, but one side of the entire length presents a succession of cut-
> ting edges, as if a number of short pieces of knife-blades had been
> cemented on a rod, in such a manner as that the cutting edges should
> be directed backwards, and overlap each other. The other lateral surface
> is plain, and both are convex in their general aspect. The appearance of
> these implements is very beautiful ...[26]

Knives sheathing knives. In striving for an accuracy and detail beyond any
previously recorded, Gosse seems to be attempting optically what George
Eliot famously described in acoustic terms in *Middlemarch*: to hear the

grass grow and to listen to the squirrel's heartbeat, arriving at the roar the other side of silence, is dangerously near to psychosis, because the descriptive language attempts to include everything.[27]

Browning's poem *Mr Sludge, 'The Medium'*, in what is perhaps a parody of Gosse's teleology, recognises the astonishing changes of proportion achieved by the atopic conditions of the lens. The speaker advises his listener to 'See the Bridgewater book', the treatises that sanctioned the revelation of God in the natural world, that are now confirmed by the microscope's action.

> Somebody turns our spyglass round, or else
> Puts a new lens in it: grass, worm, fly grow big:
> We find great things are made of little things:
> And little things go lessening till at last
> Comes God behind them …
> The Name comes close behind a stomach-cyst …
> The small becomes the dreadful and immense.[28]

The microscope takes its viewers through exhaustive phases of enlargement, contraction and enlargement again. Here it is the mediation of the microscope's optical shocks that produces God (the use of the 'Name' to signify the deity signals a form of linguistic trick), whereas for Gosse the microscope confirms a teleology of unmediated divine agency.

Gosse's sub-visible world is beautiful and terrible. On the one hand the crystal water of the rock-pool conceals a 'metropolis of the zoophytic nation',[29] teeming life operating on the same principles of chance, freedom and the struggle for life divinely appointed for the upper world:

> What microcosms are these rugged basins! … What arts, and wiles, and stratagems are being practised there! what struggles for mastery, for food, for life! what pursuits and flights! what pleasant gambols! what conjugal and parental affections! what varied enjoyments! what births! what deaths! are every hour going on in these unruffled wells, beneath the brown shade of the umbrageous oarweed, or even the waving slopes of bright green *Ulva*, or among the feathery branches of the crimson *Ceramium*![30]

On the other hand, the God of good is also a God who gives retribution for sin. In *A Year at the Shore*, Gosse attacks Coleridge's sentimental reading of prayer in *The Ancient Mariner* – 'He Prayeth best who loveth best/

All things, both great and small ...': 'It altogether ignores the awful truths of God's revelation, that all mankind are guilty and condemned and spiritually dead in Adam, that the whole world lieth in the wicked one; and that the wrath of God abideth on it.'[31] Only the Atonement can redeem the guilty. By this logic the anthropomorphised sub-visible world is a microcosm of the guilty – and certainly violent – world above it.

Lewes's popularising project had fewer scientific credentials than that of Gosse. Indeed, he mentions Gosse as an authority on a number of occasions in his *Blackwood's* articles of 1856 and 1857. Nevertheless, despite the deceptive informality of the first article, inducting the reader into the culture of rockpool hunting through descriptions of clothes, equipment, techniques of discovery and picnics on the rocks, his work has a philosophical purpose and reveals an epistemological enquiry quite different from that of Gosse. Not the discovery of detail but that of typical form is the objective of microbiology. The object of analysis in Lewes's study is not an anthropomorphised micro-world but a universe of interdependent forms (rather than interdependent parts); not the dualism of an unmediated gaze of object by subject but the microscope's function as third term. Despite his researches into the rigorous classification of specimens, Lewes is anxious to portray scientific investigation as a passion, a nervous, somatic experience of throbbing intensity that belongs as much to the body as to the mind, and where vision is inherently subjective. Paradoxically it is precisely this almost addictive and eroticised aspect of research that is the condition for untethering vision from detail so that the discovery of form can take place. It is the abstract idea of the *category of a species* that fills him with rapture. As ideal forms, species are haunting spectres.

> And now, when all is done, the microscope is taken out, and severer studies begin. The hours spent thus fled like minutes, and left behind them traces as of years, so crowded were they with facts new and strange, or if not absolutely new, yet new in their definiteness, and in the thoughts they suggested. The typical forms *took possession* of me. They were ever present in my waking thoughts; they filled my dreams with fantastic images; they came in troops as I lay awake during meditative morning hours; they teazed me as I turned restlessly from side to side at night; they made all things converge towards them. If I tried a little relaxation of literature,

whatever was read became the starting-point for wandering fancy, or more obtrusive memory; a phrase like 'throbbing heart' would detach my thoughts from the subject of the book, and hurry them away to the stage of the microscope, where the heart of some embryo was pulsating. I could not even look intently, but the chance was that some play of light would transform itself into the image of a mollusc or a polype. THE THINGS I HAVE SEEN IN TAPIOCA PUDDING ...![32]

The appropriate poetic gloss on this experience is provided not by Browning but by Wordsworth, and a passage from the 1850 *Prelude* that Lewes may have known, describing 'unknown modes of being', 'huge and mighty forms, that do not live/ Like living men, moved slowly through the mind / By day, and were a trouble to my dreams'.[33] Lewes's forms are spectres, or ghostly categories, derived from empirical research invested with the coercive power of living entities. But his point is that these do *not* live like living *men*: though, as Wordsworth's syntax suggests, they do *live*, like an uncanny return of the repressed.

Why repressed? Partly because those who 'ardently pursue' the 'exquisite delights of nature' win such sexualised experiences only through the discipline of 'patient labour',[34] thereby legitimising them. Partly because the realities of the relationship between forms of life are occluded by the very anthropomorphism that appears to link human and other organic forms. In the second, and more stringently theoretical article, Lewes spends considerable time in severing the anthropomorphic link with the sub-visible world. Molluscs do not feel pain, he insists, nor do any of the simple forms of sea creature we examine under the microscope. Perhaps even fish are exempt from pain.[35] Pain occurs when a nervous system is complex and differentiated. Molluscs can neither see nor hear: though sensate, they are blind and deaf.[36] Yet molluscs are important – Lewes thinks he has discovered a new genus of mollusc, indeed insisting, like Huxley, that the polyzoa belongs to the mollusc class.[37] Molluscs are important not because they feel but because of the specific functional work the species undertakes in the economy of the sea. The currents of the sea depend upon the mollusc – 'the mighty ocean-currents mainly depend on this said mollusc shell'. As a lime-absorbing creature, the mollusc cleanses the sea of the solid deposits that would impede its flow. 'The sea is a great lime-quarry; but the lime is arranged in beautiful forms, and subserves a great organic end.'[38] Like Huxley, Lewes wants to understand the universe as a series of fundamental morphological types.

In discussing the way we see, Lewes is implicitly justifying the microbiologist's experience as veridical. But he never argues naively that the microscope or the human eye is an empirical conduit of neutral fact, or that sight is a mere neural phenomenon. The 'image' that reaches the eye is the result of a wave of light translated into a nerve stimulus. He calls on Mueller's optics to endorse this position.[39] The eye mediates sensation, but it is as much a tactile organ as it is an organ of sight: 'We see very much by the aid of our fingers'.[40] For images are not formed on the retina, as if it were a camera obscura: they are formed as light falls on the black pigment behind the retina, which is the true recipient of light, very much as a photographic image is formed, absorbing light differentially in response to the uneven distribution of light reflected from an object. The pigment changes its temperature in response to that of light (responding to the 'touch' of heat), and the act of vision commences as the specific sensations recorded by temperature change ultimately reach the brain, which reads the configured sensations transmitted to it. Lewes goes into great detail to argue for the non-receptivity of the retina. The points to be stressed, however, are, firstly, that the 'conversion' of sensation to image is a strictly 'mathematical' process,[41] and, secondly, that the process of image creation is the result of a series of *indirect* mediations by different parts of the nerve system and not a special nerve system functioning specifically to produce sight. '[T]actile sensations and sensations of light'[42] are the optical prerequisites for image formation.

In insisting on the physiology of vision as a process that creates no direct correlation between object and image, Lewes appears to be adhering to the new optics described by Crary. However, it is a physiology that enables him to steer between a simple dualism and subjectivism. While mathematical laws establish the tactile nature of vision and establish that seeing works according to scientific principles, the *a priori* act of interpretation is still paramount as the brain construes the data transmitted to it. Thus this mediation creates the latitude for *experimental* methods, as first one solution and then another is tested, and as the testing apparatus is built in to the brain itself. When the *Blackwood's* essays became a book, Lewes interpolated a further passage at the end of the second essay. In it he defends microbiology from the charge of distortion and wilful readings of the data: 'It is further said that microscopic observation is apt to be very erroneous, and that we can see whatever we wish to see.'[43] But seeing is always inferential: rather than the instrument, a psychological anamorphosis is the cause of error. The corrective of such distortion is the self-consciousness of the scientific naturalist, aware of the possibility of error. The discipline of the experimental method is the only solution. Observation is only one aspect of research: verification and testing are its natural adjunct. Conclusions are tested less by their logical coherence than by their 'verified dependence of verified facts'.[44] Though this claim may look like a defensive empiricism, strategically offered to allay fears of relativism, this is no simple empiricism. It is itself sceptical: it recognises deconstructive interpretation as the third term that 'interrogates Nature' and the mediation of the microscope in this process. Rigorously interrogated, for instance, nature offers no 'humble mollusc' – 'I never detected any humility in my molluscs.' A note adds: 'In creation there is neither high nor low; there are only complex and simple organisations, one as perfect as the other.'[45]

Ruskin persistently attacked 'the prevailing habit of learned men ... [who] take interest only in objects which cannot be seen without the aid of instrument'.[46] His hatred of all mechanical instruments, from wheels to guns, included prosthetic optical instruments and their abolition of 'the difference between eyes and microscopes'.[47] Often read as an archaic and reactionary resistance to technology, his hatred of the mediation of the microscope is worth taking seriously. Though he refused to recognise what made their ideas *matter* to Gosse and Lewes, there is a real argument at work in his attacks on the microscope. What was at stake was an argument about ways of knowing.

The first argument is political. Ruskin connects the microscope with the many times mediated world of the urban spectacle. What I have termed the tertiary mediation of optical prosthesis is associated with the bombardment of visual media competing for the consumer's gaze, the random inscriptions that dominate the scopic experience of the city –

advertisements, bills, posters, signs, shop windows – all of which obey the principle of rapid erasure. The exhaustion of the eye requires ever more glaring visual stimuli. 'The vast extent of the advertising frescoes of London, daily refreshed into brighter and larger fresco by its billstickers, cannot somehow sufficiently entertain the popular eyes.'[48]

Philanthropists respond to 'the wearying mind of the populace' and, in particular, to the children whom 'the streets educate only into vicious misery' by educating them in further wearying mediation. Inviting these children to 'entertainment' to keep them off the streets, they produce 'scientific vision, in microscope or magic lantern; thus giving them something to look at, such as it is; – fleas mostly; and the stomachs of various vermin; and people with their heads cut off and set on again; still something to look at'.[49] But philanthropists only entangle the gaze further in the culture of spectacle and its triviality. Charitable instruction simply exposes children to more corrupt scopic experience. Ruskin's is a fiercely political argument. Educationally derelict working-class or underclass children are being bought off with trivial display posing as knowledge. The visual image independent of its source is at once placebo and distorting phantasmagoria: it is corrupt mediation. Thus the stimulus without source that Crary sees as the agent of a new control of the subject is aggressively deconstructed in Ruskin's work. He implicitly attacks Lewes's romance of the microscope through an (oddly Benjaminian) analysis that resists the view that anamorphosis can be corrected by 'interrogating' nature. Anamorphosis, Ruskin claims, is built in to culture, politics and technology, particularly in response to the latter's rapacious penetration of matter. Undistorted vision is impossible in a modern society.

In this attack on the distorting effect of the microscope and the shallow optimism of microbiology, Ruskin appears to be adopting an impossible purism, behaving as if undistorted vision were possible. This was not quite his position, but it was the case that for polemical reasons he often adopted this misleadingly simple stance. Moreover, he forgot to honour some aspects of the politics of the Lewesian argument. The morphologies revealed in the sub-visible world, Lewes suggests, are an essay in differentiated form. It is difference and not either subordination or 'progress' that is learned from physical science – the mollusc as other. Indeed, the untethered specular image precisely releases the observer into scrupulous interrogation, interrogation turned upon his own experiment as well as the natural world, and this guarantees scepticism, not acceptance. The ideology of the microscope here may be triumphalist but it is not hierarchical.

Ruskin subjects Gosse's practice of progressively minute observation to a different critique. He exposes the leakage of violence and libido into its language, and indicates the impossibility of finding a terminology that does not become a mass of heterogeneous metaphor that cannot explain proliferating scopic detail. Consider this demonstration of the breakdown of taxonomy, vision and language as the lens scrutinises the flower *Brunella*.

> I take my lens, therefore, to the little wonder of a brown wasp's nest with blue-winged wasps in it, – and perceive the following particulars.
>
> First, that the blue of the petals is indeed pure and lovely, and a little crystalline in texture; but that the form and setting of them is grotesque beyond all wonder; the two uppermost joined being like an old-fashioned and enormous hood or bonnet, and the lower one projects far out in the shape of a cup or cauldron, torn deep at the edges into a kind of fringe.
>
> Looking more closely still, I perceive there is a cluster of stiff white hairs, almost bristles, on the top of the hood; for no imaginable purpose or use of decoration – any more than a hearth-brush put for a helmet-crest, – and that, as we put the flower full in front, the lower petal begins to look like some threatening viperine or shark-like jaw, edged with ghastly teeth, – and yet more, that the hollow within begins to suggest a resemblance to an open throat in which there are two projections where the lower petal joins the lateral ones, almost exactly like swollen glands.[50]

The argument from the revelation of the divine in the natural world ends up with a hearth brush on a bonnet and a sinister pervasive sexuality. Ruskin is ruthless in analysing the ungrounded atopic image of the microscope that actually leads to disproportion and grotesque virtuality the more meticulous descriptive language attempts to be – observation goes further away from the actual the nearer it gets to it. 'We must never lose hold of the principle that every flower is meant to be seen by human creatures with human eyes.[51] To modern science 'the eye seems rather an external optical instrument, than a bodily member through which emotion and virtue of soul may be expressed'.[52]

Ruskin's defence of the innocent eye unaided and unmediated by technology is not an argument for naive immediacy, though, as we have seen, he sometimes allows that implication to stand. Instead he argues for the transposition into all scopic experience of the relations given by the eye's limits. This demands the calibration of binocular vision – its range and focus – as the governing principle of observation. For the result is a coherence frankly organised by physiological factors. The eye, in addition, expressing emotion and feeling as it does, is no more value-free than is the microscope. But its bias is regulated by recognisable physical human norms. We are not trying to see with God's eye in Ruskin's optics. His critique of Gosse's myopic teleology reasserts the human eye.

Ruskin missed the plenitude of Gosse's universe, the irreducible specificity that makes for use-value even in the sub-visible world which mimics the *laissez-faire* state, and the obsessive epistemophilia that gives the work a driving energy. In the same way he missed Lewes's democratic reading of difference. But he did see that the mechanisation of sight as a form of technology was at issue. He saw that a politics of observing governed the theories he deconstructed, including his own, depending on different accounts of mediation. The authoritarian gaze direct from God sanctions a sublime of the infinitesimal that cannot be interfered with by human act, Calvinistically free and guilty at the same time. Lewes's philosophy of tireless adjustment of the double mediating elements, whether of the eye or of the instrument, or both in conjunction, offers a paradoxically rigorous scepticism grounded in the relational truths of morphology. For Ruskin both readings technologised the eye and conferred a false objectivity on the microscope's authority, diverting attention from the needs of human species' life and refusing to understand that an innately distorting language intervenes in the representation of the seen when those needs are ignored. Forms of knowledge and forms of social organisation are equally at stake, even before Darwin's *On the Origin of Species* (1859) had intensified the social reading of natural history.

The accounts of the microscope I have discussed belong to a period prior to that in which Darwin's theory effected a transformation of the epistemological field, and as Darwin was not a populariser in the sense that Gosse and Lewes were, his work has not been central to this paper.

However, it is important to see that the social implications of Darwinism, founded in Malthusian theory as they are, are already implicit in Gosse's 'civic' reading of microscopic life in terms of the struggle for mastery, and already potentially contested in Lewes's democratic understanding of morphology. Yet Darwin's interests in microscopy seem fundamentally different from those of Gosse and Lewes. Theologically and taxonomically poles apart, both Lewes and Gosse nevertheless think of the microscope as revealing the primal form of life itself, the pure principle of being secreted in sub-visible forms, creation at last revealed because at last seen through, at last transparent. At many points in his letters Darwin rejoiced in the microscope both as the source of new information and as a means by which to celebrate the nature of creation. 'A microscope is a most wonderful instrument', he wrote in 1846, and he ordered a compound microscope soon after. As his six numbered enquiries about J. P. Hooker's drawing of a cirripede under the microscope suggest – are the bars at its jaws muscles, or a 'hard & shelly' external skeleton? – he was as sophisticated as Lewes in his understanding of the microscope's capacity for anamorphosis.[53] Nevertheless, it was variation, differentiation and transmission, and what they ultimately tell us about complex forms of life that seemed to fascinate him, rather than pure categories of being revealed through structure. In some senses 'origin' is the wrong model for his work, part of a leftover teleology. In his rather chilling notes on the pros and cons of marriage, he claimed that to marry would mean that his inability to travel would impel him not only towards zoology rather than geology, but also towards '[w]ork at transmission of species – Microscope simplest forms of life.'[54] The simplest forms of life would not be an end in themselves. They would lead to an understanding of species evolution. Marriage meant stark categorical and epistemological choices, as well as a shortage of money. As his biographers remark, 'sex and ancestry' displace pure primal form as the central consideration.[55] What seeing was did not preoccupy him and nor did the philosophical problems of the microscope. He was ready to rely on it for so long as it supplied information.

Darwin, however, is a bridge between the pre-*Origin* microscope controversy and Henry James's tale *Glasses*, which was first published in 1897 as *Embarrassments*. By then evolutionary ideas had been absorbed, and the problematisation of seeing in James's tale is also uncomfortably alive to and complicated by the feminine sexuality that Darwin's work disclosed. Sexuality, Darwin's work affirms, is one of the sites of evolutionary struggle. But it was his reading of the unisexual hermaphrodite barnacle, and its extraordinary capacity to differentiate itself from infinitesimal males lodging parasitically upon it as mere 'bags of spermatozoa', that finally convinced Darwin of this theory.[56] For it caught in the act, so to speak, the move from unisexuality to bisexuality, demonstrating the presence of reduced male organs in the hermaphrodite simultaneous with the existence of supplementary males embedded in the female. Thus adaptation was demonstrable. A corollary is the emergence of a dominant female. The dominant female is an issue for James, linked with the problem of sight.

The microscope controversy makes observation observed, as Crary noted, but its effect was to make the mechanisation of sight a contested issue rather than a *fait acccompli*. Henry James's cruel comedy, *Glasses*, makes the mechanisation of sight, the eye displaced by an external optical instrument, a test case through the acceptance or refusal of a very mundane form of the lens's prosthesis – spectacles, or 'nippers' as they were slangily described, in suggestively insectine terms: 'There are women who look charming in nippers.'[57] But Flora, the woman at the centre of the story, hates what glasses will do to her beauty, and does her utmost to disguise her need of them. It is a bizarre tale, ending with the blind Flora in an opera box momentarily mistaking the coldly amused narrator for her husband – 'she was feeling me to see who I was!' (86) One is reminded of Lewes's description of seeing by touch, but it is Ruskin's account of technologised seeing that is immediately recognisable in this story. Microscope fanatics, he had said, 'if they were permitted to make themselves to their own liking, instead of suffering the slow process of selective development, would give themselves heads like wasps', with 'three microscopic eyes in the middle of their foreheads, and two ears at the ends of the antennae' (26, 114). Flora, who finally 'went into goggles' (73), as James's narrator asserts, ends up rather like this, her face 'wholly sacrificed to the huge apparatus of sight': 'the big gold bar crossing each of her lenses, over which something convex and grotesque, like the eyes of a large insect, something that now represented her whole personality, seemed, as out of the orifice of a prison, to strain forward and press' (66); she is caged in her glasses, glazed in looking out 'from behind a mask or cage' (67). Glasses, in this story, dread 'artificial aids' (44) glitter 'like a melon-frame in August' (59), a 'great vitreous badge' (66).

Flora's suffering and anguish are carefully bracketed by the observer-narrator who is himself a professional looker-at, a painter, in his amused misogynistic mockery of her vanity (more than tinged with disgust by the woman caught in, nipped by, the hideous grip of vitreous equipment), just as his own avid curiosity about her is repressed. It is significant that the narrator seems to be dominated by the mother whose powerful friend, Mrs Meldrum, is also a friend of Flora. Mrs Meldrum, indeed, also a wearer of glasses and a hideous double of Flora, 'flattening her nose against the glass of her spectacles' (6), ensures that the artist is alive to the presence of two powerful women. It is as if the artist's resentment is turned upon Flora. At one time, with incipient violence, he likens the unthinkable idea of insulting her beauty to the experience of throwing 'a stone at a plate-glass window' (13). The idea, of course, immediately becomes thinkable. Flora ought to be transparent to him, but because she is not he sets in motion doubts about her disability by discussing her sight with the two competing males who woo her – 'I would take her with leather blinders', says one, likening her to a horse: 'I had the impression that Iffield wouldn't' (47). His innuendo and whispering campaign interferes with the 'Darwinian' struggle for Flora.

Throughout, the narrator assumes a detached demeanour while wanting control. He appears to view Flora as a scientist does his specimen, adopting the classic stance of one-way seeing sanctioned by the microscope, with its corollary of subject-object mastery. But something is back to front. It is the specimen, Flora, the flower, caught up in biology as the nineteenth-century feminine was assumed to be, who, however unwillingly, adopts the prosthesis, the vitreous goggles. It is the specimen who looks back through the heavy lens. The specimen *sees*. The looker-on sees *seeing*, and this further objectifies Flora for him. He hubristically supposes that the specimen sees in the same uni-directional way as himself. His curiosity has transformed him from looker-on to observer, with all the will to know and control that this surveillance implies. At the same time the 'specimen' escapes him, possessing an independence he has not bargained for.

James is fascinated by this power-ridden gaze: what is its issue? What more can it be than a consuming with the eye? The painter's last meeting with Flora occurs, significantly, after his mother is dead. He sees her at the opera, and this time both he and she alike are equipped with opera glasses, another mediating tool to transform the eye into an external optical instrument, but this time an undisgusting luxury item – 'the little double-barrelled ivory glass ' (83), sinisterly assimilated to a gun. They are both seemingly on the level, with the disequilibrium and distortion of one-sided optical prosthesis evened out. Through his opera glasses he sees her seeing him through hers. She smiles directly at him, a gaze of recognition meant for him. But she is blind. She has been miming the act of seeing, the 'parody' (90) of a look. The inter-personal moment of looking was illusory. In the box to which he hastens recognition comes in the shocking, farcical, blundering of bodies against one another, as Flora feels his moustache and realises that he is not her clean-shaven husband. One is reminded of Lewes's blind mollusc here. The artist has been deceived both by his own *sight* and her *looks*. The limit of the gaze is that it is not substitutable – we cannot *see for someone else* or know what they are seeing any more than we can breathe for them. The 'open' act of seeing is actually the greatest secret of life. It is also the source of freedom, since we can 'have' our vision as no one else can, even though it is predicated on solipsism. The story ceases with this *aporia*. But not before the artist has regained a certain control by commenting that Flora's beauty could now be 'seen and marvelled at ... well within her *scope*' (89; my emphasis). The rather vicious pun on 'scope', meaning both 'capacity' and 'sight', allows him to remind us that she can never see the admiration lavished upon her. But the effect of this is to turn the reader's gaze to focus upon the question of the eye and its over-determination in 'modern' *fin-de-siècle* culture. After all, operas are heard and seen, but hearing, or indeed seeing, the opera is never mentioned. The subject of the Wagner opera going on as the last meeting with Flora occurs is Lohengrin: he does not get the woman he wants. And neither does the narrator. Instead of Flora's disability, the real mystery of the story is the narrator's scopophilic act of seeing, its uncanny irrationality and obsessive nature, its occlusion of its own mediation in the act of recognising another's.[58] The lens belongs to a scopic culture whose inexorable drive to the visual makes mediation the hidden axis of nineteenth-century epistemology.

Notes

1 Adrian Desmond, *Huxley: From Devil's Disciple to Evolution's High Priest* (Harmondsworth: Penguin, 1997), pp. 43 and 61.

2 The jury commended 'low-priced instruments' exhibited by Messrs Ross and Smith and Beck. 'Philosophical Instruments' (class 10), *Exhibition of the Works of Industry of All Nations, 1851. Reports by the Juries on the Subjects in the Thirty Classes in to which the Exhibition was Divided* (London, 1852), p. 265.

3 The popularising of the microscope is heralded in David Brewster's *A Treatise on New Philosophical Instruments for Various Purposes in the Arts and Sciences* (London: John Murray; Edinburgh: William Blackwood, 1813). In a related field, see *Treatise on Optics* (London: John Taylor, 1831). The Microscopical Society of London was founded in 1839. By mid-century specialised magazines devoted to microscopy appeared, often with an appeal to an amateur as well as a professional readership. For example, *The Monthly Microscopical Journal* began publication in 1844. William Carpenter's *The Microscope and its Revelations* (London: John Churchill, 1856) went into its 8th edition by 1901.

4 For an account of the co-existence of ludic and functional optical instruments, see Barbara Maria Stafford, *Body Criticism: Imaging the Unseen in Enlightenment Art and Medicine* (Cambridge, MA: MIT Press, 1991), pp. 341–98.

5 Cf. Paul White's chapter in this volume.

6 G. H. Lewes, *Blackwood's Edinburgh Magazine*, 80 (August, 1856): 184–97; 82 (September 1857): 345–57. His *Sea-Side Studies at Ilfracombe, Tenby, the Scilly Isles, and Jersey* was published in 1858. I quote from the second edition (Edinburgh and London, 1856). Philip Henry Gosse, *Evenings at the Microscope; Or, Researches Among the Minuter Organs and Forms of Animal Life* (London: Society for Promoting Christian Knowledge, 1859); *A Year at the Shore* (London: Alexander Strachan, 1865). Gosse's *The Ocean* (London: Society for Promoting Christian Knowledge, William Clowes, 1854) is a related study.

7 Henry James, *Glasses* (London: Martin Secker, 1916). The tale first appeared under the title *Embarrassments* (London: Heinemann, 1897), and was revised for the 1916 edition.

8 *Blackwood's Edinburgh Magazine*, 80 (August 1856): 192; 82 (September 1857): 345.

9 Gosse, *Evenings*, pp. 4, 36, 48, 60.

10 Robert Hooke, *Micrographia: or some Physiological Descriptions of Minuter Bodies Made by Magnifying Glasses* (London, 1665).

11 Gosse, *Evenings*, p. 72.

12 Margaret Cavendish, Duchess of Newcastle, *Observations upon Experimental Philosophy* (London, 1668), pp. 7–9. I am grateful to Stephen Clucas for information about what he terms Cavendish's 'counter-rhetoric' of visuality. See his unpublished conference paper '"The Information of these Optick Glasses": Experiment and the Status of the Visible in Early Modern Microscopic and Anti-Microscopic Discourse'.

13 James Glaisher, 'Philosophical Instruments and Processes', *Lectures on the Results of the Great Exhibition of 1851, Delivered before the Society of Arts* (London: Royal Society of Arts, 1852) series 1, vol. 2: 323–402 and 359.

14 *Westminster Review*, new series, 8 (July 1855): 289.

15 Jonathan Crary, *Techniques of the Observer: On Vision and Modernity in the Nineteenth Century* (Cambridge, MA: MIT Press, 1990).

16 Nietzsche famously rejects linear history and substitutes a series of disjunct, often misrecognised, readings of events. See *The Genealogy of Morals* [1887], trans. Francis Golffing (New York and London: Doubleday, 1956), Preface (p. 149): 'We knowers are unknown to ourselves … we *must* mistake ourselves'.

17 Gosse, *A Year at the Shore*, p. 6.

18 *Ibid.*, pp. 324–5.

19 Gosse, *Evenings*, p. 77.

20 *Ibid.*, p. 60

21 For Huxley's interest in morphology and his archetypal theory of a basic mollusc structure, see Desmond, *Huxley*, p. 174.

22 Gosse, *Evenings*, p. 18.

23 *Ibid.*, p. 25.

24 *Ibid.*, p. v.

25 *Ibid.*, p. 49.

26 *Ibid.*, pp. 160–2.

27 'If we had a keen vision and feeling of all ordinary human life, it would be like hearing the grass grow and the squirrel's heart beat, and we should die of that roar which lies on the other side of silence.' *Middlemarch* [1872], ed. Rosemary Ashton (London: Penguin, 1994), ch. 20, p. 194.

28 Robert Browning, *Mr Sludge, 'The Medium'*[1864], in *The Poems*, ed. John Pettigrew and Thomas J. Collins, 2 vols (Harmondsworth: Penguin, 1981), vol. 2, lines 1110–4, 1117 and 1122.

29 Gosse, *Evenings*, p. 393

30 *Ibid.*, pp. 392–4.

31 Gosse, *A Year at the Shore*, p. 325

32 *Blackwood's Edinburgh Magazine,* 80 (August 1856): 196.

33 William Wordsworth, *The Prelude* [1850], ed. M. H. Abrams, Stephen Gill and Jonathan Wordsworth (New York and London: Norton, 1979), vol. 2: 51 and 398–400.

34 *Blackwood's Edinburgh Magazine,* 80 (August 1856): 197.

35 *Blackwood's Edinburgh Magazine,* 82 (September 1857): 346–8.

36 *Ibid.*: 355.

37 *Ibid.*: 349. For Huxley's simplification of types, see note 21 above, and Desmond, *Huxley*, pp. 420–1.

38 *Blackwood's Edinburgh Magazine,* 82 (September 1857): 357.

39 *Ibid.*: 352 and 352 n.

40 *Ibid.*: 354.

41 *Ibid.*: 353.

42 *Ibid.*: 354.

43 *Sea-Side Studies*, p. 39.

44 *Ibid.*, p. 40.

45 *Blackwood's Edinburgh Magazine,* 82 (September 1857): 355n. For the epistemology of the experimental method, see Simon Schaffer, 'Where Experiments End: Tabletop Trials in Victorian Astronomy', in Jed Z. Buchwald (ed.), *Scientific Practice: Theories and Stories of Doing Physics* (Chicago, IL, and London: University of Chicago Press, 1995), pp. 257–99. Schaffer's rather unsatisfactory essay argues that in terms of experimental methodology there were two rival accounts of astronomical research, one attempting to measure external phenomena, the other attempting to reproduce the conditions of astronomical phenomena in the laboratory through tabletop experiment and instruments. The emphasis moved to calibrating and standardising mediating instruments and equipment rather than 'direct' research. Schaffer argues that different class-based networks favoured the different approaches. Here his argument becomes very sketchy. It may be that the appeal of the microscope was, firstly, the relative autonomy of the viewer, who could set up his own laboratory anywhere, and, secondly, the fact that the calibration of the instrument and the process of investigation were indivisible in microscopy, as the subject had to be literally present on the stage of the instrument for investigation to take place.

46 *The Complete Works of John Ruskin*, ed. E. T.Cook and A.Wedderburn, 39 vols (London: George Allen, 1903–12), vol. 24: *Decreation – Collected Studies of the Lapse of Waves and the Life of Stones* [1879], p. 114.

47 Ruskin, *Works*, vol. 4: *Modern Painters 2*, p. 158, note added in 1883.

48 Ruskin, *Works*, vol. 23: *Mornings in Florence* [1875–77], p. 329.

49 *Ibid.*

50 Ruskin, *Works*, vol. 25: *Prosepina*, p. 469

51 *Ibid.*

52 Ruskin, *Works*, vol. 4: *Modern Painters 2*, p. 158.

53 *The Correspondence of Charles Darwin*, ed. Frederick Burkhardt and Sydney Smith (Cambridge University Press, 1985–), vol. 3: 357 and 366.

54 *Ibid.*, vol. 2: 443.

55 Adrian Desmond and James Moore, *Darwin* (London: Michael Joseph, 1991), p. 357.

56 *Ibid.*

57 James, *Glasses*, p. 47. Subsequent references to this work will be given by page number parenthetically in the main text.

58 The most obvious psychological text to associate with this story is Freud's essay 'The Uncanny' (1919). Freud's equation of fear of damaged eyesight with fear of castration might well be related to the painter–narrator's over-determined fascination with sight. But this is a little banal. What is at stake is slightly different: the inability to possess someone else's act of *looking* and what, therefore, looking really is. See Sigmund Freud, 'The Uncanny', in *Art and Literature*, Penguin Freud Library, General Editor Angela Richards (London: Penguin Books, 1985), vol. 14: 352.

3

'Thinking blues': the memory of colour in nineteenth-century photography

~

LINDSAY SMITH

Consider for a little while what sort of a world it would be if all flowers were grey, all leaves black, and the sky *brown*. (John Ruskin[1])

It is necessary to visualise a world entirely without colour, that is to say, a photographic world. (Yevonde[2])

The clothes of my school days were grey, grey flannel shirts and suits. In the 1950s everyone wore grey, the purples and reds of the Coronation were enchanting – but we saw them in grey on our televisions. (Derek Jarman[3])

Ruskin's evocation in *Modern Painters 4* (1856) of a de-saturated and near-monochromatic world, made in the context of an argument privileging colourists over chiaroscurists and Turner over other modern painters, encapsulates the effects of industrialisation upon both social and psychic life in the nineteenth century. Perhaps more implicitly it also signals the impact of photography upon Victorian culture. In one sense an extreme and pessimistic speculation designed to prove that 'innocent things' appear in 'bright colour' (the dove's neck against the grey back of the viper), in another it registers highly subtle implications for larger visual and philosophical questions of the period.[4] Ruskin's call to the reader brings to the fore a type of visual disruption central to photographic discourse, but one that might easily get lost in more seemingly obvious ways of mapping the influence of the new photographic medium upon existing ways of reproducing the visible world.

With the invention and public announcement of the *daguerreotype* in France in 1839, quickly followed by Fox Talbot's negative/positive process in England, it was not just an idea of the faithful transcription of nature that photography revolutionised, but a conception of colour in the medium's reduction to monochrome of the rainbow's spectrum, of those 'sunrises, roses, violets, butterflies, birds, gold fish, rubies, opals and corals' that Ruskin opposes to 'alligators, hippopotami, lions, wolves, bears, swine, sharks, slugs, bones, fungi, fogs and corrupting, stinging, destroying things in general'.[5] Victorian viewers of photographs did not simply read the monochrome of photography as 'natural', they registered the absence of colour as a shortfall on the part of a medium otherwise miraculous in its verisimilitude. The world upon which Ruskin reflects is one made newly and oddly monochromatic. He asks the reader to imagine a landscape drained of colour because he wants to assert in more general terms that 'colour', arguably the most abstract quality of an object, is the most dependable index both of form and of an object's essential qualities. His distinction of 1856 suggests the conceptual distance necessary to a naturalisation of black and white.

Yet the comment that 'it is necessary to visualise a world entirely without colour, that is to say, a photographic world', made almost 100 years later by the British portrait photographer Madame Yevonde , a pioneer of the Vivex – dye transfer – colour process, demonstrates the difficulty of reclaiming that conceptual space. Yevonde's viewpoint reveals the fact that because of the predominance of monochromatic photography it has become necessary to make *black and white* strange once more. Colour, absent, so to speak, since the late 1830s, cannot be simply re-introduced to representation in the 1930s. More recently still, for the film-maker and writer Derek Jarman, reflecting upon the significance of colour in different periods and contexts of his life, the 1950s appears decisively monochromatic: *colour* inhabits a realm divorced from life. It is as if in Jarman's memory of that decade, 'colour' belongs only to moments of heightened experience, accessible temporarily through fantasy, since colour is lived primarily in the inadequate embodiment of its black and white representation on the screen.

In the nineteenth century, in the wake of the invention of photography, there occurs a repeated and somewhat urgent staging in representation of such a disjunction of colour to black and white. It is a staging that will be played out in the later cultural circumstances of Yevonde's and

Jarman's work, yet which, at the time of Ruskin's writing, is already prompting him to articulate larger concerns about the nature of representation. As Ruskin's art criticism bears witness, the implications for visual perception of a new monochromatic technology for representing the visible world extend far beyond the realm of photography itself. Indeed, the very inability of photography to produce colour embodies, in some ways as if for the first time, that larger and fundamental gap between representation and reality. For what we might think of as an inadequate relationship of photography to colour harks back to more general and age-old debates about the status of visual representation: meditations embodied in the visual sphere in historical moments of the triumph of *mimesis*.

In William Dyce's *Titian Preparing to Make His First Essay in Colouring*[6] (1856–57) (figure 3.1), a young boy sits in a rural garden setting contemplating a sculpture of the Madonna and Child that is positioned on the weathered stump of an old tree. His eyes look upwards to the artefact and his expression, together with his languid pose, arm resting on the back of the chair, suggests a mixture of childish abandon and an adult purposefulness. A profusion of cut flowers spills from a wicker basket at his feet. Too full to accommodate its lid, the basket draws the eye to a flask of water close by, the function of which will be to dilute the flower juices in order to make pigments. Red and pink roses, saffron and purple crocuses, along with blue irises mark out the landscape as simultaneously an early and a late spring one. Rather in the manner of the vivid flowers in Holman Hunt's *Rienzi*,[7] Dyce's blooms catch the eye for their colour and for the variety of their detail, forming as they do a chaotic area in the bottom left-hand corner of the composition and contrasting abruptly with the white marble of the statue. The story, from Carlo Ridolfi's 'Life of Titian',[8] is that as a child Titian used the juices from flowers to colour a drawing he had made of the Madonna and Child. Such was the intensity of the colours, Ridolfi claims, it suggested the boy's future direction as an artist who would aspire to a mastery of '*colorito*'. However, in alluding to Titian's introduction to colour in painting as an experience rooted not simply in nature but in the direct application to visual representation of nature's

3.1 William Dyce, *Titian Preparing to Make His First Essay in Colouring* (1856–57)

dyes, Dyce's painting is telling a more fundamental story about the birth of colour in representation. It is a belated account both on the part of Titian and of Dyce since historically the origins of colouring in painting are established long beforehand. But the tale is very interesting for the fact that, in allegorising Titian's particularity as a colourist, it seems to aspire to a more general narrative of beginnings.

While Dyce's story does not overtly represent a classical narrative of origins in the pervasive mould of those stories of Zeuxis and Parrashios, and their extremely lifelike paintings of grapes and a curtain, respectively, or, following Alberti's treatise *On Painting* (1425), of Narcissus as the

inventor of painting, it suggests such a story while simultaneously consti-
tuting an historically topical narrative in the mid-1850s.[9] Anchored in a
classical context, it is a narrative about the place and the effects of photography – a photography that cannot yet reproduce colour. The space
occupied in the painting by the starkly monochromatic sculpture is crucial in this respect, forming such a contrast to its natural surroundings,
and reminding us, as if in short hand, of the detachment from life of
monochromatic representation. A conceptual slippage between photography and painting here is invited, not only in the sense that, at the time
of the inception of photography, iconographically the medium was frequently depicted as an infant or a child figure (as the boy Titian is por-
trayed as creator here), in order to reflect its incipient status. But also
because, in contemplating the application of colour to representation, the
child 'Titian' in Dyce's painting comes to occupy an as yet unresolved
abstract space; that which articulates the difficulty of the application of
colour to photographs. It is as if in this mid-nineteenth-century depiction
of the great Venetian colourist we find represented the lush plants (primarily in their anticipated incarnation as petal juices) of nineteenth-century photographic experiments in reproducing colour; the tools, for
example, of Sir John Herschel's many experiments in colour photography.
Titian's preparation for his 'first essay in colouring' emerges from a profound sense of the physicality of colour as an element extracted, or
pressed directly, from plants. In that sense, the painting is predicting, or
describing, in terms of its own represented historical moment, processes
of experimentation in photography. But, Dyce is also, and perhaps most
importantly, bringing to the fore the chemical fixing of the physical trace,
the 'photographicness' of photography as a pressed relation to the object,
as in the case of the contact print (or for Roland Barthes in the manner
of the death mask), rather than simply as a method of inscription, or
drawing.

Titian Preparing to Make His First Essay in Colouring represents the
introduction to Titian of colour as a highly physical and a potentially
overwhelming experience. In more general terms, Dyce's painting
assumes the status of a memorial to classical tales of the origins of colour
in painting as articulated by Pliny in *The Natural History*. Pliny discusses

colour in relationship to dyes from flowers and herbs, 'the craft and mystery of dyeing cloth, to challenge the fairest flowers in the garden, and to match, if not to surpass, the lively colours of Nature's setting',[10] and he dwells upon what he calls 'the monstrous device' of 'a new kind of artificial colouring and [dyeing] of lilies': 'a strange and wonderful matter, that any root should take a tincture so deep, as to bring forth a flower of the same dye and colour'.[11] In the thirty-fifth book of his *Natural History,* on 'discurseth of painting, colour and painters', Pliny gives an example of the origin of colour in representation. The Corinthian Cleophantus is identified as the first painter 'that took upon him to paint with colour' by using 'a piece of red potsherd, which he ground into a powder'.[12] But by introducing 'red' into painting in this way, Cleophantus remains within a paradigm of what Pliny calls 'monochromaton, that is to say, a portrait of one colour'. Yet, in the twenty-first book of *The Natural History*, which 'treateth of flowers and garlands', Pliny alludes to polychrome, citing the relationship, more crucial to my purposes in its bearing upon visual representation, of 'the artist and the Flower-Girl', otherwise the Sicyonians, *Pausias*, 'the cunning painter', and *Glycera*, 'the artificial maker' of 'garlands' and 'chaplets' from flowers:[13]

> This painter [Pausias] was wonderfully enamoured upon the said *Glycera*, and courted her by all means that he could devise: among the rest, he would seem to counterfeit and represent lively with his pencil in colours, what flowers soever she wrought and set with her fingers into garlands; and she again strived to change and alter her handiwork every day, for to drive him to a non-plus at the length, or at leastwise, to put him to his shifts; insomuch, as it was a very pleasant and worthy sight, to behold of one side the works of Nature in the woman's hand, and on the other side the artificial cunning of the foresaid painter. And verily there are at this day to be seen diverse painted tables of his workmanship: and namely, one picture above the rest, entitled Stephanoplocos, wherein he painted his sweetheart *Glycera*, twisting and braiding coronets and chaplets, as her manner was.[14]

Pausias's workmanship, driven by his desire for Glycera, results in a direct correlation of the flowers of nature 'artificially wreathed into garlands' with their representation in painting. In a further reference to Pausias, Pliny stresses the fact that it is in the artist's depiction of flowers, his desire to 'imitate with his pencil [Glycera's] handiwork', that he achieves an expression of the 'variety' of those flowers by way of a particularly fine use of 'a number of colours'.[15] It was in so using polychrome, directly measurable for its verisimilitude against the colours of the actual cut flowers that, Pliny maintains, Pausias 'brought the art [of painting] to wonderful perfection in that point'. The flower, perhaps more than any other natural object, is known by (and thus must be principally represented by) its colours. There is here a convergence of colour and object whereby the one (colour) is not extricable from the object (flower) which it determines.

While less striking than many of Pliny's stories of painters, such as that of Apelles for example, the story of Pausias and Glycera is significant for the way in which colour emerges in the context of male desire and in a competition between 'the works of Nature in the woman's hand' and 'the artificial cunning of the painter'. The ultimate test of his prowess lies in Pausias's ability to depict the infinite variety of the colours of flowers, yet he is urged on to such heights of artistic achievement by Glycera's wish 'to drive him to a non-plus' by means of her own creations. In its account of rivalry and entwined desire for sovereignty in the representation of nature's pigments, the tale contrasts two types of artifice: the wreathing and combining of actual flowers into head-dresses, and the counterfeiting in representation of those garlands and chaplets. The flowers that Pausias paints are already removed from nature to form parts of decorative objects. It is above all the truth of their colours, in their incomparable variety, that he strives to represent.

The story thereby sets up a matching of two methods of workmanship in which flowers, and their dyes as made manifest in the pigments of the painter, occupy the central role. Returning to Dyce's painting, *Titian's First Essay in Colouring* we find an equally persistent, though newly defined, emphasis on flowers as representative of colour more generally, and of the power of colour in representation. More emphatically, though, Dyce's painting, in so powerfully articulating a movement from the three dimensionality of the monochromatic sculpture, to the two-dimensional format of Titian's drawing book, partially obscured by the flowers that will colour it, encapsulates the very process of photography. In the manner of a drawing from a three-dimensional form, whose spatial short-fall in its translation of three into two dimensions might be considered redeemable by the addition of colour, the flattening of volume and the reduction in size of an object by photography, though to some extent equally compensated for by an extreme verisimilitude, are finally only compounded in their deficiency by the absolute failure of photography to harness colour *naturally*. Moreover, in Dyce's painting, the sculpture of the Madonna and Child stands in for photography – as that form of representation from nature rendered abstract by its lack of colour – that incomplete, or intermediate, stage of representation which can but suggest *mimesis* even with its glaring lack of coloration. The juxtaposition of the icon with the landscape emphasises both the very specialised representational status of the statue and also its inadequacy in terms of colour. The sculpture is present, in Dyce's narrative, to invite the occasion of its colouring, just as a monochromatic photograph, by its very absence of polychrome, alludes to that very deficiency each time it is seen. Such a connection is strengthened by knowledge of Dyce's fervent interest in the historical circumstances of coloured sculpture in churches. For in exposing a pervasive misconception and pointing out that early sculpture was in fact coloured, implicitly Dyce makes possible another kind of story for photography. It is a story in which, from the first, the monochrome of nineteenth-century photography, in addition to receiving the rather obvious embellishment of hand tinting, undergoes more subtle and profound forms of modification. By ingenious means, distinct from those of a surface application of polychrome, practitioners undermined the authority of monochromatic photography and made it represent coloration. One might go so far as to say that they made it do so by activating a type of unconscious for the photograph.

As a narrative about photography displaced to a familiar story about the Venetian master of colour, we encounter in Dyce's *Titian* a visible anticipation of the problem for photography of the colouring of objects. Ruskin admired Dyce's painting, praising its 'sculpturesque sense of grace in form'.[16] Yet, although he welcomed Dyce's reference to Titian's exemplary achievement as a colourist, Ruskin criticised Dyce's own colour as insufficiently Venetian. He also took issue with Dyce's depiction of the statue in 'the delicate-leaved twilight of a lowland garden', claiming that, detached from its context, such a sculpture would not have 'first made [Titian] dream of the Madonna', 'but rather [of] some fresco of a wayside chapel where she stood with her hands folded, and the moon under her feet, and the companions of heaven around her, crown above crown, circlet beyond circlet, – gleaming golden in the arched shade'.[17] For Ruskin, the Madonna as shown by Dyce, divorced from a naturalised and intimate symbolic context, would not hold the power to move the young artist. Yet the awkward presence of the colourless icon in the garden, itself displaced from its ecclesiastical context, precisely evokes the potential liberation of colour from line, form and perspective; an emphasis evidenced by the fresco painting of Giotto that Dyce had studied. It is a setting free from those systematic elements of visual representation of which Julia Kristeva writes in 'Giotto's Joy'.[18] Significantly, such a differently inflected and liberating relationship of colour to painting theorised here by Dyce, and demonstrated previously by Giotto, occupies a rather precarious and a difficult, historical space. As Kristeva writes:

> The symbolic necessity, or the interdiction laid down by colour, are never absolute. Contrary to delineated *form* and *space*, as well as to *drawing* and *composition* subjected to the strict codes of representation and verisimilitude, colour enjoys considerable freedom. The colour scale, apparently restricted by comparison with the infinite variation of forms and figures, is accepted as the very domain of whim, taste, and serendipity in daily life as much as in painting. If, nevertheless, the interplay of colours follows a particular historical necessity (the chromatic code accepted in Byzantine painting is not the same as that of the Renaissance) as well as the internal rules of a given painting (or any device whatsoever), still such a necessity is weak and includes its own transgression (the impact of instinctual drive) at the very moment it is imposed and applied.[19]

For Kristeva, colour enjoys a certain waywardness in spite of its circumscription by particular pictorial laws at different historical periods. Although subject to specific 'chromatic codes', there is a sense in which *colour* remains the most enigmatic element of a painting, the element least reducible to language. This enigma is important in the sense that photography is often understood to confirm the surety of geometrical perspective in the realm of the visible, but here it is as if the one blind spot of photography – colour – is always there to haunt it and to fracture that surety. The return of the repressed (so to speak) in such a context would be the return of colour long since so artfully accommodated, or so it would appear, by the seamless transparency of black and white.

Kristeva's account of Giotto's 'blue' allows us to reconsider Vasari's motive, for example, in his 'Life' of Titian, in feeling obliged to explain the painter's sovereignty over colour as simultaneously a shortcoming. In one respect, such a reaction brings to the fore a long-established distinction between drawing and colouring. By emphasising Titian's copying of 'natural objects', 'as best he knew how with colours' and 'tinting them with the crude and soft colours that Nature displays, without making preliminary drawings',[20] Vasari draws attention to the artist's lack of training in draughtsmanship as a block to the imagination, and to the requirement that, in order to privilege colour over line in such a way, Titian must always have the actual object before him. In Vasari's estimate, Titian's supremacy in matters of colour thereby makes him somewhat culpable since it suggests too close a tie to nature and a restriction of the artist's imaginative faculties. Yet, Lodovico Dolce's *Dialogo Della Pittura* of 1557, a response to Vasari and an apologia for Titian, argues the opposite view, privileging colour over drawing.[21] In maintaining that since contours of objects are themselves abstractions, and that nature is perceived in colour and tone, above all else successful artistic *imitation* must be based on colour. Dolce thus anticipates Ruskin's argument which, as we have seen, asserts *colour* as the principal index of form. With a similar sentiment, in Dyce's painting, celebrating Titian's achievement as a colourist, the idealised and glaringly monochromatic sculpture appears very much at variance with the hues that are to be extracted for dyes from the surrounding flowers. The presence of polychrome and the status of colour more generally seem to be the most important aspects of Dyce's picture. In such a way, Dyce questions the simple acceptance of black and white (monochrome) in representation as invariably natural. He opens up a space in which to re-formulate that which, by the mid-nineteenth century, had become a newly pressing issue: the very absence of colour in visual representation as laid bare by photography.

The inability of early photography to reproduce colour was a fundamental condition that led early practitioners to question the empirical status of the medium. Colour had been from the first crucial to early experiments in photography and to the pre-history of the medium. Indeed, photography was conceived, first of all, in colour, as early processes, and in particular that of the cyanotype, demonstrate. Sir John Herschel, celebrated scientist and coiner of many photographic nomenclatures including the word 'photography' itself, invented the cyanotype process outlining his discovery in his Royal Society essay of 1842.[22] The direct positive process of the cyanotype, by which the distinctive colouring of prussian blue is formed in the paper, was one of many processes and striking effects to result from early photochemical experiments, reminding us that early experimentation with colour formed an integral part of the pre-history of the photographic medium. Early photographic processes resulted in multiple monochromatic schemes, which were not simply reducible to the black and white used to describe pre-polychromatic photography. We recognise in Herschel's comments not only the legacy in colour of the black and white photograph, but the fact that when colour was invented it had the quality of a return to what had been regarded as those early potentialities of the medium. We find many experiments by Herschel, predating those with prussian blue, which suggest, in their concern for the effects given by different processes of fixing and washing out, an avid quest for colour in early photography. Recalling Pliny's discussion of dyes obtained from flowers and herbs, Herschel had been engaged during 1841 in employing juices from the petals of flowers, making hundreds of experiments in the bleaching effects of sunlight on flower juices, discovering that dyes extracted with alcohol from petals frequently produced colours different from those of the petals themselves. His method of superimposing different coloured layers with sensitivities to different primary colours produced some remarkably vivid and stable colour photographs. The Chrysotype is one such example, which gave vivid purple-coloured photographs, but did not become popular.

The cyanotype by contrast, which, rather than vegetable juices, used iron salts, was a monochromatic process distinguished by its intense blue colouring. The architectural blueprint is the sole remaining legacy of the process. The monochromatic blue of the cyanotype – and those particular theoretical issues it raises – allows us to question anew the effect of photography upon colour perception, but more importantly, perhaps, to re-think larger questions of representation that come to the fore in those philosophical and scientific debates around photography's invention. Herschel's incredible blue process provided the means by which the first photographically illustrated book was produced and, pre-dating Fox Talbot's celebrated *The Pencil of Nature* which began to appear in instalments in June 1844, it was made by a woman.[23] In October 1843 Anna Atkins (1799–1871) published *Part I of Photographs of British Algae: Cyanotype Impressions*, which ran to a ten-year span, thereby applying Herschel's process to scientific book illustrations. A keen botanist and the daughter of the scientist John George Children, Atkins took up the cyanotype process specifically in order to document specimens of algae she had collected. 'Each part [of the book] contained a number of plates that were contact prints from specimens of algae', and Atkins's motivation for using Herschel's process resulted from a desire to record minutiae which might be missed by other media. Her methods of producing cyanotypes from the seaweeds were, in their own ways, as painstaking as Herschel's chemical researches. She had to prepare thousands of sheets of cyanotype paper by hand, and 'hundreds of various and delicate specimens of algae had to be made ready, washed and arranged and dried. Each sheet took its turn in the sun, was washed, dried and flattened. Then the plates had to be collated and sewn together'.[24] Those photograms provided by the cyanotype give silhouettes, but they also lend an incomparable transparency to the objects reproduced: the fragility of seaweed and its differing levels of thickness are rendered as indelible as the creases in the clothing of a human photographic subject. The photographic process itself facilitates a sort of *seeing through* the object that, like a single-cell thick specimen prepared for a microscopic slide, invites a correspondence between the revelatory eye of a microscope and that of the camera.

I have written elsewhere about the implications for memory and for concepts of presence and absence, of Atkins's use of the monochromatic cyanotype. More recently I have considered the way in which in the 1930s, when colour photography becomes for the first time a real possibility, Madame Yevonde recreates the peculiar *monochromatic blue* of the cyanotype.[25] It is perhaps most significant that Yevonde wants to re-visit Herschel's intense blue process in the 1930s by recreating its effects, manufacturing such distinctive monochrome with materials of her day at a time when polychromatic photography is a new possibility. In her portrait, *Mrs Anthony Eden as the Muse of History*, from 'The Goddess Series' of 1935, for example, we find an incredible twinning, in monochromatic blue, of the human figure with the classical bust.[26] The monochromatic uniformity of the whole has the effect of visually correlating the human figure with the classical sculpture, of playing up their similarity as lent by the monochromatic blue itself. Similarly, in *Eileen Hunter as Dido*, the colour *blue* is used to forge a connection between the classically posed woman and the fragments of plaster casts, so that we are made to re-evaluate the position of colour more generally in Western systems of representation.

It is certain that Yevonde alludes to Herschel's cyanotype in these striking blue portraits created with the application to the lens of blue cellophane. In her lecture on women's contribution to the history of photography, delivered in Paris in 1936, Yevonde refers not only to Victorian women photographers such as Julia Margaret Cameron but to prominent nineteenth-century scientists and to the experiments of Herschel and Thomas Wedgwood.[27] In her creation of monochromatic blue, Yevonde was effectively applying cyan to the portrait, precisely that genre to which commentators maintain it could not be successfully applied. She is making her audience confront, as if for the first time, the abstraction of black and white, the partiality of its history in a wider history of polychromatic photography. In so doing, Yevonde is dramatising that what is lost in black and white may be suggested in the abstract sovereignty of 'blue'. She is making the viewer aware that monochrome is not monochrome or, as Kristeva has written in 'Giotto's Joy':'Within the distribution of colour, when black and white are present, they too are colours; that is to say, instinctual/diacritical/representational condensations.'[28]

The possibility of colour in 1935, as explored in Yevonde's self-consciously monochromatic portraits, restores to black and white photography those early nineteenth-century responses which could not but focus upon its artificiality. Between Herschel's invention of the cyanotype and the opposition to Yevonde's use of colour in portraiture there exists the complex and strategic naturalisation of black and white photography. A type of forgetting of colour has had to occur in the interim; a relatively brief, though nonetheless significant, amnesia. An ability to see the world in monochrome requires a reading of black and white as transparent; that reading is simultaneously the means by which we arrive at a supplementary relationship of colour to photography. In such a context, Yevonde's recasting of the cyanotype, as self-consciously fabricated in polychrome, questions the representational status of the photograph when historically it need no longer present a monochromatic image; when in fact it may reproduce a rainbow's spectrum. Yevonde's photographs play upon a consciousness of colour as supplementary to the photographic image, re-instating a profound awareness of that which is at stake in the naturalisation of black and white. These photographs also take us back to, and newly figure, the significance in the nineteenth century of the inability to represent *blue* photographically. The case of colour makes the viewer self-conscious, as if for the first time reading monochrome as a form of transparency.

If we merely accept that in the nineteenth century viewers of monochrome disregarded its explicit abstraction with regard to colour, that, for example, in employing the blue of the cyanotype to record algae, Atkins simply offered the most adequate match of subject to medium, what we occlude is the production by photographic representation of a specific relation to an absent object, a relation which, by definition, involves a particular condition of *dissimilarity* to a referent. Stephen Bann alludes to such a condition in *The True Vine*, referring to Roger Fenton's photographic 'still lifes' in terms of their 'comparative failure' to represent their referents.[29] Recalling Georges Didi-Huberman's 'inventive use of the theological notion of the "figure dissemblable"', Bann explores the 'figure' which, in the special circumstances of Christian art, is acclaimed as an adequate representation precisely because of its dissimilarity to its referent. Bann cites Didi-Huberman in order to register the practice of 'writing about painting' as 'inevitably' a 'figure of dissimilarity', rather than as an example of a practice that 'presuppose[s] a kind of congruity between the appearance of the work itself and the rhetorical processes used to describe it'.[30] By extension, the absolute representational inadequacy of photography with regard to colour renders the medium a consummate means of representing absent qualities. While a type of unconscious root-edness of the colour *blue* in a history of colour symbolism might be thought to prevent it from attaining the abstraction or inadequacy born of a dissimilarity to a referent, following this argument, any monochro-matic scheme would thereby constitute 'a figure dissemblable', or this type of failure. In the event, when referring to the congruence with their sub-ject matter of Atkins's cyanotypes, that blue is the perfect colour with which to represent algae, critics are too busy looking for congruity to identify the fundamental incongruence out of which photographic mean-ing is generated. Prior to the invention of photography, *blue* and white and *black* and white would equally constitute 'figures dissemblables' since both would manifest a dissimilarity to a referent. To consider thus the status of the colour *blue* provokes a need to explore further the place of colour in nineteenth-century photography.

There is, then, an important, if oblique, relationship between the cyanotype and the process of combination printing, the photographic technique which surfaced in the 1850s. The method of combination printing, the production of a print from more than one negative, provides a significant starting-point from which to pursue these concerns. Its rela-tionship to the cyanotype is evident in a shared investment in the sover-eignty of blue, both in the position of *blue* in colour theory and more generally in the history of Western art. In early photography the sky pre-sented a particular aesthetic and technical problem. Collodion emulsion was overly sensitive to blue light, to the blue parts of the spectrum. The bleaching out of skies by the collodion process, and by the narrow depth of field of early lenses, led to the creation of the technique of combina-tion or double printing, the production of a photographic image from more than one negative. Since, if a landscape were to be given sufficient exposure time it would result in a flat white sky, awkward in a photo-graphic composition, two negatives were often taken: a short exposure to record the sky and a longer one for the landscape. On the surface, photographic prints produced from combined negatives seem to hold little bearing on the phenomenon of colour. Yet since this photographic method was designed first and foremost to preserve *sky* by aspiring to a *faithful* representation of skies, combination printing (because it could not represent the colour of the sky) came to signal that very colour of the sky as a quality somehow exempt from measurement by a criterion of faithful representation. A method of photography thus designed to combat the technical inadequacies of early lenses that resulted in the effective loss of skies, combination printing emerges equally, we might say, to preserve the sky's blueness. From the time of the invention of the medium of photography, photographers clearly wanted to harness colour, as the cyanotype bears witness. But when, after a great deal of experimentation, it became clear that monochrome would be popular in spite of its inadequate rendition of colour, photographers found ways, within monochromatic schemes, of preserving colour. The most obvious of these was the practice of tinting. But I suggest that of those other less overt, more abstract, ways of registering a legacy of colour, perhaps the most curious, and the least likely, was that of combination printing.

In larger terms, combination printing thereby situates colour as a means by which photography eludes – by definition will always elude – a straightforward identification with realism. It is as if, then, the combined photographic print represents the material blueness of the sky that cannot be captured, that the cyanotype blue is standing in for Goethe's blue which draws us after it, or for Turner's sky as 'not blue colour merely' but 'blue fire' which 'cannot be painted'. 'The sky is not flat dead colour', declares Ruskin in *Modern Painters 1*, writing of Turner's skies, 'but a deep quivering, transparent body of penetrable air, in which you trace or imagine short, falling spots of deceiving light, and dim shades, faint veiled vestiges of dark vapour.'[31]

That blue remains an emotive colour for writers, photographers and film-makers should not surprise us; nor should the historical focus placed by practitioners upon blue skies. It appears that photographers need to register as lost something much greater than that which can be suggested pictorially at this point by representation, namely those transgressive elements in vision not directly reducible to language.

One such transgressive element is made manifest in the curious example of an aberrant effect to which Mark Haworth-Booth has drawn attention.[32] In the *daguerreotype* by the British photographer Horatio Ross (1801–86) *Hoddy and John Munro Fishing at Flaipool* (1847), we find the striking presence of a blue arch of sky the colour of which tinges, as if by its reflection, the water below. Haworth-Booth includes the image in his study, not only as a prototype for the later candour of the snapshot but for the very fact that the sky is oddly blue in an otherwise brown-toned *daguerreotype*. The *blue* is not the result of tinting but rather, as Haworth-Booth notes, 'a happy optical accident'.[33] For a phenomenon of solarisation occurs when there exists a high level of contrast in a subject, and 'the brighter tone can reverse, in this case into a natural blue'.

The effect of the sky is striking in this *daguerreotype*, all the more so for the fact that we have learned to disassociate colour from photographic images of this type – learned to read monochrome as transparent, that is. But the presence of colour is notable here also because, in learning to do so, we have repressed rather than simply forgotten certain fundamental qualities of visual experience and of representation. These are qualities that all photographs have immediate access to, not simply by their chemical origins, but by their suggestion of a type of unconscious for themselves. It is an unconscious echoing Benjamin's use of the term (rather than Rosalind Krauss's particular reading of Benjamin) that indicates an aspect of a photograph that is not declared but rather is present or accessible through accidents or through tricks. Nonetheless, this aspect of the medium has a coherence, an internal logic underlying its 'conscious' or more visibly organised one.

Taking the above 'happy accident' of solarisation which puts the sky back for us where it should be and, in so doing, jars us to remember what we have lost of its liquid infinity in blueness, we can read combination prints as a more subtle form of this effect. Or, put differently, we might reflect upon a combined photograph as containing such a 'happy accident' in a latent state. For, in aspiring to retain a certain *truth* of skies, combination prints contain, within their odd juxtapositions of tonally intense skies (that are equally as intense as the landscapes or seascapes that they frame) a reminder of what it is those separate parts of the print are standing in for, aesthetically, optically and unconsciously. In this respect, it would appear far from accidental that it is the blue part of the spectrum with which photography has so much trouble. Most difficult for the medium of photography is the colour most heavily invested with meaning in Western systems of representation; that colour 'blue' which, with the advent of photography, must itself come to stand for the larger absence of polychrome in early photographic representation.

Combination photographs, in the manner of the example of the *daguerreotype* with blue sky, tap into an unconscious sense, not of that which has been lost but of that which has been only forgotten, and whose absence pricks us violently once we recall it. As Wittgenstein so effectively demonstrates, we read colour into monochromatic photographs, such that in a black and white photograph of a boy with blond hair, hair *is* blond.[34] But in so doing we also fail to see colour in these same photographic places (the boy's blond hair is simultaneously shades of photographic grey) so that when colour is put there, as in the *daguerreotype* with blue sky, it leaves a monumental mark. Most significantly, perhaps, as a vehicle for remembering – and forgetting – colour comes to stand for an entire process rather than simply a phenomenon. As viewers we become aware of more than simply the fact that we have learned to read photography without colour. In its return to visual representation, so to speak, *colour* brings back with it much more than was lost, which is reciprocally much more than we might have understood ourselves to have forgotten.

Notes

1 John Ruskin, *The Complete Works of John Ruskin*, ed. E. T. Cook and A. Wedderburn, 39 vols (London: George Allen, 1903–12), vol. 6: *Modern Painters 4*: 68.
2 Yevonde, *In Camera* (London: Trinity Press, 1940), p. 185.
3 Derek Jarman, *Chroma: A Book of Colour – June '93* (London: Century, 1994), p. 53.
4 Ruskin, *Works*, vol. 6: 68.
5 *Ibid.*
6 William Dyce (1806–64) first exhibited his *Titian Preparing to Make His First Essay in Colouring* at the Royal Academy in 1857. In a long review of the

exhibition Ruskin pronounced Dyce's painting 'the only one quite up to the high-water mark of Pre-Raphaelitism in the exhibition this year' (*Works*, vol. 14: 98). He also forewarned a mid-Victorian audience: 'it will take about an hour to see this painting properly' (*Works*, vol. 14: 100).

7　*Rienzi Vowing to Obtain Justice for the Death of His Young Brother, Slain in a Skirmish between the Colonna and Orsini Factions* (1848–49) was exhibited at the Royal Academy in 1849. It was William Holman Hunt's first painting to be exhibited bearing the PRB insignia.

8　Carlo Ridolfi, 'Life of Titian', *Le Maraviglie dell' Arte* (Marvels of Art) (1648).

9　For one of the best accounts of the myths of Zeuxis and of Narcissus, see Stephen Bann, *The True Vine: On Visual Representation and the Western Tradition* (Cambridge: Cambridge University Press, 1989).

10　Pliny, *Selections from* The History of the World, *commonly called The Natural History of C. Plinius Secundus*, trans. Philemon Holland, selected by Paul Turner (London: Centaur Press, 1962), p. 191.

11　*Ibid.*, p. 190.

12　*Ibid.*, p. 400.

13　*Ibid.*, p. 188.

14　*Ibid.*

15　*Ibid.*, p. 425.

16　Ruskin, *Works*, vol. 14: 98.

17　*Ibid.*: 99.

18　Julia Kristeva, 'Giotto's Joy', in Kristeva, *Desire in Language: A Semiotic Approach to Literature and Art*, ed Leon S. Rondiez, trans. Thomas Gora, Alice Jardine and Leon S. Rondiez (Oxford: Blackwell, 1980), pp. 210–36.

19　*Ibid.*, pp. 220–1.

20　Giorgio Vasari, *Lives of the Most Eminent Painters* (London: Allen Lane, 1978).

21　Lodovico Dolce, *Dialogo Della Pittura* (1557), in M. Roskill (ed.), *Dolce's 'Aretino' and Venetian Art Theory of the Cinquecento* (New York: New York University Press, 1968).

22　For an examination of Herschel's experiments in colour in the context of his working relationship with William Henry Fox Talbot, see Larry Schaaf, *Out of the Shadows: Herschel, Talbot and the Invention of Photography* (New Haven, CT, and London: Yale University Press, 1992).

23　A. A. (Anna) Atkins, *Photographs of British Algae: Cyanotype Impressions* (Halstead Place, Sevenoaks: privately published, 1843–53), 3 vols.

24　Cited in Schaaf, *Out of the Shadows*, p. 131.

25　See Lindsay Smith, *The Politics of Focus: Women, Children and Nineteenth-Century Photography* (Manchester: Manchester University Press, 1998), and 'Photographic Portraiture and the Forgetting of Colour', *Journal of European Studies*, 30 (2000): 191–210.

26 Yevonde produced her series for the exhibition 'Goddesses and Others' that opened in July 1935 in the photographer's studio in Berkeley Square. For Yevonde's own account of the event and her opinions on colour portraiture more generally, see her *In Camera*.
27 *Ibid.*, p. 269.
28 Kristeva, 'Giotto's Joy', p. 222.
29 Bann, *The True Vine*, p. 19.
30 *Ibid.*, pp. 19–20.
31 Ruskin, *Works*, vol. 3: 345.
32 Mark Haworth-Booth, *Photography: An Independent Art* (London: V&A Publications, 1997).
33 *Ibid.*, p. 18.
34 Ludwig Wittgenstein, *Remarks on Colour*, ed. G. E. M. Anscombe, trans. Linda McAlister and Margaret Schattle (Berkeley and Los Angeles: University of California Press, 1978), section 117: 31e.

4

Cross-cultural encounters: the co-production of science and literature in mid-Victorian periodicals

‿

PAUL WHITE

In chapter 32 of Dickens's *Bleak House*, investigators enter the home of the eccentric inebriate Mr Krook, and discover unmistakable evidence of a strange and remarkable death:

> Here is a small burnt patch of flooring; here is the tinder from a little bundle of burnt paper … and here … is it the cinder of a small charred and broken log of wood …? O Horror, he is here!
> […]
>
> Call the death by any name … say it might have been prevented how you will, it is the same death … inborn, inbred, engendered in the corrupted humours of the vicious body itself, and that only – Spontaneous Combustion, and none other of all the deaths that can be died.[1]

Bleak House was first published in monthly parts, beginning in March 1852. When the account of Mr Krook's death appeared in the December 1852 instalment, objections were raised in the *Leader*, a weekly journal of politics and literature. The author of these objections was George Lewes, who had founded the journal with Thornton Hunt in 1850 and now edited the literary section, including a regular column on the progress of science. Lewes criticised Dickens for lending credence to a vulgar belief which had no scientific basis, and which he supposed Dickens must have picked up from reading novels.[2]

Indeed, a number of literary precedents existed for Krook's unusual death, such as in Frederick Marryat's *Jacob Faithful* (1834).[3] But in the next instalment of *Bleak House*, Dickens cited testimony, not from the world of fiction but from the Royal Society's *Philosophical Transactions*, from works on medical jurisprudence and from documented cases, all of which bore witness to the currency in scientific and learned circles of the theory of spontaneous combustion.[4] Called to testify at the coroner's inquest, the witnesses in the fictional Krook case confirmed the intemperate habits of the deceased, and the foetid effluvia that seeped from his premises on the evening of his death; while outside the court, men of science and philosophy discoursed on inflammable gases and phosphoretted hydrogen.

Lewes, however, remained unconvinced. If Dickens's evidence was not purely fictional, neither was it creditably scientific. In two lengthy letters to Dickens published in the *Leader*, Lewes condemned Dickens's authorities as men of 'art' and 'erudition', not of science: 'a man may be a giant among verbs "in [Greek]" yet a child among oxides and anhydrous acids', and so 'an error exploded from science, but one peculiarly adapted to the avid credulity of unscientific minds, has been seriously taken up by you, and sent all over the world with your imprimatur – an act which will tend to perpetuate the error in spite of the labours of a thousand philosophers'.[5] Displaying his own knowledge of the most recent European chemistry and physiology, Lewes countered Dickens's authorities with his own, citing, in particular, the work of Justus von Liebig on the material composition of the body. By defending the esoteric works of those whom he considered experts, Lewes tried to position himself as a scientific authority in the public sphere of print, and thereby to condemn the fiction writer's courting of public ignorance through style and dramatic effect.

Contrary to Lewes's remarks, however, Dickens had taken steps to assure a 'responsible' representation of science in Lewes's sense. His account of Krook's death was rehearsed in a piece that had appeared eighteen months earlier, in his recently launched journal *Household Words*. Here a young Harry Wilkinson lectured his uncle Bagges on the striking similarities between the human body and a taper: the body's fuel, like that of a candle, was continuously combusted through the action of oxygen, leading to the production of heat, and the exhalation of carbonic acid. Lewes's scientific authority, Liebig, appeared in the cast of characters; his pronouncements on the rate at which a human body consumed charcoal prompted the question of whether such bodies were liable to inflame occasionally: 'It is said ... that spontaneous combustion does happen sometimes; particularly in great spirit drinkers. I don't see why it should not, if the system were to become too inflammable. Drinking alcohol would be likely to load the constitution with carbon, which would be fuel for the fire.'[6] The material for this homily on chemistry and temperance had been drawn from lectures given at the Royal Institution by Michael Faraday. Apparently impressed by the 'beautiful simplicity and clearness' of Faraday's public demonstrations, Dickens had requested and received from the philosopher the notes for his lectures on the chemistry of a candle.[7]

Depending on what they chose to depict as natural, and to whom they allocated authority over the natural, periodical writers could shape the meaning of science considerably for large segments of the Victorian reading public. The question of representing science responsibly was particularly acute for scientific practitioners because of the universality of their claims to truth. Above and beyond the public sphere of the periodical, scientific practitioners had long relied on a social sphere that was highly circumscribed and policed: the scientific society and the laboratory were private sanctums in which uncertainties could be resolved before knowledge was made public.[8] The demonstrations by Faraday and others at the Royal Institution were highly orchestrated affairs. The laboratory was ostensibly opened to a select audience and experiments performed after their results were already certain.[9]

The account of combustion in *Household Words* made it possible to re-perform the reverential, transparent and character-building science of the Royal Institution in a domestic setting, through the activity of reading. Such homely, familiar accounts had disturbing implications. They held out the possibility that science could be communicated to a non-specialised readership – and, if communicated, then understood, practised and criticised outside the domains occupied by expert practitioners. As Helen Small has shown, Dickens's own dramatic readings from his novels threatened to democratise the process of participation and witnessing to a degree that contemporaries found dangerous.[10] The mid-Victorian periodical, in which Lewes's criticisms were aired, was regarded by review writers and editors as an instrument for the enlightenment and consolidation of a vast public – a reading audience that was increasingly conceived of as a real or potential citizenry – and whose ability to recognise and delegate authority had to be shaped. The ability of authors to maintain authority was a particularly troubling problem in science, which was widely presented as a truly universal knowledge from which all classes would benefit and to which any person irrespective of class could contribute.[11] The periodical was thus a highly important, if volatile, medium for the negotiation of scientific authority outside of the restricted sphere of specialist journals, societies and laboratories. As I show in what follows, Lewes's very role as a critic of scientific literature placed his authority in question – for was such a critic a 'man of science' or a 'man of letters'? Conversely, at the level of literature, distant from the sites and sources of authority of scientific practice, how were the claims of specialists to retain a different status from those of other writers?

For several decades now, accounts of science and literature in the Victorian period have been informed by assumptions about a single, overarching culture embracing and subsuming differences of profession and specialism.[12] These assumptions have drawn support from discourse models of intellectual history on the one hand, and from a range of contextualist approaches to science on the other.[13] The Victorian periodical, in which specialist scientific material famously appeared alongside works of history, drama, and fiction, might be taken to epitomise this unitary culture.[14] Although approaches that emphasise a common scientific and literary culture have proven enormously fruitful, the position articulated most famously by C. P. Snow is still prevalent in certain circles, as manifested in the recent 'science wars'.[15] Snow's 'two cultures' model remains operative in current realist assertions that science provides an account of the world which is independent of the form in which it is expressed. The main function of this chapter is to explore how the location of expert participation in science was established, and how critical commentary on science by practitioners from the humanities was invalidated. This argument to some degree problematises both views by showing how, in a continuous world of print, writers sought to differentiate themselves and their enterprises, recruit authority and fashion different sorts of publics. If debates about the existence of one or more intellectual cultures still seem

meaningful today, it is partly because the boundaries of scientific and literary culture were drawn in the Victorian period precisely in order to sustain
such views. The existence of a single culture was asserted by intellectual
elites who sought authority through the control of culture. Within that
over-arching culture, incommensurable accounts of the relations between
science and literature were fashioned and have persisted to this day.

The *Leader*'s column on the progress of science was relatively new terri-
tory for Lewes. From the early 1840s he had been an aspiring novelist,
playwright and actor, performing for several years in a theatrical troupe
under Dickens's direction.[16] He was also a full-time journalist, writing
regularly for the *Westminster Review* and concentrating chiefly on works
of fiction and history. It was in the literary circle around John Chapman,
who had purchased the *Westminster Review* in 1851, that Lewes became
acquainted with Marian Evans, the future George Eliot. Like Lewes, she
was struggling to earn a living as a journalist, being then in the employ of
Chapman as his assistant editor.[17] Lewes commenced science reviewing
as an extension of his other literary activities, and indeed as part of an
everyday life devoted almost exclusively to reading and writing. George
Eliot's journals depict the life that she shared with Lewes as one immersed
in the consumption and production of literature, describing days spent,
for example, editing typescripts and translating Spinoza, and evenings
reading aloud from Homer's *Odyssey*, Gall's *Anatomie et physiologie du
cerveau* or Carpenter's *Comparative Physiology*.[18]

Familiarity with the works of scientific specialists in comparative
anatomy and physiology became integral to the couple's sentimental self-
education, and part of the their on-going researches in organic theory, and
the relations between the sciences and the fine arts. Such topics formed the
basis of conversation in their wider social circle in London, and especially
among the group of authors and critics whom Chapman was employing
for the *Westminster Review*. This group included Charles Bray and George
Combe, well-known authors of works on phrenology, a science which pos-
tulated that the brain was composed of discrete organs the proper exercise
of which was the basis of human character and health.[19] Chapman also
solicited contributions from the aspiring man of science Thomas Huxley,

the writer on political economy Harriet Martineau, and the young philosopher Herbert Spencer, who had already published a sketch of his developmental theory in Lewes's *Leader*.[20] Many of the *Westminster Review*'s writers had shown a keen interest in the writings of the French philosopher Auguste Comte and his platform for social improvement through a progressive elaboration of the sciences.[21] Chapman's journal, in which specialist knowledge was digested for a non-specialised audience and incorporated in broad programmes for human understanding and reform, became a medium for extending the boundaries of science. The enterprise depended crucially on the authority of reviewers to span specialist domains, synthesise their contents and comment on their worth.

The members of this literary circle had similar backgrounds. Hardly any of them had attended Oxford or Cambridge. Having acquired their education at dissenting academies, at London or Edinburgh universities, or through private reading, they found that many avenues into elite circles of learning were consequently closed to them. Contributors shared a concern to reform the high culture acquired with an Oxbridge degree, which was centred primarily on familiarity with the classical canon.[22] In that respect, they were in a similar position to certain other reformist groups in the 1830s and 1840s, such as medical professionals, whose platforms were based on progressive developmental theories.[23] The science and literature presented in the pages of the *Westminster Review* were both a secular counterculture and a religious alternative to the Anglican classicism of the old universities.

The *Westminster Review*'s writers were also largely dependent on the income they derived from their articles.[24] This was not the case with some of the other literary periodicals, such as the *Quarterly Review* or the *Saturday Review*, whose contributors were largely Oxbridge-based or held positions in one of the established learned professions, such as the bar or the Church. Writing science or literature as a profession was highly problematic; those without institutional status or independent means risked being stigmatised as 'popular' writers, crass journalists, or traders in knowledge and literary fashion.[25] Unable to claim the distinction that derived from established institutions of learning or revered professions, and utterly reliant therefore on the dictates of the literary market,

Westminster Review writers nonetheless sought to present themselves as independent authorities. To do so they needed to discriminate their activities from the commercial and the popular.

In their review articles from the 1850s, Lewes and George Eliot worked to establish criteria that would demarcate serious and original writing from prose that adhered to romantic or evangelical convention. One feature that they proposed to distinguish genuine literature from merely popular fiction was pain – pain which, interestingly enough, stemmed not from the labours of composition but rather from the effect that a work had on its readers. In a *Leader* editorial from 1854, Lewes maintained: 'Authors are Teachers: they have to teach the world through severe coercive means, *constraining* the wandering attention, bending it to the laborious task of learning, a labour which is pain at first to all ... but which becomes in time a keen and eager delight'.[26] Lewes's account was underpinned by a new reflex physiology of mind that was being developed by William Benjamin Carpenter and others.[27] Such physiological models of mind had already been used by Spencer in an 1852 article in the *Westminster Review* to explain the effect of an author's work on an audience.[28] Similar accounts were given in the period of the 'sensation fiction' of Wilkie Collins and other novelists – so named because of the pronounced and immediate physiological disturbances that it produced.[29] In this instance, however, Lewes was concerned with another kind of autonomic response: complacency. Popular writers, according to Lewes's model, were those who succeeded in producing pleasure through the elaborate reflex arc that ran from the printed page to the images and thoughts called forth in the mind of the reader. The unalloyed pleasure produced by such writers was their greatest shortcoming. The authors whom Lewes and George Eliot held in disdain were those whose works merely traversed the well-worn channels of conventional taste and opinion. Similarly, 'concrete knowledge' and 'direct observation' were explicitly urged by George Eliot as an alternative to versions of rural life based on 'cockney sentimentality', and 'traditions and prepossessions'. Realist writing worked by challenging the perspective and sympathies of readers, surprising them 'into that attention to what is apart from themselves'.[30]

Lewes and George Eliot thus carved out an alternative approach to authorship, interposing citations of esoteric authorities, and descriptions and explanations drawn from a wide reading of specialists. The work of technical science was converted into style, becoming part of an array of realist devices designed to disrupt the otherwise comfortable and effortless process of reading, and to provide thereby the physiological conditions for improvement and growth. This was a risky venture; for the use of such specialist knowledge and language could be judged inappropriate. Such concerns arose over George Eliot's fiction. After the appearance of 'Amos Barton' in 1857, the first part of her *Scenes from Clerical Life*, George Eliot learned through correspondence with her publisher John Blackwood that her 'scientific illustrations' had 'obtruded themselves disagreeably' on one of her readers. Pleading her case, her identity and gender still unknown to Blackwood, she wrote: 'If it be a sin to be at once a man of science and a writer of fiction, I can declare my perfect innocence on that head, my scientific knowledge being as superficial as that of the most "practised writers".'[31] Here George Eliot assumed the role of the artist whose gift was sympathy rather than information, a role she had outlined in her criticism of women novelists.[32] The problem that faced realist writers and critics was how to present their learning as a means of enlarging the sympathies and capacities of others. To compose realistic literature required a 'moral and intellectual breadth not vitiated by a foregone conclusion or by a professional point of view'.[33] Sally Shuttleworth has explored George Eliot's natural historical and, eventually, experimental approach to fiction, bringing out the important ways in which George Eliot's novels challenged the conventions that were being set for science in other quarters.[34]

If literary figures such as Lewes and George Eliot deployed particular writerly strategies to distinguish their commentary on contemporary culture from the writings of authors who merely catered to public tastes, scientific practitioners faced a similar problem within the domain of the periodical. However, this issue of drawing and policing the boundaries between elite and popular culture was what would divide the members of the *Westminster Review*'s circle. Lewes's own scientific credentials would be condemned as exclusively literary by another review writer and aspiring 'man of science', Thomas Huxley.

Huxley was hired by Chapman at the end of 1853 to write a new column on science for the *Westminster Review*.[35] At that time, Huxley was not yet institutionally affiliated, and his own research in natural history was largely unpublished. After obtaining a degree from the University of London, he served as assistant surgeon during a survey expedition on HMS *Rattlesnake* in the South Pacific. Such a post allowed him to acquire 'expert' status as a specialist in the field of marine invertebrates. However, as Huxley was not the official naturalist on the voyage, his researches could not appear in the register of the expedition's official findings. Indeed, when Huxley returned to England, he made numerous unsuccessful attempts to obtain support from the Admiralty and the Royal Society for the publication of his work.[36]

After his return to London in 1850, Huxley spent three years applying for various university teaching positions throughout the British Empire. Even though the Royal Society had honoured him with a fellowship and its royal medal on the basis of several well-regarded publications, he was nevertheless unable to penetrate the institutional world of scientific practice until he obtained lectureships in natural history and palaeontology at the Royal School of Mines in 1854. Thus at the time of his appointment to the *Westminster Review*, despite already possessing a reputation as an expert on the comparative anatomy of marine life, he was still struggling to gain a position which would assure that reputation. All this would have been relatively unproblematic for an individual with private means, as had been the case for Charles Darwin just over a decade before. But Huxley had no private fortune, and so he was forced to move between different sources of income and authority – the state and the public sphere – during these early years. Such a situation reflected the fact that there was no established career path for scientific practitioners in this period. Even paid positions in the sciences did not enable one to support a family. Scientific practitioners often needed to supplement their salary by writing. Lacking such a position, Huxley was largely dependent on an income gained through writing for money.

There were thus good reasons why both 'men of science' and 'men of letters' were committed to a common model of culture which divided into elite and popular. It was precisely during those decades that 'popular science' was being invented as a category for excluding certain kinds of writing from the domains of proper scientific practice.[37] But a complementary strategy advanced by men of science was to refer in their writings to a set of disciplinary practices that validated their claims, but which lay outside the scope of literature, namely field and laboratory work. As a reviewer of the latest British and continental science, Huxley's role for the *Westminster Review* was comparable to that of Lewes for the *Leader*. However, the grounds on which each could claim scientific authority were quite different. Lewes lacked access to the inner social circles whose membership conferred legitimacy as a scientific practitioner. He had yet to demonstrate an expertise based on practical work. His only access to scientific authority was through reading.

Huxley's very first article attacked Lewes's recent book *Comte's Philosophy of the Sciences* (1853) for an ignorance of science that stemmed from the author's exclusively literary life. The book was a collection of papers that had first appeared in the *Leader*, in which Lewes had set out both to explicate Comte's work of the 1830s, and to bring it up to date with the latest facts and theories of chemistry and physiology. Huxley picked away at Lewes's science, alleging errors such as the insertion of 'sulphuric' for 'sulphurous' acid, and the favourable presentation of developmentalism, to which Huxley was at the time opposed. 'We are taking advantage of no accidental mistakes', he wrote, 'although those already cited would suffice to show if demonstration were needed, how impossible it is for even so acute a thinker as Mr Lewes to succeed in scientific speculations, without the discipline and knowledge which result from being a worker also'.[38] Although Huxley commended Lewes's forceful and acute forms of expression, considerations of language were outweighed in an assessment of the book as a work of science. According to Huxley, Lewes had committed errors of fact that no amount of private study or lucid style could correct. In effect, Huxley was claiming that the criteria which Lewes and George Eliot used to distinguish sound criticism and original art were inadequate for science. What one needed in order to be an authority in science was a practical training, acquired through experience in the field and laboratory.

Huxley's criticisms turned as much on the medium through which knowledge was communicated as it did on its mode of acquisition.

Original scientific work, the result of systematic observations and experimental research, was typically presented in specialised journals or monographs, in a technical language often comprehensible only to a highly select audience.[39] It was read before learned societies, or published in lengthy, expensive volumes. The periodical press was not considered the proper forum for the making public of scientific truth. Rather, the periodical was a medium for a different kind of science writing, tailored for a different audience. It was also a medium through which the distinctions between elite and popular science, and expert and lay readership, were constructed and maintained. For writers such as Huxley, it was of paramount importance to establish who had the authority to make these distinctions, and on what grounds. It was by no means certain in 1850s' Britain that the kinds of expertise being described by Huxley were those which would denote the 'man of science' for others. In this contested terrain, the authoritative status of reading and writing, of practitioners, and of the public, hung in the balance.

In their science columns, Huxley and the young physicist John Tyndall, with whom he shared the reviewing for the *Westminster Review*, drew sharp distinctions between works of genius, which produced new knowledge; works of popularisation, which disseminated knowledge; and works of popular delusion or superstitions, which debased knowledge.[40] Favourable reviews were written for works whose 'charming wonderful stories' were calculated to instil the importance of natural historical knowledge in children; or for guidebooks for the seaside collector, such as Philip Henry Gosse's *Manual of Marine Zoology for the British Isles*, which was to be read as 'an introduction rather, than a rival, to the elaborate monographs of Johnson, Busk, Forbes, Bell, Baird, and Yarrell, and other writers upon British marine zoology'.[41] By contrast, works advocating mesmerism and clairvoyance were accused of spreading a popular delirium for which there was but one remedy: 'early education, by which we mean, not mere learning, but discipline and training, in the methods of the natural sciences and the inculcation of inductive habits of mind'.[42] Such categories of authorship served to divide the readership for science into, on the one hand, an elite community of practitioners, and, on the other, a vulgar and uninstructed public. But the audience these reviews addressed lay between the extremes of expertise and ignorance. It was a readership whose rudimentary and empirical knowledge, and whose 'amateurish' contribution, would serve to confirm the authority of an elite community of specialists.

An aspiring 'man of science' such as Huxley thus depended upon periodical publication as a way of validating his laboratory expertise as cultural enterprise just as much as, he was claiming, Lewes needed to possess personal laboratory experience to validate his public statements on science. These kinds of manoeuvres were part of Huxley's broader concerns to elevate the status of the laboratory-based sciences. The cultural authority that Lewes and George Eliot claimed for the artist and the critic also rested on models of an uninstructed public and of styles of writing that catered to vulgar and conventional tastes. But the bases of scientific and literary expertise were incommensurable. Indeed, the differences were seized on and turned to advantage by both sides.

On seeing the proofs of Huxley's review of Lewes, George Eliot wrote to Chapman protesting that such a 'purely contemptuous notice' ought to be suppressed.[43] She had already written several letters to George Combe, expressing her reservations over Huxley's capacity as a reviewer, and using physiological terms to do so: 'Mr Huxley's is not the organisation for a critic, but it is difficult to find a man who combines special scientific knowledge with that well-balanced development of the moral and intellectual faculties, which is essential to a profound and fair appreciation of other men's works.'[44] Lewes himself responded to Huxley's review in a *Leader* column, objecting to being unfairly treated as a 'bookman and not even a respectable bookman' and challenging Huxley's attempt to locate the boundaries of scientific expertise outside of the world of literature.

> Appearing in the pages where it is well known I am also a writer ... this attack will have more than usual significance; and being founded on the natural but false assumption that, because Literature is my profession, therefore in Science I can only have 'book knowledge', it will fall in with the all but universal tendency of not allowing any man to be heard on more than one subject. Once for all let me say, that it is 18 years since I first began to occupy myself – practically and theoretically – with Biology, and that it is only within the last 4 years I have ventured to publish any opinions on that subject.[45]

Lewes went on to defend his scientific credentials by citing the 'best phys-iologists of the day', including Flourens, Longet and Mulder, whose pub-lications, he claimed, Huxley had evidently not read.

From the perspective of Lewes and George Eliot, Huxley's scientific expertise was merely that of a narrow specialist, selfishly defending his ter-rain against others. Lacking the perspective and sympathy that were born of broad learning, Huxley was unqualified to comment on the work of those outside of his particular field, and thus was unfit for the office of critic. On the other hand, the juxtaposition of errors promulgated in books with truths gleaned through observation and experiment remained central to arguments for cultural reform advanced by Huxley and other scientific practitioners, and would feature prominently in debates over the introduction of scientific curricula and laboratories to English schools and universities over the next several decades.[46] In some of these debates, most notably those between Huxley and Matthew Arnold, science and lit-erature assumed opposite poles, their practitioners characterised as radi-cally different types: the 'man of letters' as broad, sympathetic, humane; and the 'man of science' as brilliant, narrow and dispassionate. These stock types and boundary-drawing exchanges became a commonplace in the high-culture wars that were waged in the periodical press, much to the delight of editors like James Knowles, whose journal *The Nineteenth Century* served as a stage for debates between intellectual celebrities on such topics as 'the soul and future life'.[47]

Lewes's aspirations to creditable scientific status led him to change his lit-erary habits following Huxley's comments. Borrowing a microscope from a friend, and using funds he had obtained from his successful *Life of Goethe* (1855), he embarked on an experimental study of marine life.[48] In 1856, he took a succession of trips with George Eliot to Tenby in south-west Wales, the place where Huxley had first gone dredging only a year before while on honeymoon with his wife Henrietta. Lewes's trips resulted in a series of articles in *Blackwood's Edinburgh Magazine* between May and August 1856, entitled 'Sea-Side Studies'.[49] Here Lewes laid out his scien-tific practice before his readers' eyes, describing how, on returning to his lodgings after a day of collecting, he would display his treasures on the

table, observing the animals' habits prior to dissection. He supplied intri-
cate details of the clothes he wore and the tools with which he collected,
preserved and viewed his specimens. Lacking the institutional position or
formal training that would have authenticated his practice, he constructed a space for observation and experiment within the text itself. At
the same time, his experimental experience was supposed to precede and
validate the text. By casting himself as the leading character in a familiar
narrative, that of the heroic discovery of truth, Lewes diminished his role
as a writer, proclaiming that language was inadequate to express the
encounter with nature: 'the best description is but thin and meagre, following, beggar-like, in the footsteps of rich Fact'. Contact with the natural world and its zoological types now took on a primacy which resisted
and even excluded the literary life. 'The typical forms *took possession* of
me', he wrote. 'They were ever-present in my waking thoughts; they filled
my dreams with fantastic images; they came in troops as I lay awake
during meditative morning hours; they teased me as I turned restlessly
from side to side at night; they made all things converge towards them'. As
Isobel Armstrong points out in her contribution to this volume, Lewes's
scientific gaze, newly shaped by the microscope, transformed everyday life
and even obtruded on his literary habits:

> If I tried a little relaxation of literature, whatever was read became the
> starting-point for wandering fancy, or more obtrusive memory; a phrase
> like 'throbbing heart' would detach my thoughts from the subject of the
> book, and hurry them away to the stage of the microscope, where the
> heart of some embryo was pulsating.[50]

Appearing in *Blackwood's Edinburgh Magazine*, in the form of a first-
person narrative which emphasised inner feelings as much as disciplined
observation and experiment, Lewes's latest writings were akin to those of
Dickens in *Household Words*. They seemed to promote a non-literary
model of science, based on laboratory and field experience; yet they used
the medium of the literary periodical in a manner that was not altogether
in keeping with the 'popular science' that was sanctioned by scientific
reviewers like Huxley and Tyndall. In a second series of 'Sea-Side Studies'
published in 1857, Lewes intervened in specialists' debates on comparative
anatomy and physiology, and claimed original discoveries concerning the

nervous system of molluscs.[51] His hands-on, how-to, manner of presentation gave readers step-by-step instruction in the use of scalpel and microscope, in conjunction with book knowledge. In effect, his literary rendering of scientific practice extended a bridge across the elite–popular divide, making the tools of the expert accessible outside of the institutional structures that specialists controlled and were working so hard to extend. It also offered possibilities for the literary periodical as an alternative forum for scientific communication to the specialised journal and the private society.

Lewes's status as a comparative physiologist remained uncertain. In 1858, his paper 'On the Spinal Chord as a Sensational and Volitional Centre' was delivered by Richard Owen to the meeting in Leeds of the British Association for the Advancement of Science. Owen had urged Lewes to publish in the *Philosophical Transactions* of the Association. This prompted a letter from John Blackwood, expressing his hopes that Lewes 'would not be such a donkey as to waste [his] time on such dryasdust publications'.[52] Valued by his publisher not as a scientific practitioner but as a successful commercial writer, Lewes slipped between the standards that came to prevail in the world of journalism and that of expert knowledge. Research performed in a domestic setting, still relatively common at mid-century, was increasingly marginal and aggressively marginalized by the 1870s. As a consequence, the opportunities for practitioners outside of the institution-based sciences to make original contributions and critical interventions were greatly diminished.

In 1874, Lewes was summoned as an expert witness by the Royal Commission on vivisection, an advisory body convened amid a widespread public outcry over animal experimentation. One of the cruxes of the debate was that practitioners, in the process of acquiring scientific expertise, had lost their humanity. The very laboratory discipline that Huxley, Tyndall and others had presented as fundamental to the acquisition of scientific expertise had been purchased at the price of the capacity to sympathise with others, be they animal subjects or fellow humans. In his testimony, Lewes asserted his opposition to the proposed legislation, maintaining that such licensing and inspection procedures as were envisaged would have the effect of putting practitioners like himself, who lacked an institutional basis of authority, out of business. At the conclusion of his questioning, Lewes invited the panel members to consider the question from the perspective of literature:

> It seems to me that the vivisection of which we are now speaking is very much like vivisection in another department, that of Literature, that is to say, criticism, which is also vivisection. There is a great deal of real torture inflicted upon authors by critics, which lasts for a considerable time in sensitive minds … it is quite true that for the benefit of literature, and consequently of society, criticism is a necessity; and I suppose that everybody possessed of a right feeling, who has exercised that office, has often felt great pain in giving pain.[53]

Ironically, the self-regulating community of critics and experimenters that Lewes called for would be realised in the kind of institution that had excluded him. Independence from the dictates of the public had long been sought by literary critics and scientific practitioners alike, both of whom nonetheless claimed to serve the interests of the public as its moral conscience, its surrogate priesthood and, above all, its educators. The Royal Commission on vivisection had been convened out of pressure from influential circles of the public. On the basis of its report, legislation was enacted that would effectively enhance the authority of practitioners who worked in ostensibly public institutions – the university science departments in which the government was now beginning to invest.[54] Leading promoters of scientific instruction like Huxley spoke warmly of a 'liberal education' that would combine science with literature, knowledge in depth with a breadth of sympathy and power of expression.[55] Such an academic model extended to practitioners of the arts and humanities the kind of social sanctuary and institutional credit that had proved so effective in the sciences. At the same time, it gave an official public seal to scientific knowledge of a kind that university-based practitioners on the continent had enjoyed for decades.

In this chapter I have approached the science and literature of the Victorian period not primarily as discourses but as resources for the forging of identities and communities.[56] 'Men of science', specialists and critics emerged *alongside* 'men of letters', popular writers and novelists in the middle decades of the century. At that time, the points of identity and difference between these groups were still very much in dispute, as was the comparative currency of scientific and literary culture for Victorian readers. The periodical was an important vehicle by which scientific and literary communities were formed through the crafting of different kinds of authority, expertise and style. The presentation of science as culture in mid-Victorian periodicals was important, in turn, for the advance of scientific practitioners to prominent positions in academic institutions. The common ground of science and literature as culture was highly useful as a platform for practitioners when 'culture' was still widely regarded as universal, and when they themselves were largely excluded from the great centres of cultural production. The status of science as culture has since undergone substantial revision. It has been left for specialists in other departments to cultivate this terrain for the purposes of humanistic critique. Thus patterns that were established in the medium of Victorian periodicals have survived in the form of disciplinary traditions, which underpin our understandings of the relations of science and culture today.

Notes

For their comments on earlier drafts of this paper, I would like to thank Adrian Johns, Anne Secord, Jim Secord and Alison Winter. I am especially grateful for conversations with Emma Spary while writing this paper.

1 Charles Dickens, *Bleak House* (Oxford: Oxford University Press, 1996), p. 479.
2 *Leader*, 3 (11 December 1852): 1189.
3 G. Perkins, 'Death by Spontaneous Combustion in Marryat, Melville, Dickens, Zola, and others', *Dickensian*, 60 (1964): 57–63.
4 J. Heilbron, 'The Affair of the Countess Görlitz', *Proceedings of the American Philosophical Society*, 138 (1994): 284–316, P. Denman, 'Krook's Death and Dickens's Authorities', *Dickensian*, 82 (1986): 131–41, and E. Gaskell, 'More About Spontaneous Combustion', *Dickensian*, 69 (1973): 25–35.
5 *Leader*, 4 (15 January 1853): 64; also 4 (12 February 1853): 161–3.
6 *Household Words* (7 September 1850): 568.
7 Dickens to Faraday, 31 May 1850, in W. Dexter (ed.), *The Letters of Charles Dickens*, 3 vols (London: Nonesuch Press, 1938), vol. 2: 217. The stories in *Household Words* have been attributed to Charles Knight. See A. Wilkinson, 'Bleak House: From Faraday to Judgement Day', *English Literary History*, 34 (1967): 225–67.

8 The importance of policing spaces of knowledge production is discussed in A. Ophir and S. Shapin, 'The Place of Knowledge: A Methodological Survey', *Science in Context*, 4 (1991): 3–22; and B. Latour and S. Woolgar, *Laboratory Life: The Social Construction of Scientific Facts* (London: Sage, 1979).

9 On Faraday's command of the movement of knowledge between private and public spaces, see D. Gooding, '"In Nature's School": Faraday as an Experimentalist', in D. Gooding and F. James (eds), *Faraday Rediscovered* (Basingstoke: Macmillan, 1985), pp. 105–35. See also the account of witnessing of Royal Institution experiments in J. Golinski, *Science as Public Culture: Chemistry and Enlightenment in Britain, 1760–1820* (Cambridge: Cambridge University Press, 1992), pp. 218–35.

10 H. Small, 'The Pulse of 124: Dickens and a Pathology of the Mid-Victorian Reading Public', in J. Raven, H. Small and N. Tadmore (eds), *The Practice and Representation of Reading in England* (Cambridge: Cambridge University Press, 1996), pp. 263–90. On the implications of domesticating potentially problematic scientific knowledge, see J. Secord, 'Nature's Fancy: Charles Darwin and the Breeding of Pigeons', *Isis*, 72 (1981): 162–86.

11 On the use of 'universal knowledge' to underpin class hierarchies in Britain, see e.g. B. Barnes and S. Shapin, 'Science, Nature and Control: Interpreting Mechanics' Institutes', *Social Studies of Science*, 7 (1977): 31–74.

12 See e.g. E. Shaffer (ed.), *The Third Culture: Literature and Science* (Berlin and New York: Walter de Gruyter, 1998); S. Shuttleworth, *Charlotte Brontë and Victorian Psychology* (Cambridge: Cambridge University Press, 1996); G. Levine (ed.), *One Culture: Essays in Science and Literature* (Madison: University of Wisconsin Press, 1987); and G. Beer, *Darwin's Plots: Evolutionary Narrative in Darwin, George Eliot and Nineteenth-Century Fiction* (London: Routledge, 1983). See also the critique of the one-culture model in H. Small, '"In the Guise of Science": Literature and the Rhetoric of Nineteenth-Century English Psychiatry', *History of the Human Sciences*, 7 (1994): 27–55, and the resource model of discourse in S. Schaffer, 'Augustan Realities: Nature's Representatives and their Cultural Resources in the Early Eighteenth Century', in G. Levine (ed.), *Realism and Representation: Essays on the Problem of Realism in Relation to Science, Literature and Culture* (Madison: University of Wisconsin Press, 1993), pp. 279–318.

13 See e.g. D. Lacapra and S. Kaplan (eds), *Modern European Intellectual History: Reappraisals and New Perspectives* (Ithaca, NY: Cornell University Press, 1987); P. Dear (ed.), *The Literary Structure of Scientific Argument* (Philadelphia: University of Pennsylvania Press, 1991); and J. Christie and S. Shuttleworth (eds), *Nature Transfigured: Science and Literature, 1700–1900* (Manchester: Manchester University Press, 1989).

14 J. Shattock and M. Wolff (eds), *The Victorian Periodical Press: Samplings and Soundings* (Leicester: Leicester University Press, 1982).

15   C. P. Snow, *The Two Cultures* (New York: Mentor, 1963); P. Gross and N. Levitt, *Higher Superstition: The Academic Left and its Quarrels with Science* (Baltimore, MD: Johns Hopkins University Press, 1994); N. Jardine and M. Frasca-Spada, 'Splendours and Miseries of the Science Wars', *Studies in History and Philosophy of Science*, 28 (1997): 219–35.

16   R. Ashton, *G. H. Lewes: A Life* (Oxford: Clarendon Press, 1991), pp. 86–108.

17   On the *Westminster Review* circle, see R. Ashton, *George Eliot: A Life* (London: Allen Lane, 1996), pp. 135–63, and G. S. Haight, *George Eliot and John Chapman* (New Haven, CT: Yale University Press, 940), pp. 28–40.

18   J. Cross (ed.), *George Eliot's Life as Related in Her Letters and Journals*, 3 vols (Edinburgh and London: Blackwood, 1896), vol. 1: 193–7.

19   R. Cooter, *The Cultural Meaning of Popular Science: Phrenology and the Organisation of Consent in Nineteenth-Century Britain* (Cambridge: Cambridge University Press, 1984).

20   'The Developmental Hypothesis', *Leader*, 4 (20 March 1853): 280–1.

21   On Comtism in Victorian Britain, see P. Dale, *In Pursuit of a Scientific Culture: Science, Art, and Society in the Victorian Age* (Madison: University of Wisconsin Press, 1989). On the later Oxford-based movement, see C. Kent, *Brains and Numbers: Elitism, Comtism, and Democracy in Mid-Victorian England* (Toronto: University of Toronto Press, 1978).

22   A. Engel, *From Clergyman to Don: The Rise of the Academic Profession in Nineteenth-Century Oxford* (New York: Oxford University Press, 1983); S. Rothblatt, *The Revolution of the Dons: Cambridge and Society in Victorian England* (New York: Basic Books, 1968); F. Turner 'The Victorian Conflict between Science and Religion: A Professional Dimension', *Isis*, 69 (1978): 356–76.

23   A. Desmond, *The Politics of Evolution: Medicine, Morphology and Reform in Radical London* (Chicago, IL: University of Chicago Press, 1989).

24   N. Cross, *The Common Writer: Life in Nineteenth-Century Grub Street* (Cambridge: Cambridge University Press, 1985), p. 98. On the profession of writing in the Victorian period, see also J. Gross, *The Rise and Fall of the Man of Letters: Aspects of English Literary Life since 1800* (London: Croom Helm, 1982).

25   On the problematic relationship between scientific and commercial writing, see J. A. Secord, *Victorian Sensation: The Extraordinary Publication, Reception, and Secret Authorship of Vestiges of the Natural History of Creation* (Chicago, IL: University of Chicago Press, 2000), ch. 14.

26   *Leader*, 5 (7 January 1854): 18.

27   W. Carpenter, *Principles of Human Physiology*, 3rd edn (London: John Churchill, 1853), pp. 663–83.

28   H. Spencer, 'The Philosophy of Style', *Westminster Review*, 58 (1852): 435–59. On physiological models of reading, see A. Johns, 'The Physiology of Reading

in Restoration England', in J. Raven, H. Small and N. Tadmore (eds), *The Practice and Representation of Reading in England*, pp. 138–64; and A. Jones, *Powers of the Press: Newspapers, Power and the Public in Nineteenth-Century England* (Aldershot: Scolar Press, 1996), pp. 75–87.

29 On 'sensation fiction', see A. Winter, *Mesmerized: Powers of Mind in Victorian Britain* (Chicago, IL: University of Chicago Press, 1998), pp. 322–31.

30 (George Eliot), 'The Natural History of German Life', *Westminster Review*, 66 (1856): 51–79, reprinted in George Eliot, *Selected Critical Writings*, ed. R. Ashton (Oxford: Oxford University Press, 1992), pp. 260–95.

31 George Eliot to J. Blackwood, 4 February 1857, in G. S. Haight (ed.), *The George Eliot Letters*, 9 vols (New Haven, CT: Yale University Press, 1954–55, 1978), vol. 2: 292.

32 (George Eliot), 'Silly Novels by Lady Novelists', *Westminster Review*, 66 (1856): 442–61, reprinted in *Selected Critical Writings*, pp. 296–321, esp. 312–13.

33 George Eliot, *Selected Critical Writings*, p. 265.

34 S. Shuttleworth, *George Eliot and Nineteenth-Century Science* (Cambridge: Cambridge University Press, 1984).

35 (T. H. Huxley), 'Contemporary Literature: Science', *Westminster Review*, 61 (1854): 254–70, 580–95; 62 (1854): 242–56, 572–80; 63 (1855): 239–53, 558–63; 64 (1855): 240–55, 565–74; 65 (1856): 261–71; 67 (1857): 279–88.

36 A. Desmond, *Huxley: From Devil's Disciple to Evolution's High Priest* (London: Penguin, 1997), P. White, *Thomas Huxley: Making the Man of Science* (Cambridge: Cambridge University Press, 2002), and 'Science at Home: The Space between Henrietta Heathorn and Thomas Huxley', *History of Science*, 34 (1996): 33–56.

37 On the mutual production of popular science and the scientific professional, see R. Cooter and S. Pumphrey, 'Separate Spheres and Public Places: Reflections on the History of Science Popularisation and Science in Popular Culture', *History of Science*, 32 (1994): 237–67; A. Secord, 'Science in the Pub: Artisan Botanists in Early Nineteenth-Century Lancashire', *History of Science*, 34 (1994): 269–315; and A. Winter, *Mesmerized*.

38 (Huxley), 'Contemporary Literature: Science', *Westminster Review*, 61 (1854): 255.

39 For a bibliography of works on scientific periodicals, see W. Brock, 'Science', in J. Don Vann and R. Van Arsdel (eds), *Victorian Periodicals and Victorian Society* (Aldershot: Scolar Press, 1994).

40 For Tyndall's reviews, see 'Contemporary Literature: Science', *Westminster Review*, 63 (1855): 558–63; 64 (1855): 255–63, 557–65; 65 (1856): 254–61, 596–602.

41 (Huxley), 'Contemporary Literature: Science', *Westminster Review*, 61 (1854): 263; 65 (1856): 605.

42 *Ibid.*: 269–70.

43 Haight, *George Eliot and John Chapman*, p. 70.

44 George Eliot to George Combe, 16 December 1853, in Haight (ed.), *The George Eliot Letters*, vol. 8: 91.

45 *Leader*, 5 (14 January 1854): 40.

46 White, *Thomas Huxley*, chapter 3.

47 'A Modern "Symposium": The Soul and Future Life', *The Nineteenth Century*, 2 (1877): 329–54, 497–536. See also W. Houghton (ed.), *The Wellesley Index of Victorian Periodicals, 1824–1900*, 5 vols (Toronto: University of Toronto Press, 1966–89), vol. 2: 622–3.

48 Ashton, *G. H. Lewes*, pp. 168–94.

49 'Sea-Side Studies', *Blackwood's Edinburgh Magazine*, 80 (1856): 184–97, 312–25, 472–85.

50 *Ibid.*: 196. See also *Blackwood's Edinburgh Magazine*, 81 (1857): 680–4 and 82 (1857): 413–19. Cf. Armstrong, pp. 40–3 and also Rebecca Stott, pp. 154–5, both this volume.

51 'New Sea-Side Studies', *Blackwood's Edinburgh Magazine*, 81 (1857): 669–85; 82 (1857): 1–17 and 222–40, 345–57, 410–23.

52 Letter from J. Blackwood to G. Lewes, 30 June 1857, cited in Ashton, *G. H. Lewes*, pp. 192–3.

53 *Report of the Royal Commission on the Practice of Subjecting Live Animals to Experiments for Scientific Purposes; with Minutes of Evidence and Appendix* (London: George Eyre & William Spottiswoode, 1876), pp. 310–12.

54 W. Brock, 'Science Education', in R. Olby, G. Cantor, J. Christie and M. Hodge (eds), *Companion to the History of Science* (London: Routledge, 1990), pp. 367–78.

55 See e.g. T. H. Huxley, 'A Liberal Education and Where to Find it', *Macmillan's Magazine*, 17 (1868): 367–78.

56 Such an approach has been widely used with respect to readers. See, e.g. S. Fish, *Is There a Text in This Class?* (Cambridge, MA: Harvard University Press, 1980), and R. Chartier, *The Cultural Uses of Print in Early Modern France*, trans. Lydia Cochrane (Princeton, NJ: Princeton University Press, 1987).

5

Imitation of life: science, literature and the dissemination of culture

∽

DAVID AMIGONI

The things in play in mimesis are very cunning. (Jacques Derrida[1])

An encounter between science and culture turning on the concept of imitation occurred on 22 October 1886, when Professor Thomas Henry Huxley commented in the *Pall Mall Gazette* on the controversy that erupted following John Churton Collins's critical demolition of Edmund Gosse's literary historical scholarship. The debate became identified as 'English Literature and the Universities' in recognition of the wider issues that it raised. The newspaper's invitation to Huxley to intervene in a controversy about literature teaching and its professionalisation indicates a recognition of his legitimacy to pronounce on the relative positions of science and culture in the conceptual order of late nineteenth-century Britain. Described by the newspaper's editorial as 'hardly less distinguished for culture than for science', Huxley addressed the issue as the authoritative scientist–savant motivated by a duty to extend Matthew Arnold's account of 'culture': a task made urgent for Huxley because of the conceptual separation of *culture* from *science* which the newspaper presupposed.

This chapter explores what was at stake in the bitter quarrel that broke out between Collins and Gosse over 'English Literature and the Universities'. It establishes contexts for Huxley's foregrounding of the idea of 'imitation' in his comment on literature, science and culture for the *Pall Mall Gazette*. And it traces the idea of imitation in Gosse's *Father and Son* (1907), an acknowledged classic of literary and scientific encounter, which represents autobiographically the struggle between religious and secular temperaments in a post-Darwinian world. More specifically it relates the use of the concept of 'imitation' in *Father and Son* to contemporary scientific and sociological texts which themselves participated in textual dialogues concerning imitation as an agent of cultural evolution. Imitation was a productively unstable concept in late nineteenth-century attempts to explain, through evolutionary frameworks, the reproduction of desired cultural economies of the same. Such instability productively generated a deconstructive sense of 'literature' which differed from the pedagogic account of 'English literature' that dominated the 1886 controversy. Moreover, this deconstructive literariness troubled the avowed purposes of texts about imitation, cultural dissemination and evolution.

These texts either claim to bear philological witness to cultural evolution, as in the case of the *Oxford English Dictionary*, or they narrate autobiographical stories about cultural evolution, as in Gosse's *Father and Son*. Alternatively, they narrate macro-stories of cultural evolution through micro-observations of imitation in action, as in James Mark Baldwin's popular scientific *Story of the Mind* (1899). However, all the texts are troubled by a 'cunning' degree of play at work in the concept of 'imitation'. This was explicitly theorised in the late nineteenth-century sociological work of Gabriel Tarde, and has been recognised again in the twentieth-century philosophy of Derrida and the stylistics of Mikhail Bakhtin.

In 1885 Edmund Gosse published a book arising from the newly founded Clark Lectures in literature which he had delivered at Cambridge University. The book, *From Shakespeare to Pope: An Inquiry into the Causes and Phenomena of the Rise of Classical Poetry in England*, was published by Cambridge University Press. Both the lecture series and the book represented a triumph of social and academic recognition for Gosse which his background had hardly guaranteed. Gosse, a poet and biographer-critic who earned a secure living as a civil servant at the Board of Trade, had been educated by his strict Calvinist father Philip Henry Gosse, the naturalist patriarch of *Father and Son*.[2] Consequently Gosse did not attend the Anglican-dominated ancient English universities, and had no degree. But in the Preface to *From Shakespeare to Pope,* Gosse claimed that his literary history was rigorous, scholarly and meticulously researched.[3]

This claim was undone by a devastating critique of Gosse's book which appeared in the *Quarterly Review* for October 1886. The author was John Churton Collins, a university extension lecturer, who demonstrated that many of Gosse's facts were wrong, that he had invented evidence for his claims, that he apparently had not read some of the works on which he passed judgement.[4] But in entitling the article 'English Literature and the Universities' Collins cast his net wider, seeing the example of Gosse's dilettantism as damaging to progress on a broader front affecting his discipline: whether the ancient universities should be endowed with the professorial staff for effecting the 'dissemination of literary culture'.[5] The philological study of Anglo-Saxon and Middle English language was endowed with chairs at Oxford. Philology grew out of established traditions of teaching Greek and Latin, yet it projected itself as professional and scientific; its opponents, however, interpreted professionalism as sectarian narrowness.[6] Accordingly, Collins rejected philology, advancing instead a pedagogic vision of English literature rooted in the study of those Greek and Roman classical models of which it was substantially an imitation. For Collins it was the historical mission of the universities to 'preserve learning from extinction' and 'barbarism', or effect cultural evolution by means of an 'intellectual aristocracy', which would protect the learned core of culture from the 'contagion' of 'dilettantism' and 'the multitudes'.[7]

This was the debate about English literature on which Huxley was invited by the *Pall Mall Gazette* to comment in 1886. Huxley was one of several prominent figures – including Gladstone, Bright, Arnold and Pater – to be approached by the *Gazette*'s editor W. T. Stead, through a questionnaire prepared by Collins.[8] Huxley's perspective was particularly sought because he had already made a distinctive contribution to defining the relations between literature, culture and science in an address entitled 'Science and Culture'. That address marked the opening of Sir Josiah Mason's Science College in Birmingham, an institution which made no provision for 'mere literary instruction and education'. Huxley's lecture advanced the case for teaching natural science as a major educational refinement of Arnold's conception of culture as a 'criticism of life', by arguing that conceptions of 'life' were being radically reconfigured by natural science.[9] Huxley did not deny the importance of either literature or 'letters' to this sense of culture: but in acknowledging it he demoted the classical languages from their ascendant position. In making this move, Huxley promoted the importance of the literatures of modern languages such as French and German, but especially English: 'Every Englishman has, in his native tongue, an almost perfect instrument of literary expression; and in his own literature, models of every kind of literary excellence.'[10]

Thus, in his contribution to the debate about 'English Literature and the Universities' in 1886 Huxley responded to the terms dictated by Collins. At the same time, and for the benefit of scientific education, he renegotiated the conceptual economy that supported Arnold's literary model of culture. In his *Pall Mall Gazette* piece, Huxley acknowledges that the teaching of literature is an agent of progressive cultural evolution but, in common with Collins, refuses to endorse a model of literature teaching dominated by the narrowly professional scientism of philology, which he describes as 'a fraud practised upon letters'. Huxley advocates instead a pedagogic model of literary education based on imitation. In this model, imitation works in two senses: first, students are expected to imitate, or copy, examples of good rhetorical and stylistic practice, which echoes Churton Collins's sense of English literature's imitative relation to the classics; and, second, the examples of good expression that Huxley alludes to are all drawn from the eighteenth century: the writings of Swift, Goldsmith and Defoe are cited, all of which have in common, Huxley claims, 'clearness' and 'simplicity', or the stylistic virtues of mimetic discourse. It is significant to recall that, in defining the principles of classical literature in the Preface to the 1853 edition of his poetry, Arnold's starting point was the principle of mimesis, or imitation. But whereas for Arnold it was the Hellenic Greeks who were the masters of imitations which foregrounded action and elided expression, Huxley constructs a canonical mimesis derived substantially from the Anglo-Scottish eighteenth-century Enlightenment.[11] Huxley's definitive contribution here was his 1879 biography of David Hume for the Macmillan 'English Men of Letters' series, a work in which Hume's radically empirical philosophy became the vehicle for redefining 'criticism' – another Arnoldian term – as the scientistic police force in the world of thought, 'exterminating' contagious forms of metaphysical or superstitious rhetoric:

> It is the business of criticism not only to keep watch over the vagaries of philosophy, but to do the duty of police in the whole world of thought. Wherever it espies sophistry or superstition they are to be bidden to stand; nay, they are to be followed to their very dens and there apprehended and exterminated, as Othello smothered Desdemona, 'else she'll betray more men'.[12]

The desire to exterminate contagiously cunning and duplicitous forms of thought, to prevent their being further copied and disseminated, is gendered; indeed, the gendering of contagious cunning as waywardly feminine will be encountered again later in this chapter in a work of popular evolutionary science: Baldwin's *Story of the Mind*. Above all, the 'English Literature and the Universities' debate was preoccupied with anxieties about defending culture from contagions.

In his *Pall Mall Gazette* piece, Huxley acknowledged that his advocacy of imitation and an eighteenth-century canon would meet with detractors, for 'it has been the fashion to decry the eighteenth century, as young fops laugh at their fathers'. In order to counter this view, Huxley turns to a teleological metaphor of natural growth, insisting on the inevitability of an outcome by 'finding' in eighteenth-century English writings that 'we were there in germ'. Huxley here imagines cultural evolution in terms of developmental lines with teleological outcomes: the principal growth out of the eighteenth century being a literature premissed on mimetic, naturalistic forms of representation that disseminate an enlightened, but aggressively corrective, scientistic conception of culture at the end of the nineteenth.

However, there is another conception of 'literature' to set alongside that which Huxley advocates here, one that deconstructs the assumptions about imitation and teleological cultural evolution outlined by Huxley. This asserts itself through the textual grafts and insertions from other discourses that Huxley's text cannot keep at bay, and it frustrates Huxley's avowed logic of imitation. Huxley's view of eighteenth-century literature expresses confidence in mimetic representation as a vehicle of cultural transmission and an object of imitation in shaping human consciousness. But Huxley also acknowledges that there is a ludic tendency to diverge from the productions of previous generations in acts which he likens to 'young fops laugh[ing] at their fathers'. A remarkably similar structure of avowal and disavowal regarding the properties of imitation occurs in Edmund Gosse's *Father and Son*, as this chapter demonstrates. Thus, Huxley's and Gosse's writings glimpse a force of grafting and insertion – 'literature' in its deconstructive mode – which disrupts the assumption of high-fidelity copying or faithful imitation, and recognises the degree of contagious cunning which Jacques Derrida sees at play in mimesis.

Jacques Derrida and Mikhail Bakhtin inform my argument as theorists of the literariness generated by, on the one hand, the dissemination of textual grafts and, on the other, polyphonic and parodic texts. In texts such as 'The Double Session' and 'Psyche', Derrida generates deconstructive meditations on the concepts of mimesis and invention. For the purposes of this argument, the multiplicity of grafted discourses through which Derrida's essays move have implications for an approach to literariness as an encounter with alterity in scientific discourse.[13] Bakhtin's essay 'Discourse in the Novel' theorises the way in which parodies are culturally produced from the polyphonic arrangement of and relative authority between discourses.[14] Of course, there are differences between Derrida and Bakhtin – Derrida would be deeply sceptical about the logocentric priority that Bakhtin ascribes to 'voice' – but, as Samuel Weber has argued, 'in both [Derrida's dissemination, Bakhtin's polyphony], an irreducible alterity is shown at work'.[15] It is encounters with irreducible alterity that I explore in a selection of late nineteenth- and early twentieth-century texts. In negotiating the idea of imitation as an agent of cultural evolution these texts either explictly theorise or else open up a structural unconscious that might be called literary, against their avowed aim. Given this, perhaps Gosse's most conspicuous contribution to a theory of cultural evolution in his otherwise vilified *From Shakespeare to Pope* was his throwaway comment that literary history consists of 'blind and unconscious' movement.[16]

Edmund Gosse's *Father and Son* was published twenty-one years after his reputation had suffered as a result of *From Shakespeare to Pope* and the 'English Literature and the Universities' controversy. Gosse's text offers itself to the reader as a transparent 'document' about the mid nineteenth-century conflict between religion and science: in that sense it claims to partake of the properties of mimetic literature positively endorsed by Huxley.[17] The narrative recalls the young Gosse's relationship with his widowed father, the nineteenth-century popular naturalist Philip Henry Gosse, whose Calvinist theology and insistence on the literal truth of Creation was challenged by Darwin's theory of transmutation by natural selection.[18] Gosse's narrative presents this as a decisive moment, with Darwinism on the side of development against stagnant 'Puritanism': 'of the two human beings here described, one was born to fly backward, the other could not help being carried forward'.[19] Gosse constructs the late 1850s as the moment 'when the theory of the mutability of species was preparing to throw a flood of light upon all departments of human speculation and action'.[20] My reading of *Father and Son* focuses less on its mimetic properties, its documentary status, and concentrates instead on its textuality; that is, the way in which textual grafts link Gosse's narrative to late nineteenth-century discourses comprising those 'departments of human speculation' which were being reshaped by evolutionary theory.

The concept of imitation links these grafts, and Gosse's narrative explicitly reflects on the concept. Seeking to recover formative influences from his childhood, Edmund Gosse comments that 'the rage for what is called "originality" is pushed to such a length in these days'.[21] In order to exemplify this anti-romantic and pro-classicist view – Gosse's critical orientation in *From Shakespeare to Pope* – the narrator recalls watching and learning from his father's work as a naturalist, extolling the benefits of the act of 'healthy … direct imitation', exemplified in the way in which his younger self copied his father's work.

The narrative represents the son turning to the accumulated resources of 'human speculation' in order to learn and grow: discovering forbidden fictions, he turns to an etymological dictionary, *Bailey's 'English Dictionary'* (an eighteenth-century text), in order to learn unfamiliar words in a novel that he is reading.[22] The idea of the dictionary as an authoritative archive was a significant component of late nineteenth-century thinking about the evolution, preservation and reproduction of culture, vested in institutions such as the *New English Dictionary* or the *Oxford English Dictionary* (*OED*) from 1895. Huxley may have alleged that philology was a 'fraud practised upon letters', but the *OED* illustrated historically nuanced usage through 'letters', or the canonical works of English prose and poetry. The accumulation and collection of usages was glossed by a Darwinian rationale which had itself been shaped by philological language theory: as John Willinsky has noted, 'pursuing an evolutionary path through the archaeological record of the language ... ultimately demonstrated ... the survival of the fittest (phrase and language)'.[23] A case in point was the very term 'imitation', in which a key mechanism enabling the reproduction and dissemination of culture was itself defined and preserved in the dictionary:

> IMITATION c. *Psychol*. The adoption, whether conscious or not, during a learning process, of the behaviour or attitudes of some specific person or model. 1807
>
> (1807 WORDSWORTH *Poems* II. 153 The little Actor cons another part ... As if his whole vocation Were endless imitation.) 1895 J.M. BALDWIN, *Mental Development* xii. 351 First ... biological or organic imitation ... Second: we pass to psychological, conscious or cortical imitation ... 1903 E.C. PARSONS tr. *Tarde's Laws of Imitation* p.xiv. By imitation I mean every impression of inter-psychical photography ... willed or not willed, passive or active.[24]

This entry gathers together some of the most basic elements comprising the concept of imitation. Wordsworth's scene of imitation (from the ode 'Intimations of Immortality') captures the act of copying by heart from other sources. Baldwin's definition, taken from his *Mental Development in the Child and the Race*, distinguishes between, while seeing a route from and to, organic-biological and human-psychological processes of imitation. E. C. Parsons's usage, from the Introduction to her translation from the French of Gabriel Tarde's *Laws of Imitation* (1890), emphasises the impression that passes between two minds: the assumed fidelity of the imitation to its source is signified in its being described as 'photography' that is impressed 'inter-psychically'. Parsons's usage also distinguishes between conscious and unconscious imitation ('willed or not willed').

The entry significantly collects and preserves usages of 'imitation' which had been established in late nineteenth-century work on cultural evolution. Baldwin's work on imitation followed from his seminal 1896 paper 'A New Factor in Evolution', which conceived of culture in modified Lamarckian terms as a collective adaptive engine (which went beyond Lamarck's original individualistic sense of an organism's 'will'), and therefore as an agent of rapid species' adaptation.[25] Tarde – best known for his debates with Durkheim in the 1890s – was also active in the emerging field of criminology during that decade, where he used the concept of imitation to contest the power of the racial–determinist paradigm, arguing that 'the field of imitation has been constantly growing and freeing itself from heredity'.[26]

These entries also exemplify the *OED*'s story about the linguistic development of English, stated in the editor James H. Murray's framing 'General Explanation' and rendered in a diagram. The diagram represents vocabulary domains comprising the 'core' areas of common, literary and colloquial; these are presented as gate-keepers to the more peripheral domains of the scientific, foreign, technical, slang and dialectal. The 'Explanation' holds that 'scientific ... words enter the common language mainly through literature'.[27] According to this logic, the sense of 'imitation' illustrated from the works of Baldwin and Tarde published in the 1890s is 'psychological' or scientific; but this scientific sense is 'prepared' for entry into the common language by Wordsworth's use of the term in his 'Intimations' ode of 1807.[28]

The archival function of the dictionary accordingly sought to enshrine a set of relations between literature (as legitimator of use) and science (as the bearer of supplementary meanings). But this is a fiction which elides the tensions and struggles between signs, their multiple significations and contexts of iterability. Relocated in its poetic context, Wordsworth's deployment of 'imitation' in the 'Intimations' ode does not authorise the safe passage of the term to affirmative late nineteenth-century psychological usages; instead, 'endless imitation' of 'dialogues of business, love or strife' reproduces the 'earthly freight' which fatally obscure the 'intimations of immortality' revealed in the recollections of early childhood (stanzas VII, VIII).[29]

It was precisely that semiotic variation, nuance and struggle which was theorised in Tarde's sociology of imitation in ways which make the 'unconscious' a leading concept. In conceptualising the 'field of imitation', Tarde formulated a theory of cultural space structured by signs organised in '*diametrical* oppositions', as he states in a formulation congruent with Saussure's theory of binary oppositions. Cultural sign-space, he argued, 'is so constituted as to admit an infinity of couples whose members are opposed to each other in direction, and our consciousness is so constituted as to admit of an infinity of affirmations opposed to negations, or an infinity of desires opposed to repugnances, each having precisely the same object.'[30]

Tarde argued that imitation had to be seen in the context of linguistic rivalry in which signs and accents of 'affirmation', 'negation', 'desire' and 'repugnance' contest the same referent:

> Linguistic progress is effected first by imitation and then by the rivalry between the languages and dialects which quarrel over the same country, and one of which is crowded back by the other, or between the terms or idioms which correspond to the same idea. This struggle is a conflict between opposite theses implicit in word or idiom.[31]

Tarde thus goes beyond Saussure by advancing a position on the contestation of the sign which bears comparison with the linguistics of the Bakhtin circle. Reflecting on different categories of 'belief' – religious, moral, juristic and political – Tarde claims that these are inseparable from 'linguistic beliefs', for 'what an irresistible although unconscious power of persuasion our mother tongue ... exerts over us'.[32] Tarde here contributes to the late nineteenth-century pursuit of the unconscious, in which Freud's psychoanalytic 'discovery' was only one episode. Tarde's sense of the unconscious is less the Freudian account of depth-psychological sublimated motive, and more a Derridean sense of the unconscious as a structural necessity which eludes total epistemological mastery of a field.[33]

Tarde's sense of a linguistic unconscious as a structural necessity in the field of cultural imitation is glimpsed in the 'General Explanation' to the *OED*. In seeking to represent the 'core' of English vocabulary, the 'Explanation' grafts into its rationale a classificatory biological discourse that simultaneously defines and undermines the dictionary's archivising enterprise by finding at the margins of the 'core' a blurring of delineations through which an irreducible alterity is encountered:

> That vast aggregate of words and phrases ... may be compared to one of those natural groups of the zoologist or botanist, wherein typical species forming the characteristic nucleus of the order, are linked on every side to other species, in which the typical character is less and less distinctly apparent, till it fades away in an outer fringe of aberrant forms, which merge imperceptibly in various surrounding orders, and whose own position is ambiguous and uncertain.[34]

My focus is on aberrant forms, ambiguity and uncertainty in my readings of scenes of imitation narrated in Gosse's *Father and Son*, and Baldwin's *The Story of the Mind*, through which the play of 'literariness' is encountered.

James Mark Baldwin narrates a scene of imitation in his popular work *The Story of the Mind* in which he describes a young child in the act of copying an original. For Baldwin the subject is a 'socius', which he defines as 'a normally educated person'.[35] Accordingly, imitation becomes a mechanism in the service of normalisation, or the replication of the same: 'Beliefs are contagious, ideas run from mind to mind, imitation produces sameness', he states in a formulation which implies the 'photographic' quality of inter-psychic imitation.[36] This sense of the contagious basis of sameness frames Baldwin's ideal scene of imitation, in which the male child 'looks at the copy before him; sets all his muscles of hand and arm into massive contraction ... holds his breath and in every way concentrates his energies upon the copying of the model'.[37] Although Baldwin stresses the trial and error nature of the practice of imitation – that the child will, necessarily, have to experiment and initially produce low-fidelity imitations – the goal must still be accurate copying, getting it 'right'.

This can be contrasted with Gosse's commentary extolling the benefits of 'healthy ... direct imitation' in *Father and Son*. Despite the commentary, this scene can be juxtaposed to Baldwin's in the way that it raises questions about the extent to which sameness can be reproduced: the sovereignty of intention and consciousness is challenged by the parodic and the ludic – in other words, by play. As we have seen, Gosse looks back to the time of his childhood when his father was composing *Actinologia Britannica* (1860), the work on the marine life of Britain's coasts, and a point at which Gosse's younger self was imitating his father's work, 'preparing little monographs on seaside creatures'. Looking at the preserved remains of his copies, consisting of words and water-colour pictures, Gosse is struck by 'the perseverance and the patience, the evidence of close and persistent labour'. Yet, comparing the copies he produced to his father's originals, Gosse is perplexed by what he sees and, perhaps more significantly, recalls the extent to which these productions perplexed his father, for the imitations were

> ludicrous pastiches ... they were, moreover, parodies, rather than imitations of his writings, for I invented new species, with sapphire spots and crimson tentacles and amber bands, which were close enough to his real species to be disconcerting ... If I had not been so innocent and solemn, he might have fancied I was mocking him.[38]

Philip Henry Gosse is confronted with imitations of his observations of nature which are similar enough to their object to claim fidelity, and yet which are sufficiently divergent from and subversive of the original representations they purportedly imitate to be 'disconcerting'. It is 'disconcerting' for the father – that is to say his masterful self-possession is disturbed, put out of concert – precisely because the imitations are unconscious parodies, for Edmund's solemn and innocent demeanour indicates that there is no intention to mock or to laugh at the father.[39]

Significantly, 'disconcert' is produced as a consequence of Gosse's shift from imitation to parody, which is represented as an inventive move ('I invented new species'); for 'invention' has implications which disrupt the logic of imitation. As Derrida argues in 'Psyche: Invention of the Other', invention is an enigmatic concept which is radically distinct from copying ('a copy can never be an invention'), and yet which depends on an established cultural fabric to make it intelligible.[40] Commonly

authorised categories of invention are, as Derrida points out, stories –
the fictional or fabulous – and machines, which Derrida defines as
devices which generate 'new operational possibilit[ies]'.[41] As Derrida's
performance progresses, he grafts together the characteristics associated
with these conventionally different categories of invention in order to
draw analogies between them.[42] This grafting draws attention to the
mechanical unconscious inventiveness of narrative and textual systems,
which, in their openness to the other produce 'new operational possibilities', the contours of which cannot consciously be grasped in advance.
For Derrida, the unconscious 'machinery' of written texts generates an
inventiveness and openness which, 'through a merging of chance and
necessity, produce[s] the new of an event' that can move beyond 'the
economy of the same'.[43]

Philip Henry Gosse's moment of 'disconcert' from *Father and Son*,
read through Derrida, enables a re-reading of the exemplary stories in
Baldwin's *Story of the Mind*. In other words, this graft produces a mode of
reading which can open up a generically non-literary popular scientific
text about cultural evolution to the play of the literary; a play which disrupts the economy of the same that one of Baldwin's exemplary stories
seeks to uphold. In this episode, Baldwin reflects on children learning
through their observation of parental behaviour, which the children then
imitate through play: 'if a man study these games patiently in his own children ... he gradually sees emerge from within the inner consciousness a
picture of the boy's own father, whom he aspires to be like, and whose
actions he seeks to generalize and apply'.[44]

Baldwin goes on to narrate, in detail, an episode that he has witnessed
in which his daughters act out a little maternal scene with a doll: Baldwin
poses a rhetorical question: 'what could be a more direct lesson – a lived
out exercise – in sympathy, in altruistic self-denial, in the healthy elevation of her sense of self to the dignity of kindly offices?'[45] The answer to
this question is, however, put in doubt when, in the middle of the episode
of playful domestic imitation that Baldwin narrates, one of Baldwin's
daughters invents a supplementary father figure (so marginalising the one
standing by, watching the play). She fashions the supplentary patriarch
from an ornamental column standing in the corner of the living room.

Although Baldwin's text inscribes the daughter in the language of the passive, obedient feminine, it also records her ventriloquial imitation of a deep masculine voice which supposedly emanates from the column: if Baldwin speaks for her 'type' and its replication, the child has pre-emptively spoken for his. Baldwin's mastery within what Tarde would describe as the field of imitation is here rendered uncertain as he encounters a voice which is not conscious of its parodic effect, yet can be read as parodic. This accords with Bakhtin's account of parody, which is conceptualised in terms of dialogic tensions and conflicts between voices, a (persuasive) authoritative 'word of the father' being relativised by other, competing, voices that play for the subject's attention.[46] Baldwin's indirect response to his daughter's invention is to warn the reader that 'play has its dangers also – very serious ones. The game gives practice in cunning no less than forbearance'.[47] Baldwin's text here unconsciously anticipates Derrida's observation that 'the things in play in mimesis are very cunning'. For the 'contagion' of sameness that Baldwin claims to find in thoughts passing 'photographically' between minds is undone by the cunning of 'contamination' that Derrida finds at play in his account of the condition of impurity which haunts classificatory drives.[48]

Baldwin's text produces 'new operational possibilities' through contact with Derrida's texts, an encounter with alterity of which it itself could not be 'aware'. The extent of this alterity goes beyond simply this graft. For it is possible to read Baldwin's account of his daughters at play through Jacques Lacan's psychoanalytic account of the symbolic order, the Law of the Father, and the phallus as transcendental signifier; and to claim, despite the text's avowed intentions, that it has glimpsed the politics of the reproduction of contingent gender differences otherwise projected as natural. This reading is certainly not indifferent to 'public tradition[s]' of discourse in history:[49] Lacan's discourse is a variation on Freud's writings on the unconscious, which were themselves derived from traditions of evolutionary anthropology.[50] But that is not precisely the point, for it is above all important to stress that Baldwin's moment of disconcertion is not the discovery of *the* unconscious as a domain of mind or thing; rather, we find in Baldwin's textual system, and the grafts through which it can be read, a manifestation of the unconscious as a structural necessity: it generates an inventiveness producing the 'new of an event', open to the other and breaking the economy of the same. Nonetheless, the reading that follows from this event, and which generates critical insight, has a content. The content relates to gender politics, and the unconscious parody of masculine mastery that Baldwin's text represses and brings forth can be read in opposition to Huxley's gendering of science's drive to exterminate what it takes to be 'feminine' superstition and sophistry.

Gabriel Tarde's late nineteenth-century sociology struggled to conceive and theorise the terms in which new events steered culture in unforseen directions. Tarde was sceptical of the capacity of a Darwinian evolutionary paradigm to account, universally, for every cultural event. In an effort to conceptualise the new – which draws upon the concept of invention, bringing forth the very difficulties that Derrida was later to encounter – he called for a philosophy of 'insertion' which could grasp the nature of revolutionary changes in cultural direction.[51] Darwinian evolutionary theory is premissed on mechanistic totality, even though it can acknowledge, indeed needs, multiple lines of development on which selection can work. In the sphere of culture there is a contrary need to theorise the role of a multiplicity of diversely constituted mechanisms – texts as themselves highly complex and varied inventions – which can be inserted into openings for change in the conceptual order.

Adapting Henry James's famous description of Edmund Gosse as a writer with a genius for inaccuracy, it might more charitably be said that Gosse had a genius for invention. The literary historian who fabricated the circumstances surrounding the Cavalier-poet Sidney Godolphin's death in *From Shakespeare to Pope* transmuted into the autobiographer who invented a colourfully dramatic life script for himself in *Father and Son*.[52] Perhaps Gosse's story about his childish attempts to imitate his father's natural history illustrations, attempts which turn unconsciously into parodic inventions, was itself an invention: whether it was, or not, Gosse certainly wrote a self-deconstructing allegory about the virtues of imitation which opens up the productive instability around this concept. Gosse's story also takes us back to our starting point of T. H. Huxley's foregrounding of imitation in his *Pall Mall Gazette* piece of 1886, in which imitation figured as a solution to the 'English Literature and the Universities' question and a pedagogic strategy for restructuring the relations between literature, science and culture.

A controversy turning on the issue of professionalising the teaching of literature drew a reaction from Huxley which curiously side-stepped the issue of professionalisation; yet this still tells us something important about the relations between literature, science and culture. In his *Pall Mall Gazette* piece of 1886 Huxley, who probably achieved more than any nineteenth-century scientist towards the goal of professionalising his field, notably rejected the most self-consciously professional position in the teaching of English philology, as a 'fraud practised on letters'. While Huxley sought an important position for science in the reformed conceptual order supporting culture, culture remained for him a many-sided process of humanising which raised itself above narrow professionalism. Although Arnold and Huxley differed in their respective conceptions of the authority of science within a new conceptual order, they actually shared a broad sense of that conceptual order's outline. In 1873, Arnold wrote to Huxley referring to their joint commitment to a critique of theological orthodoxy which was 'as great as that which happened at the Reformation'. For Arnold, this critique was broadly to the good, but also dangerous because it was popular and embraced 'numbers of men ... [and therefore] will carry with it a large part of blunder and misconception'.[53] While Arnold and Collins were advocates of an elite culture with the classics at its core, and Huxley by contrast lectured to working-class audiences about a culture with enlightened science at its core, all feared contagions which might disintegrate what they took to be the core of culture, and constructed traditions which would legitimise their elimination (or even 'extermination', to use Huxley's language). Despite these avowals, the deconstructive play at work in grafts encountered between late nineteenth-century literary and scientific writings on imitation are fascinating precisely because of the way in which they arrest the authority and teleology of traditions, and advance a cunning and contagious stylistics of parody. Despite their best intentions, they can be read against the grain, inserting new modes of critical thought into the process of cultural dissemination.

Notes

Thanks to Fred Botting, Roger Luckhurst, Jo McDonagh and Barbara L. Kelly for helpful comments on earlier drafts of this essay.

1 '"This Strange Thing Called Literature": An Interview with Jacques Derrida', in Derek Attridge (ed.), *Jacques Derrida: Acts of Literature* (New York and London: Routledge, 1992), p. 57.

2 Gosse's version of his childhood and education is narrated in *Father and Son*; for the best and most recent account of Gosse's life, see Ann Thwaite, *Edmund Gosse: A Literary Landscape 1849–1928* (Oxford : Oxford University Press, 1985).

3 Edmund Gosse, *From Shakespeare to Pope: An Inquiry into the Causes and Phenomena of the Rise of Classical Poetry in England* (Cambridge: Cambridge University Press, 1885), p. vi.

4 For instance, Gosse implies that Sidney's *Arcadia* is a work of poetry rather than prose. See *From Shakespeare to Pope*, pp. 25–6. For John Churton Collins on this point, see 'English Literature and the Universities', *The Quarterly Review* (October 1886): 296.

5 Churton Collins, 'English Literature and the Universities', p. 328.

6 On the other hand the appreciation of English literature as such was viewed suspiciously as amateur and intellectually second rate, as Gerald Graff argues in *Professing Literature: An Institutional History* (Chicago, IL, and London: University of Chicago Press, 1987). Graff is writing specifically about the development of higher-education literature teaching in United States' cultural history, but his anatomy of the conflict between scientistic philological researchers and generalist critic-teachers expresses the divisions which drove the 'English Literature and the Universities' debate in Britain. So much so that Churton Collins's book of 1891, *The Study of English Literature: A Plea for its Recognition and Reorganization at the Universities*, which addressed the situation in Britain, was debated extensively at Modern Language Association gatherings during the 1890s. See Graff, chapter 5, p. 72.

7 Churton Collins, 'English Literature and the Universities', pp. 290 and 294.

8 This amounted to a well-organised campaign; Collins launched his damaging salvo against Gosse from the *Quarterly*, and then, with Stead's assistance, sustained the debate in the newsapaper columns of the *Pall Mall Gazette*. See Anthony Kearney, 'Literary Journalism and the English Debate in the 1880s', *Durham University Journal*, 54, 1 (January 1993): 40–1.

9 T. H. Huxley, 'Science and Culture', in Huxley, *Science and Culture and Other Essays* [1881] (London: Macmillan, 1888), pp. 6 and 15.

10 *Ibid.*, p. 19. Arnold responded to Huxley in 1882 with his own address to Cambridge University entitled 'Literature and Science', which restated the case for a literary and humanistic understanding of culture rooted in the classics.

11 'We all naturally take pleasure, says Aristotle, in any imitation or representation whatever; this is the basis of our love of poetry', according to the Preface of 1853 in *The Poems of Matthew Arnold*, ed. Kenneth Allott (London: Longman, 1965), p. 591. For the point about action over expression, see p. 595.

12 T. H. Huxley, *Hume*, English Men of Letters series (London: Macmillan, 1879), p. 58.

13 These performances are primarily literary and philosophical in orientation: 'The Double Session' deconstructs assumptions of presence in the idea of *mimesis* by reading a text by Plato against a text by Mallarmé; and 'Psyche' reads a poem by Francis Ponge to unweave the concept of invention. In 'The Double Session', Derrida's sense of 'grafting' works with a rhetoric of texts as organisms, and is a play upon Gaston Bachelard's sense of the graft in his work on the relationship between science, culture and literature in *Water and Dreams*; see *Dissemination*, trans. Barbara Johnson (London: Athlone Press, 1981), p. 203. For a discussion of the way in which Derrida has drawn on ideas of vegetal and animal grafting to arrive at his textual sense of the graft, see Jonathan Culler, *On Deconstruction: Theory and Criticism After Structuralism* (London: Routledge & Kegan Paul, 1983), p. 135. Derrida's 'Psyche: Invention of the Other', in exploring the issue of iterability, signifies the text as 'machine' in ways which connect with work on artificial intelligence; see the edited version of Catherine Porter's translation in *Acts of Literature*, p. 335.

14 See M. M. Bakhtin, 'Discourse in the Novel', in Bakhtin, *The Dialogic Imagination*, trans. Caryl Emerson and Michael Holquist (Austin: University of Texas Press, 1981). The linguistics of the Bakhtin circle can be seen in the context of early twentieth-century debates about the relationship between theories of consciousness and the natural sciences. Bakhtin conceptualises the place of discourse in scientific thought on p. 351; see also V. N. Voloshinov's *Freudianism: A Marxist Critique*, trans. I. R. Titunik (New York: Academic Press, 1976), p. 76, which situates twentieth-century understandings of consciousness in the context of 'post-Darwinian biology'.

15 Samuel Weber, 'The Intersection: Marxism and the Philosophy of Language', *Diacritics* 15, 4 (1985): 111, quoted in Robert J. C. Young, 'Back to Bakhtin', in Young, *Torn Halves: Political Conflict in Literary and Cultural Theory* (Manchester: Manchester University Press, 1996), p. 36.

16 Gosse, *From Shakespeare to Pope*, p. 21.

17 E. Gosse, *Father and Son: A Study of Two Temperaments* (Keele: Keele University Press, 1994), p. 29.

18 Compare Isobel Armstrong's discussion of Gosse in chapter 2, this volume, pp. 36–9.

19 Gosse, *Father and Son*, p. 31.

20 *Ibid.*, p. 86.

21 *Ibid.*, p. 122.

22 *Ibid.*, p. 51. The work referred to is Nathan Bailey's *Universal Etymylogical Dictionary* (1721).

23 John Willinsky, *Empire of Words: The Reign of the OED* (Princeton, NJ: Princeton University Press, 1994), p. 202. An important work of popular philology which drew connections between Darwin's work and the history of the language was Friedrich Max Müller's *Lectures on the Science of Language: First and Second Series* (1862–64); for a contemporary commentary, see Gillian Beer, 'Darwin and the Growth of Language Theory', in John Christie and Sally Shuttleworth (eds), *Nature Transfigured: Science and Literature 1700–1900* (Manchester: Manchester University Press, 1989).

24 *Compact Oxford English Dictionary*, 2nd edn (Oxford: Clarendon Press, 1991). All references to this edition.

25 J. M. Baldwin, 'A New Factor in Evolution', *American Naturalist*, 30 (1896).

26 Gabriel Tarde, *The Laws of Imitation* [1903], trans. Elise C. Parsons, in Terry N. Clark (ed.), *Gabriel Tarde: On Communication and Social Influence* (Chicago, IL, and London: University of Chicago Press, 1969), p. 190.

27 *OED*, p. xi.

28 Murray's governing framework was in place when the dictionary first appeared. However, the *OED* was initially published in serial parts: the parts covering IJK (which would have included the entry on 'imitation') were in preparation and appearing between 1899 and 1901. The entry from Baldwin (1895) could have been included, though not the entry from Parsons translation of Tarde (1903), which would most likely have been collected in preparation for the *Supplement* (1928–33), when many additional 'scientific' usages were included.

29 William Wordsworth, *Poetical Works*, ed. Thomas Hutchinson and Ernest de Selincourt, new revised edn [1936] (Oxford: Oxford University Press, 1981), p. 461.

30 Tarde, *Laws of Imitation*, pp. 166–7. Saussure's theory is set out in the *Course in General Linguistics* (1916); it should be added that Tarde's texts are replete with formulations which cannot be reconciled with Saussure's theory and its implications – particularly in respect of Tarde's view of the origin of meaning, which held (p. 186) that ideas and their meanings had to have been formulated before being cast in oral expression.

31 Tarde, *Laws of Imitation*, p. 182.

32 *Ibid.*, p. 178.

33 'Contrary to the terms of an old debate full of the metaphysical investments that it has always assumed, the "unconscious" is no more a "thing" than it is any other thing, is no more a thing than it is a virtual or masked consciousness'. See Derrida's discussion of Freud and Nietzsche in 'Différance', *Margins of Philosophy*, trans. Alan Bass (Brighton: Harvester, 1982), p. 21. For a discussion of the place of the 'unconscious' as a strategy in Derrida's thought, see Christopher Norris, 'Deconstruction, Ontology and the Philosophy of Science' in his *New Idols of the Cave: On the Limits of Anti-Realism* (Manchester: Manchester University Press, 1997), pp. 84–5.

34 *OED*, p. xi.

35 J. M. Baldwin, *Darwin and the Humanities*, 2nd edn, The Ethical Library (London: Swann Sonnenschein, 1910), p. 50.

36 *Ibid.* p. 54.

37 Baldwin, *Story of the Mind*, Library of Useful Stories series (London: Newnes, 1899), p. 94.

38 Gosse, *Father and Son*, pp. 123–4.

39 *Ibid.*, p. 123.

40 Derrida, 'Psyche', p. 310.

41 *Ibid.*, p. 322.

42 *Ibid.*, p. 333.

43 *Ibid.*, p. 340.

44 Baldwin, *Story of the Mind*, p. 111.

45 *Ibid.*, p. 115.

46 Bakhtin, 'Dialogic Imagination', pp. 342ff.

47 Baldwin, *Story of the Mind*, p. 116.

48 Jacques Derrida, 'The Law of Genre', in *Acts of Literature*, p. 225.

49 Derrida, 'Psyche', p. 333.

50 See for instance Sigmund Freud, 'Totem and Taboo' (1912–13), in *The Penguin Freud Library*, vol. 13: *The Origins of Religion*, General Editor Angela Richards (Harmondsworth: Penguin, 1985).

51 According to Tarde (*Laws of Imitation*, p. 184): 'When a new invention, an invisible microbe at first, later on a fatal disease, brings with it a germ which will eventually destroy the old invention to which it attaches itself, how can the latter be said to evolve? Did the Roman Empire evolve when Christianity inoculated it with the virus of radical negations of its fundamental principles? No, this was counter-evolution, revolution perhaps ... it is a great mistake to consider the sum formed by these elements as a single evolution.'

52 For Gosse's romantic account of the death of Godolphin, see *From Shakespeare to Pope*, p. 109. Churton Collins takes particular pleasure in exposing the level of fabrication involved; see 'English Literature and the Universities', p. 300. For an analysis of Gosse's invention of a dramatic sense

of an ending in *Father and Son,* see Peter Allen, 'Sir Edmund Gosse and his Modern Readers: The Continued Appeal of *Father and Son*', *English Literary History*, 55, 2 (1988): 494.

53 Letter from Matthew Arnold to T. H. Huxley, 13 February 1873), in *The Letters of Matthew Arnold*, vol. 4: *1871–1878*, ed. Cecil Y. Lang (Charlottesville and London: University of Virginia Press, 2000), p. 143.

6

Passages in the invention of the psyche: mind-reading in London, 1881–84

⌒

ROGER LUCKHURST

In May 1884 at the offices of the *Pall Mall Gazette* a group of thirty people assembled to witness an event that was something between an experimental demonstration, an entertainment and a séance. Those attending included the zoologist Edwin Ray Lankester, the medical doctor Bryan Donkin, the editor of the *British Medical Journal* Ernest Hart, the businessman and newspaper proprietor Andrew Carnegie, the theosophist Colonel Henry Steele Olcott, the *belle lettriste* Edmund Gosse, the scientific journalist Grant Allen, and the aesthete Oscar Wilde. Both the conjuror, John Neville Maskelyne, who performed at the Egyptian Hall in Piccadilly, and John Tyndall, professor of physics at the Royal Institution and leading ideological proponent of scientific naturalism, sent letters regretting their absence. This group had been invited by the *Gazette*'s new editor W. T. Stead, who was transforming the evening paper into the most influential radical journal of the 1880s. In mid-1884, Stead was at the apex of his influence over government policy, with direct lines of communication into Gladstone's cabinet. This impressive group had gathered at the *Gazette*'s offices to examine the alleged 'faculties' of a certain Stuart Cumberland.

Cumberland was a mind-reader. He could discern the numbers on a bank-note sealed in an envelope, seen and memorised by only one person at a gathering. If a person either hid something or agreed to concentrate exclusively on an object in the room, Cumberland, blindfolded, could find the object. He could locate a pain in the body of a person who agreed to focus his or her thoughts upon it. More playfully, if someone was asked to imagine both a victim and a means of murder, Cumberland would 'read' that crime, identify the victim, and act out the method of dispatch.

The session at the *Gazette* was typical of his performances in many respects. It began with Cumberland blindfolded and Stead's hand pressed to his forehead. The nervous indications he 'read' from his subject enabled him to locate an object, a pin, hidden in the room. Next, Cumberland placed his hands 'nervously' on Andrew Carnegie's body, correctly isolating a pain. He then singled out Lankester, but the location of his pin could not be 'read' from the robust nerves of the naturalist. Wilde, 'who had seen where the pin was hidden, then took Professor Ray-Lankester's place, and Mr. Cumberland struck a bee-line and had the pin in no time at all'.[1] This must have amused the gathering, for Wilde had refused to be the first for experiment, declaring 'that he was not a good subject'.[2]

Halfway through the soirée Cumberland rested, and Wilde took centre-stage, delivering a 'free-and-easy' lecture on aestheticism, reported in the *Gazette* with some bewilderment. Wilde shook his green silk handkerchief at the offence of Stead's office décor, and his discourse was replete with his typical inversions of nature and culture ('There was something wrong with the Atlantic, and Niagara was not quite up to the mark'[3]). After half-an-hour, Cumberland returned, having agreed as a final test to attempt to locate an object beyond the confines of the room. The sensitive hand to be read in this instance belonged to Grant Allen. Once blindfolded, and holding Allen's hand, Cumberland plunged into the street, to the consternation of passing 'hansoms, foot-passengers, policemen, open-mouthed waiters'.[4] The object was found in interview rooms further down the street. The report ended with the news that Cumberland was likely to appear on public platforms soon, but that it would be 'difficult to give more conclusive demonstrations of his ability to "read thought" by the delicate muscular action of the hand'.[5]

Cumberland did indeed give further performances in London that season. A few days later the Chief Rabbi Dr Adler, the theologian Moncure Conway and the evolutionary biologist George John Romanes were among members of a committee overseeing a set of tests arranged at the Charing Cross Hotel. A crowd of fifty people followed Cumberland through the streets, this time bound to his subject, 'the eminent classical scholar, the Rev. Dr. Holden', by a silk handkerchief rather than by direct touch.[6] This last detail had no doubt been prompted by the latest trick of

Cumberland's mind-reading rival, the American performer Washington Irving Bishop. Bishop was also in London in the summer of 1884, extending the range of his mind-reading performances.

Bishop had first gained note in England in 1881, when his 'remarkable power of "thought-reading"' was attested to by William Carpenter and T. H. Huxley, the leading physiologists of the age.[7] This prompted a gathering of men of science, which included Lankester and Hart, the politician and campaigner for science education Lyon Playfair, the Queen's personal physician Dr Andrew Clark, the alienist Dr Daniel Hack Tuke, the evolutionary theorists Francis Galton and George Romanes, and several leading medical men.[8] As reported by the London *Standard*, Bishop began with a successful 'reading' of Lyon Playfair, and so consistently hit the mark that 'scepticism began to give way, if not to faith, at least to something approaching sympathetic curiosity'.[9] In early June 1884, the *Pall Mall Gazette* reported on his séance at the Westminster Palace Hotel, in which Bishop had read the mind of Canon Harford despite blindfold, a black sack over his head, and being connected to his subject only by seven feet of copper wire loosely attached to his fingers. Bishop read the nervous indications conducted along the wire from his subject and, followed by some 500 people, left the hotel, moved into Victoria Street, and then into Dean's Yard in Westminster, eventually arriving at the statue Harford had chosen in a second-floor room.[10] Bishop was always a flamboyant performer: one American commentator recalled that his most spectacular trick had been 'driving a team of horses, while he was ostensibly blindfolded, at break-neck speed by a circuitous route, through crowded streets, and finding, at a distant point, an object'.[11] Not to be outdone, on the same day that the *Gazette* reported on Bishop's experiments, Cumberland claimed in a 'chat' with the editor that his largest audience had been some 20,000 people, gathered in Princes Street, Edinburgh.[12]

A month after these rival meetings, the radical MP and editor of *Truth* Henry Labouchère, having been 'read' himself, arranged for Cumberland to do some mind-readings in the strangers' smoking-room of the House of Commons.[13] The *Illustrated London News* carried front-page portraits of Cumberland and his parliamentary subjects.[14] Cumberland successfully read the minds of T. P. O'Connor and Lord Lewisham, and then of Prime Minister Gladstone, 'plucking' the number 366 from Gladstone's mind (even remarking correctly on Gladstone's irresolution about choosing 365 or 366). Cumberland commented in his first set of memoirs that Gladstone was 'one of my most remarkable "subjects"', 'a magnetic man' to the extent that 'were Mr. Gladstone to try his hand at physical mesmerism with those whom he now politically hypnotises, his success would be equally marked'.[15] This reading in the House of Commons helped consolidate a remarkable *fin-de-siècle* career, in which Cumberland travelled the world, wrote several gothic novels, and read the minds of many leading British politicians and men of empire, like Lord Curzon, Lord Cromer, Sir Wilfred Laurier, Lord Milner and Lord Kitchener, leading artists, such as Gilbert and Sullivan, Rudyard Kipling, Arthur Conan Doyle, Marie Corelli and Hall Caine ('the most intense I have ever experimented with', he claimed), and the royal families and political leaders of world powers, including Baron Bismarck, the Tzar and the Khedive of Egypt.[16]

What was the status of these events? Why did performers like Bishop and Cumberland attain such celebrity at the *fin de siècle*? These questions are what this chapter examines. My suggestion is that these events were over-determined moments, in which scientists and supernaturalists, materialists and those holding that the mind or spirit was irreducible to bodily mechanism, struggled to impose incommensurable meanings on 'mind-reading'. These demonstrations can come to be seen as instances of controversy at a critical stage in the emergence of a recognisably modern scientific profession. But they were also more than moments of demarcation: 'mind-reading' was caught on the cusp of rival conceptions of mind, proving an unlikely site for both men of science and men of letters to articulate new possibilities of psychical action. It is precisely in this conjuncture, I want to argue, in the messy and confusing overlay of discourses at such events, that something like a modern subjectivity begins to be articulable.

To what genre, then, did a Bishop or a Cumberland mind-reading belong? In one sense, it was merely an entertainment which followed the course of the 'willing game', a popular middle-class pastime in which

one of the party, generally a lady, leaves the room, and the rest determine
on something which she is to do on her return ... She is then recalled, and
one or more of the 'willers' place their hands lightly on her shoulders.
Sometimes nothing happens; sometimes she strays vaguely about; sometimes she moves to the right part of the room and does the thing, or something like the thing, which she has been willed to do.[17]

Yet the presence of so many eminent men, the detailed press reports,
the attention of serious radicals and reformists like Henry Labouchère
and W. T. Stead, and the essays of leading intellectual contemporaries,
clearly wanted to ascribe to these events a *gravitas* beyond mere vulgar
entertainment.

Were they experiments, then? In a certain sense, they were.
Washington Irving Bishop's first demonstrations in May 1881 resulted
in an exchange of views in the columns of *Nature*. George Romanes, at
work on mental evolution in animals and men, reported that he had,
with Francis Galton, Lankester and George Croom Robertson (the editor
of the journal *Mind*), conducted a series of further experiments on
Bishop. Bishop, entering into the spirit of inductive inquiry, 'professes
that he is himself ignorant of his *modus operandi*, and merely desires
that this should be adequately investigated and satisfactorily explained',
Romanes reported.[18] The investigators used William Carpenter's theory
of unconscious cerebration – that Bishop's subjects unknowingly gave
muscular cues of their thoughts – and tested for the extent of his sensitivity. They deemed it 'a remarkable thing that such precise information as to a mental picture of locality should be communicated so
instantaneously', yet concluded that Bishop had no unusual physiological sensitivity to raise his experimental demonstrations beyond 'ordinary drawing-room amusement'.[19] Croom Robertson noted that the
leading American nerve specialist George Beard had already published
a physiological explanation of Bishop's talents, following his own investigations.[20] Beard considered Bishop's entirely explicable talents of use
to 'physiologists and students of diseases of the nervous system', given
the demonstration of exalted 'modes of vibration of the nerve-force'.[21]
This was essentially what Carpenter and Huxley claimed to be of interest in their testimonial for Bishop.

For the *Saturday Review*, however, any attention paid to such 'crazes' and 'modern wonders' was not worthy of the name 'experiment'. It thundered at the 'folly of bringing a dozen scientific men together to investigate what is, after all, a very common conjuring trick', claiming that 'scientific men do not make at all good observers at such exhibitions'.[22] For the *Review*, Bishop was another symptom of a rampant supernaturalism at work in England, evidence of a dangerous primitivism, no different from the claims of mesmerists and spiritualists. 'Such exhibitions', the article concluded, 'are in every way unwholesome; they encourage a misguided hankering after notoriety in the performer, they suggest a fresh means of imposture to professional charlatans, and, worst of all, they bring science and scientific evidence into ridicule and disrepute'.[23] Henry Labouchère, too, used the columns of *Truth* to expose the 'humbug' Bishop, contemptuously offering a famous '£1,000 Thought-Reading Wager' for a successful séance, then lambasting Bishop as a charlatan and thief. He warned that 'persons of position should hesitate before they allow themselves, through idle curiosity, to slip into a connection with rogues of this description'.[24]

This response showed the contradictory nature of what was understood to be at stake in such gatherings, for Bishop and Cumberland had promoted their displays as containing an educative function beyond mere frivolous entertainment, allying their demonstrations with the demystificatory project of modern science. Bishop had written a pamphlet in 1880, entitled *Second Sight Explained*, which revealed the simple techniques of music-hall clairvoyants for convincing 'weak people that there is something supernatural in the matter'. Addressing a popular readership, Bishop warned: 'The fact that a person does not comprehend the cause of a given result is evidence rather that he does not know everything, than that the cause is supernatural or even abnormal. The Conjuror, like the Spiritual Medium, comes upon the scene with his conditions and his preconcerted arrangements.'[25] Stuart Cumberland, in the same way, had begun the meeting at the *Gazette* by stating: 'I do not profess ... to give any illustrations of the supernatural'. He offered instead a physiological explanation of his talents: 'If a person will concentrate his or her mind entirely and earnestly on a given object, I claim that the thought is conveyed to any person of sufficient quickness of perception by the action of the physical system.'[26]

Cumberland, in fact, had first risen to notice in 1880 as a result of a famous disruption of a spiritualist séance in Bloomsbury, at the heart of London's spiritualist community. Amid the darkness of this séance with a highly regarded medium, Cumberland had squirted a materialised visiting spirit with cochineal, stubborn traces of which remained on the face of the medium after the lights had come up. 'All my life', he stated later, 'I have been out to find something to which a purely supernatural origin could be applied, and up to the time of writing I have not seen anything which was not explicable on a mundane basis.'[27] It was this early anti-spiritualist tone of his thought-reading performances that led to the support Cumberland received from some men of science. The alienist James Crichton-Browne presided over one performance in May 1882, praising Cumberland's 'salutary work in exposing the impositions of charlatans, and the superstitions of weak-minded enthusiasts'.[28] This applied both to spiritualists and to adherents of thought-transference. Cumberland stated: 'I have no more belief in the marvels of so-called thought transference than I have in supernatural phenomena. Thought transference has its limits, and, beyond a certain point, there is nothing doing.'[29] Thus, at the height of his fame in the 1880s, Cumberland told the readers of *The Nineteenth Century* that the talent was merely 'an exalted perception of touch'.[30] He always supported such assertions by emphasising that he was 'on excellent terms with the leaders of scientific thought', naming Carpenter, Huxley, Lankester, Crichton-Browne and David Ferrier.[31]

This ostensible demystifying function explained the presence of a number of scientific men at Bishop and Cumberland's performances. Lankester and Donkin had together launched the prosecution of the American spiritualist medium Henry Slade in 1876. Slade held private séances, at which the spirit of his wife inscribed messages to earnest seekers on a slate, a practice known as 'psychography'. Slade had been lauded by London spiritualists on his arrival, one proclaiming: 'Bring Huxley, Tyndall, Carpenter, Clifford, I care not which of them, face to face with Slade, and I maintain the scientist will be "beat."'[32] A month later, in the middle of a séance, Lankester and Donkin seized a slate with pre-prepared writing and successfully sued Slade under the Vagrancy Act, through which a conviction for gaining money under false pretences by fortune-telling could result in three months' imprisonment with hard labour. On this occasion, the *Saturday Review* had been happy to take the opportunity of the judgment to declare Slade 'a rogue and a vagabond', and hoped the prosecution would 'do good in imposing and unmasking one of the most disgraceful and degrading superstitions of modern times', while asserting the value of 'ordinary science'.[33] The prosecution's star witness had been John Maskelyne, the 'Royal Illusionist' whose Egyptian Hall show at the time included 'exposures of so-called spirit media'.[34] That explained why the *Gazette*'s report of Cumberland's demonstration included reference to his letter regretting his absence: Cumberland was a fellow debunker. After Labouchère had so insistently attacked Bishop, he also took up Cumberland as an honest debunker, praising 'this gentleman's candour' in helping expose the 'wretched nonsense' of thought-reading as 'nothing more than a sleight of touch'.[35] All of these men, it seems, attended Cumberland performances because his stage show offered a populist version of modernity's war on superstition. This was scepticism, 'the highest of duties' as T. H. Huxley had termed it, but without the austerity often associated with the scientific clerisy.[36]

The doctor Ernest Hart was present at both Bishop and Cumberland events in a slightly different, boundary-policing, role. After first witnessing Bishop, Hart composed a lengthy editorial for the *British Medical Journal*, lambasting the 'unpardonable hyperbole' of calling a 'common parlour-trick by the title "thought-reading"'.[37] The more serious aim was to give 'no uncertain verdict on an alleged discovery for which scientific patronage has been sought', warning the 'leaders of the medical profession' not to give their sanction to a performer whose performances could be misunderstood by non-professional audiences, and which gave 'free play to credulity'.[38] Hart would later declare war on 'the new witchcraft', trouncing the claims of hypnotists and neo-mesmerists that they could mesmerise at a distance, or transfer symptoms and thoughts between patients. He was more outraged that respectable English publications like *The Times* published such reports. This was all evidence, Hart held, of a 'pandemic' of credulity, an 'occultation of common sense'.[39]

As the *Saturday Review*'s fulminations at the 'unwholesome' demonstrations of Bishop revealed, and as Hart feared, neither Bishop and Cumberland nor their scientific advocates could control the meanings ascribed to these 'experiments'. One of the letters printed in *Nature* interpreted Bishop's act against its declared intention, claiming that 'there seems to be strong proof of Mr. Bishop's power of *will-compelling*, a power which, as far as I have heard, Mr. Bishop has not yet publicly claimed to possess'.[40] A pamphlet also appeared in 1883, which laboriously revealed the purely physiological means by which Bishop read minds. This was offered in order to 'make plain to the credulous and the superstitious the apparently mysterious and miraculous powers attained by Mr. Bishop' – despite the fact that the theory presented, 'unconscious muscular indication', was frequently adopted by Bishop himself.[41] Cumberland, too, unable to defuse supernaturalist accounts of his behaviour, remarked on 'folk crediting me with powers that not only I did not possess, but that I never had the remotest idea of laying claim to'.[42] At the *Gazette*'s offices, the theosophist Colonel Olcott emphatically denied Cumberland's mundane explanations of his own actions in favour of Madame Blavatsky's theories of astral travel and thought transference. Since Olcott displayed 'a ring which Mdme. Blavatsky, by her occult power, had caused to grow in the middle of a rosebud, and carried in his pocket a portrait of a seer which the same remarkable woman had willed out of the "astral light" upon a piece of cardboard', the reporter admitted that Cumberland's mind-reading tricks would be unlikely to impress such marginal adherents of magical powers. Yet Prime Minister Gladstone was also spooked by Cumberland. 'Somewhat superstitious, and not a little nervous', Gladstone had been terrified, Cumberland later revealed, by his throwaway 'shilling shocker' about mesmeric murder, *A Fatal Affinity*.[43]

Gladstone had another framework: a competing set of terms for what Cumberland had done to him in the House of Commons. Gladstone was an early honorary member of the Society for Psychical Research, an institution founded in 1882 by a number of scientists and academics antipathetic to reductively materialistic explanation. The Society had declared its primary object of research to be 'an examination of the nature and extent of any influence which may be exerted by one mind upon another, apart from any generally recognised mode of perception'.[44] What Cumberland and Bishop called mind- or muscle-reading, psychical researchers began to call *telepathy*, a term coined in December 1882 by one of the founding members of the Society, Frederic Myers. Telepathy, meaning literally 'distant touch', was premissed on the very absence of what Cumberland and Bishop insisted was necessary for their displays – physical contact with their subjects. Unwittingly, the debunking performances had fuelled the conceptual elaboration of telepathy, as an experimentally proven instance of a hitherto unregarded force in nature. After Bishop's public display in May 1881, the professor of physics William Barrett contributed to the debate in *Nature* by revealing his own tests on a particular family, 'all of whom are able to go through the ordinary performances of the "willing game" rapidly and successfully, without the contact of hands'.[45] The absence of contact was the defining tele-effect. It was only a few months later that Barrett organised the conference from which the Society for Psychical Research emerged.[46] Later, in 1884, Barrett wrote an attack in the opening edition of the *Journal of the Society for Psychical Research* on the 'epidemic delusion' surrounding Cumberland and Bishop. 'Sedate and distinguished citizens, clutched by the arm of the so-called Thought-reader, have been dragged hither and thither, indoors and out of doors, amid breathless throngs of sight-seers, in a heroic and successful search for a hidden pin', Barrett wryly commented.[47] Barrett dismissed the mere 'muscular interpretation' of these acts (even 'gentle contact' was outlawed under the rubric of telepathy), and he used these public performances to restate the experimental rigour of psychical research, which eschewed such platforms for the 'calmness and privacy needful for scientific investigation'.[48]

This was a reference to the Society's own set of experiments in mind-reading, first with over 1,000 trials of the 'willing game' in the respectable home of a family of 'sensitive' girls, and then, in an impromptu laboratory at the Society's headquarters in the winter of 1882–83, with a young stage mesmerist and thought-reading performer, George Smith. Smith and his partner Douglas Blackburn claimed to have developed a close 'mental sympathy' through which thoughts and simple mental images could be transferred without any material support. As Blackburn described it in his book *Thought Reading or Modern Mysteries Explained*, this was an unexceptional skill, being 'purely and simply illustrations of Will-power, the *soi-disant* Thought-reader being generally a person whom a natural sensitiveness, enhanced by practice, has rendered exceptionally susceptible to the active Will agency of another'.[49] A 'prominent American exponent' of this skill – Bishop was left unnamed – was dismissed as 'mediocre'.[50] The Society tested, and affirmed, this power through trials in the transference of words, numbers, and simple drawings.[51] These experiments looked exactly the same as the trials set up for Bishop and Cumberland. They also shared some of the same audience: Francis Galton, George Romanes and Sir James Crichton-Browne attended some sessions. These experiments could claim, if anything, more rigour. They were test sequences in a controlled experimental environment, subject to pioneering statistical analysis, with reports passed through peer review in an official journal rather than played out in the sensationalising press.[52] But the experiments had a diametrically opposed object from those with Bishop and Cumberland. They aimed to determine a supra-materialistic residue, the fleeting evidence of thought transference materially unsupported. One proven instance, the Society averred, would break the grip of the bleak physiological determinism and materialism that drove scientific naturalism.

Psychical research, therefore, sought to positivise the *super*-natural. Although the results of such tests were bitterly contested by sceptical naturalists,[53] the Society premissed all of its work for the next twenty years on the findings of the experiments with Blackburn and Smith. Thus, when Cumberland came to the *Pall Mall Gazette*'s offices in May 1884, the secretary of the Society, Edmund Gurney, refused the invitation to attend, remarking that since touch was involved it added little of value to an established body of scientific knowledge. An exchange of letters left Bryan Donkin fulminating

> What Mr Cumberland and many others in greater or lesser degree can do in their way has nothing whatever in common with the pretended experiments of the Psychical Research Society. So-called 'thought-reading without contact', or 'thought-transference', exists only in the minds of mystics and mystery-mongers.[54]

What had started out as scientific support for an entertaining but educative demystification in 1881 had become, by 1884, a site from which challenges to the limits of materialistic explanation could be launched. It was now difficult to discern how Donkin was distinguishing 'pretended' experiments on telepathy from 'real' experiments on mind-reading against Gurney's claims for scientific authority, or how Barrett could mark off 'pseudo thought-transference' (with Cumberland and Bishop, mere stage-performers) from the real thing (with Smith, also a stage-performer). Personnel overlapped confusingly between the camps. This was exactly what Ernest Hart had feared: if medical men gave their sanction by appearing on stage with Cumberland, there was nothing to stop an ignorant crowd from mistaking causation and believing 'that there exists a new form of mental power which has hitherto escaped the observation of scientific men'.[55] Perhaps the greatest conjuring feat of these performers was to ensnare such an impressive section of the intellectual elite in a debate over their status. This was the result, one contemporary analyst remarked, of basic 'errors of inference' by audiences, a skilful concealment of simple methods of apprehension, which 'create[d] the impression that one is possessed of a weird power'.[56] Thus did some remarkable careers bloom at the *fin-de-siècle*.

These episodes can be inserted into recent revisionist histories of Victorian science. Historians are now more suspicious of the trajectories men of science themselves gave in outlines of scientific progress. There was no monolithic transfer of cultural authority from religious or broadly supernaturalist claims to scientific rationality. The relation of science to theology was frequently less one of war than of quiet accommodation.[57] There was no progressive move through Auguste Comte's epistemological hierarchy, from primitive theological belief, through metaphysics, to the triumphal arrival of positive knowledge, which dispensed with all 'supernatural agents' or 'abstract forces' for scientific reasoning.[58] Even after the 1870s – which in Britain saw the Royal Commission on Scientific Instruction and the Advancement of Science (1872–75), the beginnings of public endowment for scientific research, the establishing of a chain of technical and scientific institutes, and dedicated research laboratories in

Cambridge, Edinburgh, Glasgow, London, Manchester and Oxford – the nascent profession was fragile, however essential it claimed to be to the national good, and however far it expanded its rights of explication and inquiry into the cultural sphere.[59] Instead of this clear-cut transfer, the extension of scientific authority produced a diffuse and uncertainly bounded 'field of scientificity' to highly unpredictable effect. The late century was awash with unforeseen knowledges, hybrid and ephemeral notions, ingenious couplings which emerged as compromise formations melding apparently discrete discourses. It was an era which, for the scientific ideologue Karl Pearson, was dominated by a provoking paradox: 'the highest intellectual power accompanied by the strangest recrudescence of superstition'.[60] Such hybrid forms engendered strenuous attempts to demarcate the sphere of proper science, both discursively but also spatially. Sophie Forgan, for instance, has traced a conceptual shift from the *juxtaposition* of scientific sites with other cultural institutions in London at mid-century to an accelerating *separation* towards the end of the century, reflecting a concern to isolate scientific practice, exemplified by the laboratory, from all manner of social and cultural contaminations.[61] These exertions, however, only tended to embed scientific discourse further within contested cultural dynamics. They gave scientific authority more allure, and thus more reasons for its 'improper' appropriation. With Cumberland and Bishop, what had begun as displays of demystification, a populist alliance of music-hall debunking with scientific rationality, could end up contributing to the production of rigorously formulated experimental objects like 'telepathy'. Such a sequence upholds the view that lines of demarcation are never final, but are rather invitations to transgression.

The debate over the precise status and legitimacy of Cumberland and Bishop's performances can also be illuminated by recent work on the role of experiment in science. Experiments, James Secord has observed, are usually thought of as 'the products of individuals in conceptually defined traditions'.[62] They are also regarded as autonomous self-regulating disciplinary procedures, and thus remain, as the editors of *The Uses of Experiment* observe, a 'neglected activity', seemingly transparent and self-evident.[63] Sociologists of science have begun to interrogate these assumptions in recent years. Bruno Latour and Steve Woolgar's *Laboratory Life* tracked the messy and argumentative route from instruments and annotations on the bench, through piles of printouts and disorderly office desks, to the finished product of the scientific paper, concluding that experimental practice, 'widely regarded by outsiders as well organised, logical and coherent, in fact consists of a disordered array of observations with which scientists struggle to produce order'.[64] Where Latour and Woolgar analysed 'normal' science, the work of Harry Collins and Trevor Pinch has focused on experiment at the contested frontiers of science. 'In controversial science', they suggest, 'no one can agree on a criterion of competence.' Therefore, 'scientists at the research front cannot settle their deep disagreements through better experimentation, more knowledge, more advanced theories, or clearer thinking', but rely instead on contingent social factors like reputation, institutional locus and authority, and the degree of the claimants' 'integration into various scientific networks'.[65] Latour's more recent work has also argued for the acculturation of science, an analysis which attempts to reconnect experiment to the wider social spheres in which it subsists. In this view, experiment is never autonomous, but is part of a highly socialised network.[66]

Passages in the history of science can offer other ways of reconnecting experimental rationality to social agency. James Secord's case history of the amateur scientist Andrew Crosse, who appeared to produce living mites by electrolysis in his private laboratory in 1836, 'the most famous experiment in the first half of the nineteenth century',[67] is meant to display both the fluidity of the epistemic spaces in which the experiment could be placed, but also the intrinsic connections between scientific practice and social interest. Crosse's experiment was situated between geology, biology and electrical science, and as a point of contest between emergent definitions of amateur and professional science, between elite and artisanal electrical institutions, between local and metropolitan periodical presses, and, given the apparently spontaneous generation of life in the experiment, between religious and radical atheistic constituencies. Similarly, Simon Schaffer has examined the controversial attempts of mid-Victorian astronomers to re-negotiate their place in the hierarchy of knowledge, to re-assign astronomy from a purely observational to an experimental science, and, most radically, to extend the limits of experimentation itself. When spectroscopic analysis of starlight brought celestial bodies into the observatory and onto the table-top, astonomers hooked up a new network of instrument-makers, opticians, chemists and photographers, and brought the isolated gentleman's observatory into contact with new public institutions. 'In these enterprises', Schaffer concludes, '"experiment" is best understood as a label applied to complex arrays of personnel, technique, hardware, and social institutions.'[68]

Cumberland and Bishop appeared across a diversity of spaces – in private laboratories, drawing-rooms, in theatres and music-halls, in the street – and before a bewildering collocation of experimentalists – biologists, chemists, alienists, academic psychologists, medical men, journalists, politicians, lawyers, novelists and aesthetes. They constitute an exemplary instance of the open, disordered and socially riven manner of experimentation at a critical phase of science's professionalisation. They were occasions for demarcation, because their displays took place on the vital line separating science and superstition, and scientists could stamp rational exposition over apparent supernatural agency. Yet they became sites of proliferating explanation, not because the scientists were ineffectual, or the 'criteria of competence' for experimentation were improperly controlled, but rather because the very object of the trials was hybrid, unformulated, in dispute. For scientific naturalists and materialists, mind-reading was physiologically determinable 'unconscious cerebration'. For others, including members of the scientific community like William Barrett, mind-reading was valuable precisely as supra-materialist evidence of the 'veritable exoneural action of the mind'.[69] If the word *psyche* is missing in these disputes, falling between physiological and transcendental attribution, that is because it was not really a respectable or distinctive disciplinary object.

In the final two sections of this essay, I argue that these mind-reading experiments display how notions of the 'psyche' and the 'psychical' were being transformed in the late nineteenth century. The experiments are rich sites for analysis because of their hybridity, and the disparate resources brought to them from biology, theology, medicine and aesthetics helped to elaborate conceptions of subjectivity. After a final excavation of the transitional meanings of 'psyche' at work by the beginning of the 1880s, I then circle back to a last examination of the conjuncture that occurred around Stuart Cumberland in the offices of the *Pall Mall Gazette*.

In 1876, in the 'Prefatory Words' to the new journal *Mind: A Quarterly Review of Philosophy and Psychology*, George Croom Robertson confessed that psychology, 'pursued as a positive science ... has been far from as fruitful as could be wished'. He hoped that the journal would 'procure a decision as to the scientific standing of psychology'.[70] Three years later, the academic psychologist James Sully, again in *Mind*, wrote: 'Psychology must be said just now to be in a fluent condition. The old conception of the science as limited to the introspective study of the human mind is fast disappearing, and it is as yet difficult to say what new shape this department of knowledge is destined to take.'[71] Charles Darwin had held out the promise of integrating psychology into scientific legitimacy through the synthesising power of the evolutionary hypothesis: *On the Origin of Species* had projected that '[p]sychology will be based on a new foundation, that of the necessary acquirement of each mental power and capacity by gradation'.[72] Developmental theories of human psychology had been influential through the mid-century, as in Herbert Spencer's fusion of neurology, biology and mind in *The Principles of Psychology* or the 'mental physiology' of alienists like Henry Maudsley and Thomas Laycock and neurologists like John Hughlings Jackson. Yet when Darwin died in March 1882, and *Nature* ran a series of essays assessing his impact on scientific disciplines, psychology was dealt with last. 'The truth of the matter', the essayist argued, 'is that psychology, in being the science furthest removed from the reach of experimental means and inductive method, is the science which has longest remained in the trammels of an *a priori* analysis and metaphysical thought.'[73]

At the beginning of the 1880s the legitimacy accrued from entraining mental development to evolutionary trajectories had not secured psychology in either conceptual or disciplinary terms. It remained uncertainly located between the subjective moral sciences and the objective, natural sciences, and fractured between the disciplines of medicine, neurology, alienism, asylum treatments and academic philosophy of mind, itself divided between idealist and empiricist camps. One of the essential problems was that 'psychology' retained a residual sense of being the 'science of souls' (*psyche* meaning 'breath' or 'soul' in Greek). It was the implied dualism of body and mind which a monistic scientific naturalism sought to interrogate by reducing mind to an epiphenomenal effect of brain physiology, at least in its most extreme forms. Darwin, followed by George Romanes, had spent the 1870s attempting to trace the most complex human emotions back to their evolutionary origins, often as physiological reflexes.[74] In the late 1870s, however, a number of prominent scientists began to explore mental phenomena which had long been rejected as fraudulent imposture. In 1876, Jean-Martin Charcot, the eminent Paris neurologist and hero of the anti-clerical rationalists, began to investigate the claims of Victor Burq that hysterical patients in somnambulistic states could be affected by magnets. Burq demonstrated that with magnets he could transfer somatic paralyses around the body, a mobility which severed symptom from simple physiological causation. Burq's later 'metallotherapy' also claimed to effect a transfer of symptoms between patients. Charcot confirmed these test results in 1878, and again to the austere Académie des Sciences in 1882. This is often regarded as the moment at which the 'rejected knowledge' of mesmerism became a scientifically legitimated study of hypnotism.[75] At about the same time, trance states revealed peculiar disturbances of memory – hidden memory strands, inaccessible to the conscious self, which seemed to constitute second selves, double or even multiplex personalities. These maladies of memory required a new diagnostic language of amnesia, hypermnesia and cryptomnesia, and a reconceptualisation of mental topography. For Ian Hacking, the decade between 1875 and 1885 was the time when 'the sciences of memory firmed up, and when the idea of trauma, previously used only for a bodily wound or lesion, came to apply to psychic hurt'.[76] In these shifts, what was beginning to emerge was the sense of a distinctive dynamic psychology – that is, a conception of mind as never simply reducible to physiological processes.

The mind-reading performances of Bishop and Cumberland resonate with these disturbances. The 'fluent condition' of the discipline accounted to some extent for the multifarious and cross-disciplinary audiences at the experimental gatherings. The disputes over the nature of the phenomena witnessed centred on where to locate psychical activity and whether it was reducible to or independent of physiology. The psychical researcher William Barrett had in fact first coined 'thought transference' as a way of theorising the 'community of sensation' claimed to occur between patient and operator during mesmeric sleep, and many of those attending Bishop's and Cumberland's trials had direct experience of anomalous trance states.[77] The dispute was reduced to science versus superstition, however, because in England the transitional de-spiritualised meanings of 'psyche', 'psychical' and even 'psychological' were still felt to have emerged from a decidedly spiritualist context.

A key context for the mind-reading performances of Bishop and Cumberland was the theory of *psychic force*. This had been coined by the journalist, lawyer and sergeant-at-arms Edward Cox in 1871 as a term to explain the phenomena at the core of some of the most controversial scientific experiments of the 1870s. In 1870, Cox had joined the vice-president of the Royal Society, the astronomer William Huggins, and the chemist and editor William Crookes in an investigation of alleged spiritualist phenomena. Crookes had announced in his own journal, the *Quarterly Journal of Science*, that he intended to settle the question of spiritualism by sweeping away the 'pseudo-scientific' jargon of claims to 'electro-biologise' or 'psychologise', in order to replace it with the sound theoretical principles of the natural sciences.[78] He was well placed to do so, as a leading chemical spectroscopist and fellow of the Royal Society, awarded for his discovery of the element Thallium. Much to the consternation of the scientific community, however, Crookes's report in July 1871, after a year of inquiry into spiritualist mediums, announced that 'these experiments appear conclusively to establish the evidence of a new force, in some unknown manner connected with the human organisation, which for convenience may be called the Psychic Force'.[79] Crookes attributed the coinage to his fellow experimentalist Edward Cox. Cox had sought a term which refused to acknowledge the 'spirit hypothesis', and which attributed séance phenomena not to spirits of the departed, but to a force 'generated in certain persons of peculiar nervous organisation in sufficient power to operate beyond bodily contact'.[80] He coined another term for such sensitive people: 'psychics'. For Cox, the 'virulence of hostility' which had met Crookes's experiments and the proposed theory of psychical action was the result principally of ideological factors: 'Psychic Force is a *fact* which ... *does* go very far indeed to disturb the Philosophy of Materialism which has taken so strong a hold of the scientific world'.[81] Psychic force thus aimed to lever open a space between reductive physiology and spiritualist belief, a scientised supra-materialist energy modelled on 'electricity, magnetism, and other invisible and intangible forces of nature'.[82]

While Crookes's utterances in scientific contexts were vigorously policed by his fellow scientists, Cox went on to found the Psychological Society of Great Britain, which ran until his death in 1879. The Society's resolutions declared its 'object' to be 'the scientific investigation of psychology in all its branches', with the rider that all theological questions were 'to be strictly excluded'.[83] A formal council was set up, and Cox ensured that the Society met 'in season' and at venues not identified with the spiritualist community. He proposed periodical publication, in order to develop 'a storehouse of *facts* to which Psychologists everywhere may refer'.[84] The one collected volume published showed through its lectures (on 'The Psychology of Memory', 'On Some Phenomena of Sleep and Dream', 'Primitive Psychology of the Aryans', and so forth) that it was reaching for legitimate areas of study. Mention of 'spiritualism' was actively avoided, while apparently naturalist arguments were constant. 'We do not concern ourselves with the *super*natural', Cox promised. 'It is not within our province. We list to Nature only – to the *living* man – to the *actual* world.'[85] By the third season of meetings, in 1876, Cox claimed that no scientific society, other than the Royal Geographic Society, was gaining larger audiences in London. Cox also wrote a vast two-volume synthesis of current work at the limits of the physiological explanation of psychical action, entitled *The Mechanism of Man*. In these volumes, Cox traced out the lineaments of a system which began with sleep and dream states, and passed through delirium and catalepsy before treating the uncanny phenomena associated with natural and artificial somnambulism. At a vanishing point, beyond the gravitational pull of physiology, these 'states' passed over into the super-sensuous perception associated with *psychism*, the force that 'radiates from the nerve centres'.[86] And, by 1879, Cox could cite the experimental proofs then being claimed by Jean-Martin Charcot at the Salpètrière Hospital in Paris, a report on which he included in the appendix of the second volume. Cox was becoming an expert at binding his notion of 'psychic force' into legitimate, if controversial, frontiers of the new experimental psychology.

The effect of Cox's attempt to de-spiritualise 'psychology' produced a conflicted response among spiritualists. *The Psychological Review* opened in 1878, its title placed in unproblematic opposition to a materialism which failed 'to get beyond the outward form, the mere shell, husk, and envelope of things'.[87] 'Psyche' and 'spirit' were interchangeable here. Yet *Spiritual Notes* which ran between 1878 and 1880, and was subtitled 'A Monthly Epitome of the Transactions of the Spiritual and Psychological Societies', began by being 'undecided' on the relative virtues of the terms 'spirit' or 'psyche',[88] before rapidly retreating from Cox's 'psychism'. One writer warned that psychism was 'only the porch of Spiritualism', and was dangerously snared in materialist explanations, the enemy of faith.[89] For many orthodox naturalists, on the other hand, Cox was merely an untrained amateur, 'the most gullible of the gullible', a spiritualist transparently affecting to transpose soul into the language of science.[90] Cox had therefore rendered 'psyche', 'psychism' and 'psychic force' highly charged, unstable and transitional terms.

The influence of the trials of Crookes, Cox and Huggins in detecting 'psychic force' inevitably hung over the mind-reading performances of Bishop and Cumberland. Prominent men had elaborated a theoretical armature of psychism in the 1870s, and to Lankester and Donkin, at least, public performances of mind-reading might explode their illogical basis and reconfirm the demystifying practice of scientific common sense. Yet William Crookes was also a respected figure, and his experimental practice was rigorous enough to impress many. Crookes's private laboratory was the site of intensive experimentation, in which a battery of knowledge and techniques was directed at isolating fugitive instances of psychic force. Crookes's own precision work reading chemical spectra and tracking elusive streams of 'radiant matter' *in vacuo* was joined to the observational and spectroscopic expertise of the astronomer William Huggins.

These skills were combined, on occasion, with those of the electrical engi-
neer Cromwell Varley, one of the fêted telegraphic pioneers who had laid
the successful transatlantic telegraph cable in 1866. A spiritualist, Varley
saw clear analogies between electricity and spirit forces: both the tele-
graph-room and the séance involved securing unbroken lines of communication and instruments of sufficient sensitivity to detect faint signals. In
one experiment with Crookes, Varley wired a medium into an electrical
circuit, the medium taking 'the place of the telegraph cable, under electrical test'.[91] The polymathic talents of Francis Galton were also put to use
by Crookes. Galton crawled beneath tables to ensure no physical forces
were being mistaken for the action of psychic force.[92] Galton told his
cousin Charles Darwin: 'Crookes is working deliberately and well.'[93] At
another experimental séance recorded by Cox, the medium Eva Fay was
wired into a circuit in Crookes's library, separated from his laboratory by
a heavy curtain. The wires led back into the laboratory, and to a 'detective
light', which would signal any break in the circuit, and thus any illegal
move of the medium. The experimentalists Crookes, Cox, Galton and
Huggins watched the light 'burn steadily', as a spirit hand passed them
copies of their own books from the library shelves.[94] Huggins had
described the impact of the spectrosope on astronomy as opening 'the veil
and the door behind which lay the unknown mystery of the true nature
of the heavenly bodies'.[95] Here was a domestic version of the veil being
parted, affording a glimpse at previously hidden *psychic* forces.

It is the transgression at this doorway, on the threshold between the
laboratory and the library, the world of science and the world of letters,
that symbolises for me the kind of hybrid site in which notions of the
psyche were being reinvented in the late Victorian era. The resources
bound in to this private experiment were extraordinary: they stretched
from the farthest limits of the visible universe (Huggins) to the microscopic particles in evacuated tubes (Crookes), from electrical technologies communicating across the Atlantic (Varley's test device) to the puzzle
of inheritance and the limits of the human faculties (Galton). Cox and
Crookes were also journalists and proprietors, and therefore able contro-
versialists, riding the wave of growing mass readerships. This was only a
small circle of men: once we return to the offices of the *Pall Mall Gazette*,

with Stuart Cumberland and his audience of thirty, the hybrid elements bound in to the construction of his 'psychic' talents multiply powerfully.

We have a sense, now, of the scientific resources and controversial issues at work behind Cumberland's hunt for a hidden pin. This complex and riven picture becomes more over-determined if we consider the resources brought to the *Gazette* by the several men of letters in attendance. Scientific discourse on the psyche held no monopoly: indeed, Regenia Gagnier has argued for the powerful influence of a specific notion of a 'literary subjectivity' on the sense of Victorian selfhood. If this solitary, 'internalised, self-reflexive subjectivity' was under pressure from scientific discourse late in the century,[96] Cumberland's mind-reading performances again provide an exemplary site for analysis.

Let us take Grant Allen, who stepped up to be the test-subject for Cumberland, in the experiment to seek an object beyond the confines of the office. Allen was known, by 1884, as a scientific journalist, a disciple of Herbert Spencer, and the author of *Physiological Aesthetics*, whose object was 'to exhibit the purely physical origin of the sense of beauty'. This treated the 'intellectual faculties and the higher emotions, which, until the rise of Physiological Psychology, were usually considered as purely and exclusively mental', and reduced them to reflexes of pleasure and pain.[97] In this schema, refined aesthetic taste came with extreme nervous sensitivity, feeling 'every delicate thrill of harmony, every minute twinge of discord, which our nervous organisation renders us capable of perceiving'.[98] His naturalistic explanation of Cumberland's 'psychic' talent was anticipated here: nerves can be refined to exquisite sensitivity, 'but we can never get beyond this natural barrier, or transcend our own organic capacities'.[99] In a memoir, his friend Edward Clodd noted that Allen refused to 'use time in discussing the validity of a heap of trivial pseudo-mysteries loosely grouped under the term "supernatural"'.[100] Yet, in 1884, Grant Allen also dropped the pseudonym that he had used for a number of gothic short stories, publishing *Strange Stories* under his own name, with an apology for his tendency to 'stray surreptitiously and tentatively from my proper sphere into the flowery fields of pure fiction'.[101] What prompted him to fiction writing (apart from finances) was a ghost

– or, rather, the realisation that a refutation of ghosts was better done in narrative form. A number of his first stories attempted to puncture supernaturalism, one of them including a comically mundane explanation for a phantasm reported by a gullible believer in 'psychic force' in the pages of a barely fictionalised 'Proceedings of the Society for the Investigation of Supernatural Phenomena'.[102]

Allen went on to publish novels like *The Great Taboo*, which explored anthropological theories of ghost-worship in primitive religion.[103] Other tales, however, positively exploited the superstitious thrills of the gothic, capitalising on literature's suspension of the 'thetic' thrust of science. In a later story, for instance, Césarine Vivian, a Haitian quadroon, mesmerically exerts a 'strange and weird fascination' on our hapless English hero, who is commanded, against his will, by her 'terrible influence' into an ecstatic but horrifying miscegenate marriage.[104] There is no voice of the rational physiologist to ground the occult and sexual fantasies operating here, in a text which contributes fully to the fictional exploration of the uncanny influences of mesmerism and hypnotism.[105] Therefore, as the mind-reader Stuart Cumberland was led towards a hidden object by Grant Allen's 'nervous' indications, Allen was in a critical year of transition, caught between scientific naturalism and the ludic potential of gothic fiction. Allen's emerging hybridity – Edward Clodd remarked on a 'bewildering' career following subjects of 'strange incongruity and divergence'[106] – made him ideally situated for exploring the psyche.

This is because gothic fiction, as Robert Miles has argued, has always 'found itself embroiled within a larger, theoretically complex project: the history of the "subject"'.[107] The topographies of the modern mind were, for many literary historians, elaborated in the gothic narratives of the late eighteenth century. While much criticism of late-Victorian gothic has concentrated on its degenerate bodily horrors, the transitional state of the psychical in the 1880s suggests that Terry Castle's readings of early gothic still hold force. Castle argues that Gothic fictions dramatise modern subjectivity as constituted by a 'spectralisation or "ghostifying" of mental space', in which the discourse of the supernatural is displaced into the language of haunting memories and phantom thoughts, the states of reverie, dream and nightmare typical of gothic fiction.[108] Thus, she argues, the 'explained supernatural' pioneered by Anne Radcliffe, as a popularised version of the demystifying project of Enlightenment thinkers, 'was peculiarly compromised from the start. The rationalists did not so much negate the traditional spirit world as displace it into the realm of psychology'.[109]

This transaction, in which the attention of demystificatory rationalism actually only intensifies uncanny effects, haunted Cumberland's mind-reading performances and the discourse around them. Cumberland presented himself to the public and the scientific world in these displays as a rationalist and debunker of superstitions, reducing psychic powers to the grooves of nervous action. Yet Cumberland also began to use gothic fiction as a different mode of articulation, investigating the 'vasty deep' of the mind and, in *The Fatal Affinity*, the occult psychic powers of the orient.[110] Here, foul murders in London are directed mesmerically, across the astral plane, by servants of Hindoo devils – an enemy that can be fought only by the enigmatic Colonel Mansfield, who 'had dipped deeply into the sacred writings of the Hindoos, and was greatly learned in what is termed the Occultism of the East'.[111] In this text, full of entranced cataleptic states, unbounded psychic power and the attribution of magical vengeance to a colonised race, Cumberland exploited, rather than dismissed, a strong locus of late imperial anxiety and superstition. His fellow stage performer and debunker John Maskelyne had railed against the 'meretricious glamour' of tales of oriental magic, complaining that 'it occasionally happens that some writer of fertile imagination evolves from his inner consciousness a romance embodying suppositional incidents and fictitious miracles. This, on being published, is seized upon with avidity by those in search of the marvellous, and repeated as a record of something which actually occurred'.[112] The confusion of fictive and real, rational and oneiric, conjured in the ghostly 'inner consciousness', was precisely what Cumberland affected in his gothic fictions, and this must have inevitably bled into his mind-reading performances. This elision left Cumberland closer to Colonel Olcott, the unimpressed theosophist in the audience at the *Gazette*'s offices, than any of his scientific supporters could have countenanced.

The gothic becomes a means of hollowing out new topographies of the psyche, a subject typically 'in a state of deracination, of the self finding itself dispossessed in its own house, in a condition of rupture, disjunction, fragmentation'.[113] What is specific to late-Victorian gothic is a highly localisable language of psychic force, telepathy, hypnotic states and occult influence, but also of split and multiplex personalities. Aside from Jekyll and Hyde, the other enduring late-Victorian gothic figure of psychic splitting is Oscar Wilde's Dorian Gray. And when Cumberland picked Oscar Wilde to be 'read', other aspects of the gothicised self were invoked.

Wilde, it will be recalled, initially refused to be read by Cumberland, claiming to be a 'poor subject', but nevertheless stepped in for the resistant Lankester, and proved to be an open book. The proximity of these figures is neatly representative of the hybrid and contradictory elements at work in the *Gazette*'s offices. Lankester had recently published his lecture *Degeneration: A Chapter in Darwinism*, in which the biological retrogression of primitive sea squirts was the model for the decline of civilisations, and their slide into decadence.[114] Since Wilde was fast becoming the emblem of 'decadence', and because the decadent was frequently identified with morbidly over-sensitive nerves, his readability would have confirmed naturalist prejudices. What is perhaps more interesting, though, is Wilde's intial refusal to offer himself for mind-reading. This reluctance is echoed, if at some distance, in his tale 'Lord Arthur Savile's Crime', first published in 1887.

Lord Savile, attending a mixed party, 'a wonderful medley of people', has his palm read by a foreign 'chiromantist'.[115] The palm-reader is so appalled by the secret crime he sees written in the palm that he initially refuses to tell Savile what he has read there. Savile postpones his wedding in order to live out his destiny, to commit murder. The chiromantist, in some way, has given Savile his first sense of interiority, of mysterious and obscure destiny. After a series of failed attempts to murder aged relatives, Savile conveniently kills the messenger himself, tipping the palmist into the Thames, thus fulfilling his duty and sealing up his pre-marital secret. The palmist is not missed: his patron, Lady Windermere, comments: 'I go in for telepathy now. It is much more amusing.'[116] After the impact of queer theory, it is tempting to read this comic–gothic tale as an allegory of a 'homosexual' secret, read in the grain of the body by an expert who is initially paid for his silence, and is then killed off, with the hero left to masquerade successfully within a heterosexual marriage.

Wilde was 'read' by Cumberland only a few days before his marriage to Constance, on 29 May 1884. If there was no 'homosexual' secret as such to be uncovered, Wilde's dysphoric gender performances as the effete dandy had already met with strong disapproval. Wilde's frequent use of gothic narratives and tropes was arguably because the psychic topographies of the genre in the late nineteenth century had also become imbricated in the relatively new discourse of sexology, in which sexuality was the organising 'secret' shaping the subject. Eve Sedgwick has argued, influentially, that the gothic can articulate a homosexual panic, a reiterated plot in which a man is harried by his double, a man who is 'persecuted by, *but considers himself transparent to* and often under the compulsion of, another male'.[117] And when Edward Carpenter in 1896 defined 'the intermediate sex', he noted of the Uranian man that 'the logical faculty may or may not, in their case, be well-developed, but intuition is always strong; like women they read characters at a glance, and know, without knowing how, what is passing in the minds of others'.[118] Was Wilde's masquerade under threat by being an open book to a mind-reader wielding a hypersensitivity to the secret signals of the body? This encounter might therefore also be read within Michel Foucault's analysis of the growing surveillance of sexualities at the end of the century.[119] The ironies are indeed manifold, given Henry Labouchère's concurrent involvement with Cumberland. Wilde's private life would eventually be rendered readable to all, when tried and imprisoned for acts of gross indecency under Labouchère's clause added to the Criminal Law Amendment Act of 1885. This Act had precipitately passed into law as a result of the purity campaigns of the *Pall Mall Gazette*'s editor W. T. Stead. By the time of Wilde's prosecution, Stead had become the leading advocate for the 'scientifically proven' facts of telepathy, messages from the dead, astral travel and the photography of materialised spirits.[120]

Literary and cultural narratives of selfhood therefore brought their own conceptual resources to the frameworks intended to comprehend Cumberland's mind-reading act. The gothic form hollowed a sense of interior mental space which could be the stage for the obscure psychic forces and pulsions of the nervous body that were being engineered by the disciplinary transformations of psychology. Such a minor incident as a mind-reading in a newspaper's offices thus becomes a highly over-deter-mined instance, in which scientific materialism, theosophy, astronomy, spectroscopy, psychical research, telegraphy, orientialism, music-hall con-juring, sexology, hypnotism, physiology, spiritualism and gothic narra-tives constellated themselves in shifting formations around the body of Stuart Cumberland. This complex, knotted event deserves disentangling. Cumberland may have largely disappeared from the historical record, because it is difficult to know which disciplinary narrative he might best serve, whether in histories of psychology, or of psychical research, or of Victorian conjuring, or as just a footnote to any number of biographies. But this lack of place is precisely the point. It is only at such sites, I would argue, that the full sense of the networks of knowledge at work in trans-forming notions of selfhood in the late Victorian period can begin to be recovered. Literary historians, as well as historians of science interested in shifting formations around conceptions of subjectivity, might well find new interconnections and pathways by attending to events which seem so initially impoverished and marginal – or just frankly bizarre.

Notes

1 'Muscle-Reading by Mr. Stuart Cumberland', *Pall Mall Gazette* (24 May 1884), p. 2.
2 *Ibid.*
3 *Ibid.*
4 *Ibid.*
5 *Ibid.*
6 'Pin-Finding and Thought-Reading at Charing Cross', *Pall Mall Gazette*, 5 June 1884, p. 10. Citation from Stuart Cumberland's recollection of the test in *A Thought-Reader's Thoughts* (London: Sampson Row, 1888), p. 29.
7 Carpenter's letter was cited in 'Thought-Reading', *British Medical Journal* (14 May 1881): 777. Carpenter and Huxley understood thought-reading to be explicable entirely by mundane physiological mechanisms, as will become clear below.
8 For the most complete list of those who attended this gathering, see 'Thought-Reading', *Lancet* (14 May 1881): 795.
9 'Thought-Reading', *Standard*, 10 May 1881, p. 5.

10 'Mr. Irving Bishop's "Thought-Reading" Experiments', *Pall Mall Gazette*, 4 June 1884, p. 10.

11 Dr Charles Gatchell, 'The Methods of Mind-Readers', *Forum*, 11 (1891): 197.

12 'A Chat with Mr. Stuart Cumberland', *Pall Mall Gazette*, 4 June 1884, p. 11.

13 See the 'Scrutator' columns, *Truth* (19 June and 26 June 1884): 917–18 and 954–5.

14 'Politicians at Play: "Thought-Reading" in House of Commons', *Illustrated London News*, 28 June 1884, p. 622.

15 Stuart Cumberland, *A Thought-Reader's Thoughts*, pp. 69, 71 and 73.

16 Stuart Cumberland, *People I Have Read* (London: C. Arthur Pearson, 1905). Citation, p. 176.

17 William Barrett, Edmund Gurney and F. W. H. Myers, 'Thought-Reading', *Nineteenth Century* (1882): 890.

18 George Romanes, 'Thought-Reading', *Nature* (23 June 1881): 171.

19 *Ibid.*: 172.

20 George Croom Robertson, 'The Physiology of Mind-Reading', *Nature* (14 July 1881): 236.

21 George M. Beard, 'The Physiology of Mind-Reading', *Popular Science Monthly*, 10 (February 1877): 170.

22 'Thought-Reading', *Saturday Review* (21 May 1881): 652–3.

23 *Ibid.*: 653.

24 'Entre Nous' column, *Truth* (2 August 1883): 153. Labouchère was responding to a rather remarkable action by Bishop. His career had clearly been so affected by the campaign in *Truth* that Bishop decided to defend himself by issuing a one-off copy of a newspaper, *The Truth* (subtitled 'Mr. Henry Labouchère, M.P., *versus* Mr. W. Irving Bishop'), which looked identical to Labouchère's journal, and which carried an eight-page refutation of the charges of fakery, collusion and embezzlement of money. Labouchère (unusually for him) decided not to sue. See *The Truth* (26 July 1883).

25 Washington Irving Bishop, *Second Sight Explained: A Complete Exposition of Clairvoyance or Second Sight, as Exhibited by the Late Robert Houdin and Robert Heller, Showing How the Phenomena May Be Produced* (Edinburgh: John Menzies, 1880), pp. 8 and 77.

26 'Muscle-Reading by Mr. Stuart Cumberland', *Pall Mall Gazette*, 24 May 1884, p. 2.

27 Stuart Cumberland, *Spiritualism – The Inside Truth* (London: Odhams Ltd., 1919), p. 15. The opening chapter includes a narrative of Cumberland's cochineal trick.

28 'Thought-Reading', *British Medical Journal* (13 May 1882): 710.

29 Stuart Cumberland, *That Other World: Personal Experiences of Mystics and their Mysticism* (London: Grant Richards, 1918), p. 170.

30 Stuart Cumberland, 'A Thought-Reader's Experience', *Nineteenth Century* (1886): 883.
31 Stuart Cumberland, *People I Have Read*, p. 188.
32 Rev. Stainton Moses, *The Spiritualist* (11 August 1876): 22.
33 'A Rogue and Vagabond', *Saturday Review* (4 November 1876), p. 561. Slade fled the country, although the Court of Appeal later overturned the verdict.
34 See John Neville Maskelyne, *Modern Spiritualism: A Short Account of its Rise and Progress, with Some Exposures of So-Called Spirit Media* (London: Frederick Warne & Co., 1876). This pamphlet contains advertisements for the twice-daily Egyptian Hall shows of 'MASKELYNE & COOKE, THE ROYAL ILLUSIONISTS AND ANTI-SPIRITUALISTS'.
35 'Scrutator', 'Sleight of Touch', *Truth* (26 June 1884): 954.
36 T. H. Huxley, 'On the Advisableness of Improving Natural Knowledge', *Lay Sermons, Addresses and Reviews* (London: Macmillan, 1870), p. 21.
37 'Thought-Reading', *British Medical Journal* (21 May 1881): 814.
38 *Ibid.*: 815.
39 Ernest Hart, *Hypnotism, Mesmerism and the New Witchcraft*, 2nd edn (1896, New York: Da Capo Reprint Series, 1982), p. 166.
40 Thomson Whyte, 'Thought-Reading', *Nature* (7 July 1881): 211.
41 T.E. and F.N., *Exposition of W. Irving Bishop's Thought-Reading with Explanations How to Attain this Wonderful Power* (7-page pamphlet, not dated [1883]), p. 7.
42 Stuart Cumberland, *That Other World*, p. 183.
43 *Ibid.*, p. 180. *A Fatal Affinity: A Weird Story* appeared in 1889 (Blackett's Shilling Novels, London: Spencer Blackett, 1889). Cumberland claimed that Gladstone's wife had had to check beneath her husband's bed for several weeks after he had read the book.
44 'Obects of the Society', *Proceedings of the Society for Psychical Research*, 1, 1 (1882): 3.
45 William Barrett, 'Thought-Reading', *Nature* (7 July 1881): 212.
46 Standard histories of the Society include John Cerullo, *The Secularisation of the Soul: Psychical Research in Modern Britain* (Philadelphia, PA: Institute for the Study of Human Issues, 1982); Alan Gauld, *The Founders of Psychical Research* (London: RKP, 1968); Janet Oppenheim, *The Other World: Spiritualism and Psychical Research in England, 1850–1914* (Cambridge: Cambridge University Press, 1985).
47 Willam Barrett, 'Pseudo Thought-Reading', *Journal of the Society for Psychical Research*, 1 (1884): 10.
48 *Ibid.*: 11.
49 Douglas Blackburn, *Thought-Reading or Modern Mysteries Explained, Being Chapters on Thought-Reading, Occultism, Mesmerism, etc.* (London: Field & Tuer, 1884), p. 27.

50 *Ibid.*, p. 28.
51 For the full details, see 'Third Report on Thought Transference', *Proceedings of the Society for Psychical Research*, 1 (1882–83): 161–215.
52 The historian of science Ian Hacking, argues that these experiments were formative in the development of probabilistic experiment with randomised and double-blind testing, and reflected 'the highest standards of positivist scientific methodology'. 'Telepathy: Origins of Randomisation in Experimental Design', *Isis*, 79 (1988): 437.
53 In 1907, from South Africa, Blackburn revealed that the tests had been tricks to dupe the eminent men of the Society, although Smith continued to affirm their soundness. Crichton-Browne was prompted by Bryan Donkin to record his own, highly contemptuous view of the experiments in a long letter, 'Occultism and Telepathic Experiments', *Westminster Gazette*, 29 January 1908, p. 3. This was re-cast in his memoirs under the heading 'TELEPATHY', in *The Doctor's Second Thoughts* (London: Ernest Benn, 1931), pp. 58–65. These keystone experiments for psychical research were demolished in Trevor Hall's highly partisan book, *The Strange Case of Edmund Gurney*, 2nd edn (London: Duckworth, 1980).
54 HBD (Donkin), 'Mr Stuart Cumberland's Muscle-Reading', *Pall Mall Gazette*, 30 May 1884, p. 2.
55 'Thought-Reading Demonstrations', *British Medical Journal* (23 February 1881): 383.
56 Charles Gatchell, 'The Methods of Mind-Readers', p. 201.
57 On accommodation not war, see James R. Moore, *Post-Darwinian Controversies: A Study of Protestant Struggle to Come to Terms with Darwin in Great Britain and America 1870–1900* (Cambridge: Cambridge University Press, 1979) and Ruth Barton, 'Evolution: The Whitworth Gun in Huxley's War for the Liberation of Science from Theology', in D. Oldroyd and I. Langham, *The Wider Domain of Evolutionary Thought* (London: D. Reidel, 1983).
58 Auguste Comte, *Introduction to Positive Philosophy*, translated Frederick Ferré (Indianapolis, IN: Hackett Publishing, 1988), p. 2.
59 For helpful general context, see particularly Frank Turner, *Contesting Cultural Authority: Essays in Victorian Intellectual Life* (Cambridge: Cambridge University Press, 1993). For specifics see, Roy MacLeod, 'Resources of Science in Victorian England: the Endowment of Science Movement, 1868–1900', in Peter Mathias (ed.), *Science and Society* (Cambridge: Cambridge University Press, 1972). For development of the 'industrial-scientific complex', see Crosbie Smith and M. Norton Wise, *Physics of Empire: A Biographical Study of Lord Kelvin* (Cambridge: Cambridge University Press, 1989). For rise of the laboratories, see Romauldas Sviedrys, 'The Rise of Physics Laboratories in Britain', *Historical Studies in the Physical Sciences* 7 (1976); and Frank James

(ed.), *The Development of the Laboratory: Essays on the Place of Experiment in Industrial Civilisation* (Basingstoke: Macmillan, 1989).

60 Karl Pearson, *A Grammar of Science* (London: Walter Scott, 1892), p. 4.

61 Sophie Forgan, '"But indifferently lodged … ": Perception and Place in Building for Science in Victorian London', in Crosbie Smith and John Agar (eds), *Making Space for Science: Territorial Themes in the Shaping of Knowledge* (Basingstoke: Macmillan, 1998).

62 James Secord, 'Extraordinary Experiment: Electricity and the Creation of Life in Victorian England', in David Gooding, Trevor Pinch and Simon Schaffer (eds), *The Uses of Experiment* (Cambridge: Cambridge University Press, 1989), p. 339.

63 Gooding, Pinch and Schaffer, 'Introduction: Some Uses of Experiment', p. xiii.

64 Bruno Latour and Steve Woolgar, *Laboratory Life: The Construction of Scientific Facts*, 2nd revised edn (Princeton, NJ: Princeton University Press, 1986), p. 36.

65 Harry Collins and Trevor Pinch, *The Golem: What You Should Know About Science*, 2nd revised edn (Cambridge: Cambridge University Press, 1998), pp. 3, 142–3 and 101. Their discussion of 'contingent' as opposed to 'constitutive' fora for scientific disagreement is in the influential essay 'The Construction of the Paranormal: Nothing Unscientific is Happening', *On the Margins of Science: The Social Construction of Rejected Knowledge*, Sociological Review Monograph 27 (Keele: University of Keele, 1979), pp. 237–70.

66 Bruno Latour, *Science in Action: How to Follow Scientists and Engineers through Society* (Cambridge, MA: Harvard University Press, 1987).

67 Secord, 'Extraordinary Experiment', p. 338.

68 Simon Schaffer, 'Where Experiments End: Tabletop Trials in Victorian Astronomy', in Jed Z. Buchwald (ed.), *Scientific Practice: Theories and Stories of Doing Physics* (Chicago, IL: University of Chicago Press, 1995), p. 299.

69 William Barrett, 'Thought-Reading', *Nature* (7 July 1881): 212.

70 George Croom Robertson, 'Prefatory Words', *Mind*, 1 (1876): 3.

71 James Sully, Review of Grant Allen's *The Colour Sense*, *Mind*, 4 (1879): 415.

72 Charles Darwin, *The Works of Charles Darwin*, volume 15: *On the Origin of Species by Means of Natural Selection, or the Preservation of Favoured Races in the Struggle for Life* [1859], ed. Paul H. Barrett and R. B. Freeman (London: Pickering, 1989), p. 445n.

73 *Nature* (22 June 1882): 169.

74 Charles Darwin, *The Works of Charles Darwin*, vol. 23: *The Expression of the Emotions in Man and Animals* [1872], (London: Pickering, 1989)

75 For details of specific experiments, see Eric J. Dingwall, 'The Metalloscopy Controversy', *Abnormal Hypnotic Phenomena: A Survey of Nineteenth-Century Cases*, 4 vols (London: J. & A. Churchill, 1967–68), vol. 1: 254–63;

and Anne Harrington, 'Metalloscopy and Hemi-Hypnosis', *Medicine, Mind and the Double Brain: A Study in Nineteenth-Century Thought* (Princeton, NJ: Princeton University Press, 1987). For Charcot's place in the development of hypnotism, see Alan Gauld, *A History of Hypnotism* (Cambridge: Cambridge University Press, 1992).

76 Ian Hacking, *Rewriting the Soul: Multiple Personality and the Sciences of Memory* (Princeton, NJ: Princeton University Press, 1995), p. 128.

77 William Barrett's formative essay 'On Some Phenomena Associated with Abnormal Conditions of Mind' was first delivered, controversially, to the British Association for the Advancement of Science in 1876. It was eventually published in *Proceedings of the Society for Psychical Research*, vol. 1 (1882–83). Francis Galton recorded in *Memories of My Life* (Methuen: London, 1908), p. 80, that he had seen Mesmeric performances in the 1840s, and went on to mesmerise eighty persons himself, before giving it up as an 'unwholesome procedure'. The alienist Daniel Hack Tuke published *Sleepwalking and Hypnotism* in 1884, a pioneering fin-de-siècle account. Hack Tuke worked with a number of psychical researchers in the 1880s to investigate hypnotic effects, and Croom Robertson gave space in *Mind* in the mid-1880s to the Secretary of the Society for Psychical Research, Edmund Gurney, for his essays on Hypnotism. Ernest Hart was more typical of the English suspicion of trance-states, and was the scourge of 'neo-Mesmerism'. He immediately suspected Bishop of feigning a trance state at the end of the May 1881 trial. See 'Thought-Reading', *British Medical Journal* (21 May 1881): 816.

78 William Crookes, *Researches into the Phenomena of Spiritualism* (London: J. Burns, 1874), p. 5. This is a useful collection of Crookes's various reports on his investigations between 1870 and 1874, published by the Spiritual Institute.

79 *Ibid.*, p. 9.

80 Edward Cox, 'What is Psychic Force?', *Spiritualism Answered by Science* (London: Longmans, 1871), p. 34.

81 *Ibid.*, p. 13.

82 *Ibid.*, p. 29.

83 Introduction, *Proceedings of the Psychological Society of Great Britain, 1875–9* (London: privately published, 1880), pp. v–vi.

84 Edward Cox, 'The Province of Psychology', *ibid.*, p. 34.

85 Edward Cox, Fourth Sessional Address, *ibid.*, p. 237.

86 Edward Cox, *The Mechanism of Man*, 2 vols (London: Longmans, 1876 and 1879), vol. 2: 309.

87 John Page Hopps, 'Modern Materialism', *Psychological Review*, 1 (1878): 34. The *Review* closed in 1883.

88 J. J. Morse, 'Notes by the Way', *Spiritual Notes* (Sept 1878): 31

89 'Mr Serjeant Cox on "Psychism"', *Spiritual Notes* (May 1879): 139.

90 'Spiritualism and its Recent Converts', *Quarterly Review*, 131 (July–October 1871): 343. This all-out attack on Crookes, Huggins and Cox for their declaration of the reality of 'psychic force' was soon ascribed to the mental physiologist William Carpenter.

91 Richard Noakes, 'Telegraphy Is an Occult Art: Cromwell Fleetwood Varley and the Diffusion of Electricity to the Other World', *British Journal of the History of Science*, 32 (1999): 455. Richard Noakes also deals in absorbing detail with William Crookes in his doctoral thesis '"Cranks and Visionaries": Science, Spiritualism and Transgression in Victorian Britain', Cambridge University, 1998. I am immensely grateful to Richard for his generosity in sharing his research with me.

92 See Crookes's notebook for the experiment of 16 April 1872, reprinted in R. G. Medhurst, *William Crookes and the Spirit World: A Collection of Writings Concerning the Work of Sir William Crookes, O.M., F.R.S., in the Field of Psychical Research* (London: Souvenir Press, 1972), p. 208.

93 Letter from Galton to Darwin, 28 March 1872, cited in Karl Pearson, *The Life, Letters and Labours of Francis Galton* 3 vols (Cambridge: Cambridge University Press, 1924), vol. 2: 63.

94 Edward Cox, 'Other Phenomena of Psychism', *The Mechanism of Man* (1879), vol. 2: 446–9.

95 William Huggins, 'Historical Statement', *The Scientific Papers of Sir William Huggins* (London: William Wesley & Son, 1909), vol. 2: 6.

96 See Regenia Gagnier, *Subjectivities: A History of Self-Representation in Britain, 1832–1920* (Oxford: Oxford University Press, 1991), p. 223.

97 Grant Allen, *Physiological Aesthetics* (London: Henry S. King, 1877), p. 2.

98 *Ibid.*, p. 50.

99 *Ibid.*

100 Edward Clodd, *Grant Allen: A Memoir* (London: Grant Richards, 1900), pp. 194–5. Clodd served as president of the Folk-Lore Society in the 1890s; its journal at the time collected and analysed examples of superstitious belief.

101 Grant Allen, *Strange Stories* (London: Chatto & Windus, 1884), p. iii.

102 Allen's first story was 'Our Scientific Observations on a Ghost'. The satire on psychical research was the story, 'A Mysterious Occurrence in Piccadilly'.

103 *The Great Taboo* was published in 1890, and is, along with Allen's contributions to anthropologies of the ghost, discussed in David Amigoni's essay 'Ghosts, Anthropology and Cultural Evolution in the Writings of Grant Allen and His Contemporaries' (forthcoming).

104 Grant Allen, 'The Beckoning Hand', in *The Beckoning Hand, and Other Stories* (London: Chatto & Windus, 1887), pp. 2 and 11. Fortunately, Césarine catches yellow fever after sacrificing a child in a 'Voudaux' ceremony, leaving the hero to return to his initial Aryan object of desire.

105 I have explored this in 'Trance-Gothic, 1882–1897', in Ruth Robbins and Julian Wolfreys (eds), *Victorian Gothic* (Basingstoke: Palgrave, 2000).

106 Edward Clodd, *Grant Allen*, p. 205.

107 Robert Miles, *Gothic Writing 1750–1820: A Genealogy* (London: Routledge, 1993), p. 2.

108 Terry Castle, 'Phantasmagoria: Spectral Technology and the Metaphoric of Modern Reverie', *Critical Inquiry*, 15 (1988): 29.

109 *Ibid.*, p. 52. For further analysis in the same vein, see her 'The Spectralisation of the Other in *The Mysteries of Udolpho*', in Felicity Nussbaum and Lara Brown (eds), *The New Eighteenth Century* (London: Methuen, 1987), pp. 231–53.

110 Cumberland's first novel *The Vasty Deep* appeared in 1885, as did *The Rabbi's Spell: A Russo-Jewish Romance* which relies on the association of Jews with the exercise of mesmeric power. *A Fatal Affinity* appeared in 1889.

111 Cumberland, *A Fatal Affinity*, p. 39.

112 John Maskelyne, 'Oriental Jugglery', in Lionel A Weatherly (ed.), *The Supernatural?* (Bristol: Arrowsmith, 1891), p. 161.

113 Robert Miles, *Gothic Writing*, p. 3.

114 Lankester's lecture was delivered initially to the British Association in 1879. It is sampled in Sally Ledger and Roger Luckhurst (eds), *The* Fin de Siècle: *A Reader in Cultural History* c.*1880–1900* (Oxford: Oxford University Press, 2000), pp. 3–5.

115 Oscar Wilde, 'Lord Arthur Savile's Crime: A Study of Duty' [1887], *The Complete Works of Oscar Wilde* (London: Collins, 1986), p. 168.

116 *Ibid.*, p. 192.

117 Eve Kosofsky Sedgwick, *Between Men: English Literature and Male Homosocial Desire* (New York: Columbia University Press, 1985), p. 91 (my emphasis).

118 Edward Carpenter, 'The Intermediate Sex' (originally published in 1896 as 'Homogenic Love'), *Love's Coming-of-Age* (London: Methuen, 1914), p. 129.

119 See Michel Foucault, *An Introduction to the History of Sexuality*, trans. Robert Hurley (London: Pelican, 1979).

120 See, for instance, Stead's occult journal *Borderland*, which ran from 1893 to 1897.

7

Darwin's barnacles:
mid-century Victorian natural history and
the marine grotesque

∽

REBECCA STOTT

For historians studying the cultural assimilation of evolutionary theory it is the figure of the ape as human ancestor which has come to embody the nineteenth-century fears and imaginings occasioned by Darwin's species theory. But I argue in this chapter that in the 1850s, for Victorian scientists and readers of Victorian science of all kinds, it was the marine invertebrate that dominated imaginative evolutionary speculation, the marine invertebrate conceived of as the primary or 'parent' life-form. These two evolutionary icons, the marine invertebrate and the ape, do of course shadow each other from the earliest evolutionary narratives of the eighteenth century, but my argument here is that as proposed 'parent' life-forms they carried very different meanings and associations, particularly in satire, fiction and popular science. They were used in different ways. It is not surprising perhaps that, with the publication of Darwin's *On the Origin of Species* (1859) and Huxley's *Evidence as to Man's Place in Nature* (1863), and the public and journalistic fascination with du Chaillu's gorillas in the early 1860s, the ape tended to dominate the latter part of the century. This 'gorilla craze' pushed popular evolutionary speculation, particularly in fiction, into a later stage, characterised by anxieties about race and degeneration which persisted throughout the *fin de siècle*. But the marine invertebrate imagined as prototype for human anatomy and behaviour provided a much more comic, absurd and less-troubled series of popular imaginings at mid-century. This is partly perhaps because the idea of any kinship between humans and tentacled sea-creatures is inherently more absurd and because the anatomical forms were so remote, unlike that of the ape. This shift of attention from the marine invertebrate to the ape as imagined 'missing link' between the animal and human worlds marks a significant moment in the history of the popular reception of evolutionary theory, a transition from comic fantasy to tragic nightmare, from slime to fur.

The marine invertebrate had a special place in morphology, comparative anatomy and early evolutionary science in the first half of the nineteenth century. Jean-Baptiste Lamarck, the French evolutionist who specialised in invertebrate anatomy (he coined the term 'invertebrate'), claimed in *Philosophie zoologique* (1809) that invertebrates, because of their multiplicity and diversity of form, provided a key to the evolution of higher forms.[1] Marine invertebrates proved more resistant to classification than other invertebrates because of the intensity of variation within the sub-groups.[2] Invertebrate classification systems had become the subject of public disputes in 1830, in which the French comparative anatomist Georges Cuvier contested Etienne Geoffroy St Hilaire's theories about the unity of structure (homology) between vertebrates and cephalopods (squids, cuttlefish and octopi). Throughout the 1830s Richard Owen, Hunterian professor of comparative anatomy, dominated these debates in Britain, arguing passionately for unity within species of the vertebrate embranchement; he and Cuvier argued that there could be no common unity of design among any of the five embranchements. When Robert Chambers published anonymously the controversial and widely read *Vestiges of the Natural History of Creation* (1844), his evolutionary narrative proposed that the earliest life-forms were the 'unpretending forms' of sea-creatures such as zoophytes, molluscs and polyps. Satirisers of Chambers's book made much of this implied evolution of man from primitive sea-creatures.

A number of important specialised monographs on marine zoology were published in the 1840s and 1850s. T. H. Huxley, who specialised in squids, crayfish and jellyfish, published papers on jellyfish in the 1840s, two memoirs on sea-squirts in 1851 and his first monograph, *Oceanic Hydrozoa*, in 1859. Edward Forbes, a lecturer in botany at King's College

London, published *A History of British Starfishes* in 1841. Like Darwin, both Forbes and Huxley drew extensively on the research they had undertaken and the collections they had put together during their sailing voyages of the 1840s – Forbes to the Mediterranean (1841–42) and Huxley to Australia (1846–50). The 1850s was also a key period in research into the anatomy and classification of the infusoria, a term used to describe microscopic invertebrate animalcules found in pond water. Such research was made possible by developments in microscopes and microscopal techniques from the 1830s. In 1838 Christian Gottfried Ehrenberg, Berlin's leading invertebrate taxonomist, had published the classic textbook of infusoria,[3] in which he had overhauled Cuvier's hierarchical system of classification arguing that the 'infusorian has the same sum of organisation-systems as a man'.[4] Ehrenberg further threatened the absolute demarcations of Cuvier's embranchements by placing a new emphasis on function as the explanation of the adaptation of form. Ehrenberg's claims were closely debated in comparative anatomy throughout the 1840s.[5] When Charles Darwin in 1846 decided to dedicate himself to an eight-year research project to classify the barnacle (cirripede), then, it was with the knowledge that such a classification exercise would keep him at the centre of these overlapping international debates about homology, taxonomy, species and morphology – debates critical to his developing ideas about natural selection.

In 1835, while on the *Beagle* voyage, Darwin discovered a 'most curious', aberrant and parasitical barnacle on the shore of southern Chile. Eleven years later, in 1846, after he had spent ten years unloading and cataloguing the *Beagle*'s specimens, it was to this 'illformed little monster', the size of a pinhead, that he turned. He would write a short paper on it, he decided, before moving on to his book on species, but the 'beautiful structure' of the barnacle's tiny and puzzling anatomy absorbed him for much longer than he had anticipated. He began to send for specimens from other barnacle groups in specialist collections and to look at the various growth stages. Later he said, 'I had originally intended to have described only a single abnormal Cirripede, from the shores of South America, and was led, for the sake of comparison, to examine the internal parts of as many genera as I could procure'.[6] In consulting the relevant marine invertebrate literature, Darwin also realised that the classification systems for barnacles were in 'chaos' because barnacles had recently been reclassified; they had been classified as molluscs in the Linnaean system until the early nineteenth century when Jean-Baptiste Lamarck questioned their place in the mollusc group.[7] In 1830, experiments with the free-swimming larvae by an army surgeon, John Thompson, had suggested that they were in fact crustaceans. Darwin committed himself to setting the barnacle record straight. What was initially supposed to have taken less than a year took him *eight* years, during which he dissected thousands of barnacle specimens sent to him by naturalists throughout the world. He began in 1846 and the last of the four volumes on cirripedes was published in 1854, by which time he had demonstrated the community of descent between barnacles and crustaceans. In 1853 he was given the royal medal of the Royal Society of London for the work.

Darwin published his specialised work on marine invertebrates in the 1850s, the decade of the public craze for marine zoology and drawing-room aquaria. Robert Warrington, a chemist, had outlined the principle for an aquarium in a paper delivered to the Chemical Society in 1850, stressing the need for aeration through the addition of water plants, but it was the naturalist Philip Gosse who popularised the aquarium in several books published in the early 1850s. Gosse also assisted in the construction and stocking of the new aquarium in London Zoo which was opened in 1853. A large number of seaside manuals were produced in that decade to cater for public demand: G. H. Lewes was writing his 'Sea-Side Studies' for *Blackwood's Edinburgh Magazine* in the summers of 1856 and 1857; Philip Gosse published his best-selling books *The Aquarium* and *A Manual of Marine Zoology* in 1854 and 1856; and Charles Kingsley published *Glaucus, or the Wonders of the Shore* in 1854. By the mid-1850s aquarium stockists and suppliers had sprung up in many seaside towns, a number of them also offering catalogue purchases. The microscope too became much less costly in the 1850s: 'a good one cost about 4 guineas, an adequate one thirty shillings'.[8] The sea-creatures kept in drawing-room aquaria were both aesthetic exotic objects and used for dissection. G. H. Lewes, for instance, wrote in 1856 about the sea-anemone: 'At once pet, ornament, and "subject for dissection", the Sea-anemone has a well established popularity in the British family-circle; having the advantage over the hippopotamus of being somewhat less expensive, and less troublesome, to keep.'[9]

Darwin's barnacle research has tended to be relegated to the sidelines of the history of evolution, seen as a minor phase in his development as a scientist, even as a distraction from the more important business of producing his species book. Yet, as he said of himself in 1853: 'I have become a man of one idea – cirripedes morning and night'.[10] Barnacles provided one of the primary anatomical forms on which during these eight years he tested out his speculations on development and natural selection. Most historians of science follow Darwin's own lead in assigning the barnacle research to his need to win his spurs in large-scale scientific systematising. He needed a specialism. But why barnacles in particular?

Darwin became interested in marine zoology when he was a student at the University of Edinburgh (at the time *the* British centre for the study of marine invertebrates) through the influence of the sponge expert, lecturer in comparative anatomy and local physician, Robert Edmond Grant, an outspoken Lamarckian and evolutionist. In his *Autobiography* Darwin claimed to have been 'astonished' by Grant's views on evolution at this time.[11] Grant's shocking evolutionism was focused primarily on marine zoology – he maintained that primitive sea-creatures like the sponge were the 'parent' of higher animals and that all animals shared basic anatomical structures, blueprints in accordance with which later forms had evolved.[12] Grant's interest in marine invertebrates concerned their 'power as analytical models for the solution of major questions of form and function'.[13] Phillip Sloan has shown, however, that his research in the late 1820s was pulling away from Lamarck towards new German theories of comparative anatomy, in particular those of Frederick Tiedemann who claimed that the zoophytal form was a unifying point for plant and animal kingdoms.[14] By 1828 Grant was arguing that plants and animals were 'so intimately blended at their origins' that certain well-known forms, such as barnacles and zoophytes, presented insurmountable problems of classification to the modern systematist.[15] Darwin absorbed these radical new cosmologies during his informal apprenticeship to Grant in walks across the Firth of Forth shoreline and in the seminar rooms and societies of Edinburgh. His first scientific paper, presented before the Plinian Society in 1827 through

Grant's support, announced his discovery that the so-called ova of the bry-ozoan *Flustra foliacea* (sea-mat) were in fact larvae of the leech Pontobdella.

Darwin worked on barnacles, then, not only because he wanted extended experience of dissection and classification, but because the marine invertebrates were central to his introduction to transformism at Edinburgh and to key debates in zoology, morphology and comparative anatomy. When Darwin returned to marine invertebrates with the bar-nacle project in 1846, after the *Beagle* journey, he took up many of the homological principles and questions left behind in Edinburgh.[16] By choosing the barnacle, a creature more varied and peculiar in its anatomy and life-cycle than almost any other invertebrate, he was able to demon-strate that diversity was not the exception but the rule in nature. He may have begun with the intention of systematising the barnacle record, but the enormous variation in the form and the parts of the barnacle drove him to distraction, as he wrote to Hooker towards the end of the project in September, 1853:

> After describing a set of forms, as distinct species, tearing up my M.S.,
> & making them one species; tearing that up and making them separate,
> & making them one again (which has happened to me) I have gnashed
> my teeth, cursed species, & asked what sin I had committed to be so
> punished.[17]

He had complained earlier in 1850 in another letter to Hooker:

> You ask what effect studying species has had on my variation theories; I
> do not think much; I have felt some difficulties more; on the other hand
> I have been struck (& probably unfairly from the class) with the variabil-
> ity of every part in some slight degree of every species: when the same
> organ is *rigorously* compared in many individuals I always find some
> slight variability, & consequently that the diagnosis of species is always
> dangerous ... Systematic work [would] be easy were it not for this con-
> founded variation, which, however, is pleasant to me as a speculist though
> odious to me as a systematist.[18]

Darwin describes himself as both systematist and speculist, drawing attention to an important tension in his work. He was trying to fix and classify and erase difficulty through systematic description, and at the same time *speculate* on the 'how' of this creature. Darwin had chosen his specialism well: the barnacle's grotesque and amorphous anatomy proved that 'the diagnosis of species is always dangerous'. It also forced him to review those ideas about homology, inherited from Robert Grant, Richard Owen and Henri Milne-Edwards, with which he had begun the project. He came to reject an Owenite definition of divine and *fixed* archetypes in favour of types '*undergoing* further development'.[19] By 1854 he was arguing that 'it is hopeless to find in species ... any one part or organ ... absolutely invariable in form or structure'. Instead, where there is some variation between parts or organs within a species, such parts will 'be found eminently variable'.[20] However, the scientific importance of Darwin's barnacle research has been well documented elsewhere. My interest here is in the imaginative potential offered to mid-Victorian writers by the grotesque morphological liminality of the marine invertebrate.

A large part of Darwin's problem with systematising was created by the need to put barnacles and barnacle body parts *into words*. Naming the body parts of marine invertebrates produced predictable problems for Victorian marine zoologists searching for homology. If marine invertebrates like polyps and sponges represented the 'parent' of higher forms then it was important to search for the source of the anatomical features found in higher forms in the body of the marine invertebrate. Comparative anatomists were also forced to speculate on how the body parts of a barnacle might have evolved into the body parts of higher forms. Take the case of the barnacle as represented in Darwin's monographs (see figure 7.1). In its adult form it is attached to a rock by its 'head' and waves its 'feet', or tentacles, in the air, has a 'mouth' situated between its 'legs' in its larval form and a double 'eye' attached to fibrous tissue on the upper part of the 'stomach' deep within the body. As soon as you apply to the marine invertebrate terms which are common to human anatomy (mouth, legs, eye, anus, feet), as Darwin did, two things happen. A grotesque distortion of the human form is conjured up, much more grotesque than that imaginable by a Mary Shelley – upside-down, mouth between its legs, eyes inside its stomach. Second, the superimposition of anatomical forms makes a nonsense of any attempt to find a *primary* anatomical form, for any perceived similarity between an eye in a head and an eye inside a stomach is outweighed by the grotesque and comic *dissimilarities*. Borderlines and distinctions between forms disappear until mouths and orifices of all kinds seem to be merged into one grotesque palimpsest.

7.1 Charles Darwin, Plate IV *Anelasma: Ibla* (1851), *A Monograph of the Sub-Class Cirripedia, Vol. 1: The Lepadidaeii*

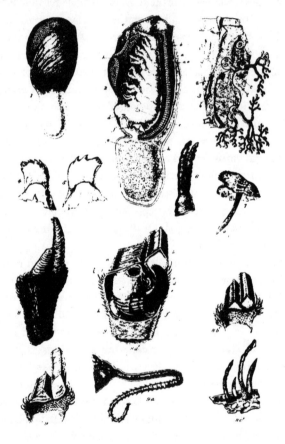

PLATE IV

Anelasma: Ibla

334

The problems created by eight years of struggle to put barnacles into words within a homological framework are, I am convinced, part of the process by which Darwin came to form the distinctive vision of fragmented and grotesque body parts so characteristic of *Origin*. Yet how aware was he of the anatomical absurdities his barnacle book conjured, and what was of interest to him in this creature? Here Darwin's use of the word 'curious' as applied to the barnacle in the letters and the monographs is, I think, crucial to moments at which his imaginative speculation begins and momentarily exceeds his systematising impulse.

In April 1853 Darwin wrote to T. H. Huxley to offer help with Huxley's study of the *Ascidae*, or sea-squirts. At the end of the letter he asked Huxley to review and publicise his books on barnacles. In November 1853 Huxley was asked to write for the *Westminster Review*, a journal purchased by John Chapman in 1852 and dedicated to a developmental philosophy of progress. His review of Darwin's barnacle monographs would come out in the *Westminster Review* the following year. In the letter to Huxley, Darwin drew attention to the 'curiosities' offered by the barnacle, suggesting by doing so that these were features to which Huxley should draw attention in his review:

> Upon my honour I never did such a thing before as suggest (not that I have exactly suggested this time) a review to any human being. But having done so, I may mention that in my own opinion, the Limulus-like larva in 1st stage; – the mouthless pupa; – especially the method of cement with its modifications; – the senses; – & homologies & sexual peculiarities, – are the most curious points, – but I daresay I greatly exaggerate their curiosity, for I have become a man of one idea – cirripedes morning and night.[21]

Huxley's 1854 review even further exaggerates the comic potential of the anthropomorphised barnacle by comparing it to Mr Punch. Furthermore, for Huxley, who had been engaged for seven years and would marry in July 1855, the barnacle's chief curiosity seemed to reside in its comic resemblance to his own impending metamorphosis from free-swimming bachelor to sedentary married man:

> [T]hese animals in their young state are active, sharp-sighted creatures ... A time comes, however, when they know they have to settle down in life; they adhere to some fixed or floating body by their sucking-cups; then a

long hump – we can call it nothing else – somewhat like that with which Mr Punch is provided, only ten times as long, grows out of their backs. From the end of the hump sticky cement is poured out, which glues them firmly to their support … they remain during life the witnesses of a different state of existence.[22]

In reviewing Darwin's very specialised book for an audience of non-specialists, Huxley anthropomorphises the barnacle as a means of satirising human domestic arrangements.

By 1854 *Punch* too had realised the comic potential of marine zoology, publishing a series of cartoons about the public craze for seaside tourism and natural history. John Leech's cartoon of 1857 was particularly popular (see figure 7.2) in which the female rock-pool collectors are made to look as strange as the sea-anemones themselves. However, while *Punch* cartoons made much of the visual comparison between women's fashions and the anatomy of marine invertebrates, in Darwin's work and Huxley's review the comic potential of the comparison between marine invertebrate and human anatomy is focused upon the adult human *male* – at the point at which he 'settles down'.

7.2   John Leech, 'Common Objects at the Sea-Side' (1857), *Punch*

Darwin persistently drew attention, in letters to scientific colleagues, to the 'eminently curious' *general* sexual peculiarities of the barnacles. As the research progressed, however, it was the parasitism and diminished scale of the male barnacle in particular that attracted most of his attention. Most barnacles are hermaphrodite; but, as Darwin dissected, he discovered variations on this pattern. Some barnacles, he noted (namely the *Alcippe, Ibla* and the *Scalpellum*), were not hermaphrodite, but contained small rudimentary males, parasitic upon a much larger female, embedded in her flesh. Then he found another variation, with what he called 'complemental males' attached not to a female but to a hermaphrodite. Darwin realised that from this he could speculate on the question of sexuality and its evolution. In his early notebook studies of hermaphrodite plants Darwin had worked from the premiss that evolution had moved from hermaphroditism in 'lower' forms to separate sexes in the 'higher' forms, and here was a form of proof found significantly in the animal kingdom. The *Ibla* genus that he dissected was in a *transitional* state: the male organs of the hermaphrodite were degenerating, and the barnacle was compensating by producing separate but rudimentary males. Literally, these were primitive males in the making.

In the monographs, Darwin continually apologises for spending so much time speculating upon the sexual peculiarities of his barnacles and relegates much of this speculation to lengthy footnotes. He never directly anthropomorphises the barnacles except in the application of human anatomical terms to the barnacle anatomy. However, in letters to scientific colleagues he seems to be interested *only* in barnacle sexuality, presenting the barnacle as a figure of sexual comedy in which the parasitical characteristics of the adult male barnacle in particular take on increasingly human form. The hermaphrodite anatomy causes Darwin no disturbance; it is the parasitical nature of the male upon the female that compels his interest. As Huxley may have glimpsed his own comic reflection in Mr Punch, the barnacle, Darwin seems amused by what he perceives as similarities to aspects of Victorian male behaviour. In some letters, for instance, Darwin moves seamlessly between reference to cirripedal reproduction and reference to his own sexual reproduction without drawing direct connections between the two. To Henslow, he wrote:

I must tell you a curious case I have just these few days made out: all the Cirripedia are bisexual, except one genus, & in this the female has the ordinary appearance, whereas the male has no one part of its body like the female & is microscopically minute; but here comes the odd fact, the male or sometimes two males, at the instant they cease being locomotive larvae become parasitic within the sack of the female, & thus fixed & half embedded in the flesh of their wives they pass their whole lives & can never move again. Is it not strange that nature should have made this one genus unisexual, & yet have fixed the males on the outside of the females; - the male organs in fact being thus external instead of internal.

We are all well here, & a sixth little (d) expected this summer: as for myself however, I have had more unwellness than usual.[23]

Unlike some of his contemporaries, Darwin did not work in a separate scientific sphere – his study, placed at the centre of Down House, meant that domestic and family life and scientific work seeped into each other in interesting and sometimes useful ways.[24] His letters reveal constant slippage between the domestic and the scientific. Darwin began work on barnacles soon after he had become a father for the fourth time: William (1839), Annie (1841), Henrietta (1843) and George (1845). In the eight years between starting his work on the barnacles and the publication of the final volume in 1854, his wife Emma bore four more children: Elizabeth (1847), Francis (1848), Leonard (1850) and Horace (1851), and the Darwins lost their 10-year-old daughter Annie in 1851. From 1847 to 1848 his father, who suffered from gout, was dying from an illness that swelled him up and brought out boils on his body. Obese and immobile, he couldn't turn himself over in bed and was confined to a wheelchair or a bed in his home in Shrewsbury. Darwin himself was, of course, plagued with illness, digestive problems, 'boils & swellings'.[25] It was immediately after the death of his father that Darwin began the water cure in March 1849, returning to Down in June 1849 where he had a miniature hut built in the garden to contain a huge cistern holding 640 gallons of water, which was designed to fall on him through a two-inch pipe every day. He also underwent shallow baths, dripping sheets, heat lamps, these periods of immersion in alternately hot and cold water punctuated only by barnacle dissection.

Given such a domestic context, it is perhaps not so surprising, then, that in the description of the barnacles in Darwin's letters between 1848 and 1853 male reproduction and masculinity generally, particularly in relation to parasitism and invalidism, become more and more of an issue. In a letter to Charles Lyell in 1849, for instance, the barnacle female is the dominant comic image, carrying her husbands in her pockets. The picture is curious, even charming, but not grotesque:

> I work now every day at the Cirripedia for 2½ hours & so get on a little but very slowly – the other day I got the curious case of a unisexual, instead of hermaphrodite cirripede, in which the female had the common cirripedial character, & in two halves of the valves of her shell had two little pockets, in each of which she kept a little husband; I do not know of any other case where a female invariably has two husbands. – I have one still odder fact, common to several species, namely that though they are hermaphrodite, they have small additional or as I shall call them Complemental males: one specimen itself hermaphrodite had no less than seven of these complemental males attached to it. Truly the schemes and wonders of nature are illimitable.[26]

But Darwin's interest in the reproductive modes of the barnacles is also very much of a piece with other kinds of zoological research in the 1850s. Frederick B. Churchill argues that in the 1850s 'the hypothesized overt sexuality of infusorians became a respected, even dominant, perspective of infusorian natural history … at a time when the range of reproductive modes was being expanded throughout both animal and plant kingdoms'.[27] In fact, Churchill even suggests that this 'mid-century penchant' for plotting a 'spectrum of generative capacities throughout the living world' prevented microscopists from attending to the other important questions which would in turn lead towards Weismann's concept of the germ plasm.[28]

By 1853 the barnacle is well established as a grotesque in Darwin's letters as he begins to focus on the anatomical form as a site for absence of orifices such as the rectum, for instance. At a time when he was himself constantly vomiting and anxious about the labours of his wife, this transition from vomiting barnacles to childbirth has a comic poignancy:

> I have this morning been dissecting a most abnormal cirripede, which after a good meal has to vomit forth the residuum, for there is no other exit [no rectum]!

> I heard yesterday from Mr Hooker, who married Henslow's eldest daughter, of the birth of a son under Chloroform, at Hitcham.[29]

There are few references to female barnacles in the later letters, where the enlarged and polygamous female has been usurped in Darwin's interest by the male grotesque, distinguished both by the diversity of its appearance and by the absence of anatomical features:

> You may imagine how peculiar the appearance of the male Alcippe is, when I mention that, though I had experience of how diverse an aspect the males put on, I now know that I looked at a Male, during the first day or two, & never dreamed it was a cirripede![30]

> The male is transparent as glass … In the lower part we have an eye, & great testis & vesticula seminalise: in the capitulum we have nothing but a tremendously long penis coiled up & which can be exserted. There *is no mouth no stomach no cirri, no proper thorax!* The whole animal is reduced to an envelope (homologically consisting of 3 first segments of head) containing the testes, vesticula, & penis. In male Ibla, we have hardly any cirri or thorax; in some male Scalpellums no mouth; here both negatives are united … I believe the males occur on every female: in one case I found 12 males & two pupae on point of metamorphosis *permanently* attached by cement to one female.[31]

> I have just finished dissecting a curious cirripede, which is female & has successive corps of males attached to her: I found one with 12 males so fixed to her! These males I suspect are the most negative creatures in the world; they have no mouth, no stomach, no thorax, no limbs, no abdomen, they consist wholly of the male reproductive organs in an envelope.[32]

These 'negative' creatures, minute, transparent, immobile, embedded in their wives' flesh or pockets, offer Darwin the prospect of a masculine archetype, the 'parent' of higher forms, as nothing but a reproductive organ situated in the place of a head, with no independent existence. They are defined entirely by the absence of all other significant organs beside the reproductive organs. But while Darwin stresses the negativity of these creatures, he offers them to his colleagues as creatures of high comedy and as a grotesque challenge to natural theology.

In *Rabelais and His World*, Mikhail Bakhtin has formulated a theory of the grotesque which is of some use in examining Darwin's marine grotesques. He argued that the grotesque could be traced to the preclassical Western visual arts, characterised by fantastic and monstrous transformations of animate and inanimate forms. He maintained that grotesque realism, a genre prevalent in folk cultures and in medieval and Renaissance culture in particular, had been marginalised by the emergence of classical realism in the eighteenth and nineteenth centuries with the rise of bourgeois individuality and of science. Bakhtin calls classical realism 'the new canon' and at its centre, he argues, is a classical conception of the body – entirely finished, completed, individualised, sealed off from the world, all its orifices closed. All attributes of the unfinished world are carefully removed in the construction of the fully completed individualised self.

Bakhtin celebrates grotesque realism as a form of representation that, unlike classical realism, emphasises becoming, process and change, and argues that the comedy it produces is subversive in that it stands in opposition to the social values embodied by contemporary representational norms. In grotesque realism (Bakhtin draws on the work of Bosch, Rabelais and Cervantes but modern theorists have added the work of Sterne and Joyce), the body at the centre of the writing is a grotesque body – it protrudes, seeps, outgrows itself. It is a body in the act of becoming; its outlines and edges are indistinct for it merges with the rest of the world. Its bowels, genital organs and mouth are prominent as places of entrance, for in the grotesque anatomy the points of contact with the outer world are predominant. Grotesque art, Bakhtin claims, is an art of transitional spaces in which the

> borderlines that divide the kingdoms of nature in the usual picture of the world were boldly infringed … There was no longer the movement of finished forms, vegetable or animal, in a finished and stable world; instead the inner movement of being was expressed in the passing of one form into the other, in the ever incompleted character of being.[33]

And what of the barnacle? In Darwin's monographs, descriptions of barnacles oscillate uneasily between an anatomical structure which in Bakhtinian terms might be called 'classical' (fixed, sealed off, named) and one which is 'grotesque' (always slipping or seeping out of categories). This is perhaps due to the opposing drives in the book, which Darwin himself draws attention to: the impulses of the systematist and the speculist. As systematist Darwin is concerned with classical bodies, and as speculist he describes a grotesque body of possibility and becoming. This is also perhaps why Darwin is so preoccupied with orifices, because it is these orifices or borderlines that define and categorise the barnacle, borderlines between gland and ovary, stomach and eye, legs and mouth, male and female, borderlines that, in this topsy-turvy body, at once offer and deny classification. Over and over again in his letters and notes, Darwin describes his attempts to trace one part of the anatomy to its mergence in another, only to find himself 'lost' and the borderlines impossible to retrace.

Far from being a *cul-de-sac*, then, Darwin's barnacle books, eight years in the making, may have contributed to a distinctive way of seeing, born out of this collision between the impulses of systematist and speculist, expressed in part in the grotesque and fragmented images characteristic of *On the Origin of Species*. James Krasner has described Darwin's impulse in *Origin* as

> to create a welter of whirling animal parts that constricts the possibility of imagining a whole form. Teeth, hair, feathers, wings, and feet from various creatures are jumbled before the reader's vision in a witches' brew of fragmented zoology from which no fully formed creature can emerge … a visual field so crowded with body parts that everything seems to be linked to everything.[34]

Krasner argues that this characteristically Darwinian vision was formed by Darwin's reading of Malthus, Paley and Lyell. It is the influence of Malthus in particular, he argues, that accounts for the grotesque in Darwin's writing, especially Malthus's grotesque fantasies of overpopulation, bodies expanding and contracting, multiplying to cover the universe.[35] Although this Malthusian way of seeing must have seemed particularly apposite to Darwin during his barnacle research – because of the reproductive peculiarities of the barnacles, his own rapidly expanding family and his increasing certainty about archetypes in movement – I would argue that he finds in the barnacle's splitting and swelling anatomy, not Malthusian nightmare but a figure of comic and celebratory possibility.

Darwin's instinct to anthropomorphise the marine invertebrate and his fascination with its sexual peculiarities are common to other 1850s' works of marine zoology. Barnacle males, parasitical, diminutive and immobile, offered a comic vision of domestic co-existence, an alternative model of social-sexual arrangements. But there were other grotesques to be found in the bizarre anatomies and behaviours of sea-squirts, cuttlefish and octopi. In the 1850s and early 1860s, the period during which marine biology was at its most popular, and in which more and more of the middle classes purchased for their drawing-rooms aquaria stocked with the sea-creatures they collected in glass jars during seaside holidays, and as microscopes came down in price, there was a corresponding demand for popular guides to marine forms. These books (some of them best-sellers for a time) and journal articles written by Philip Gosse, George Henry Lewes and Charles Kingsley, among others, used every possible opportunity to anthropomorphise in order to entertain their readers. They transformed these drawing-room aquaria into mini-domestic theatres (see figure 7.3). These little glass stages, peopled by the strangest forms, offered a way of imagining human–animal kinship without the disturbing racial and sexual implications suggested by the anatomy of the ape.

7.3   John Leech, 'Valuable Addition to the Aquarium' (1860), *Punch*

VALUABLE ADDITION TO THE AQUARIUM.

TOM (WHO HAD A VERY SUCCESSFUL DAY) PRESENTS HIS SISTERS WITH A FINE SPECIMEN OF THE CUTTLEFISH (*OCTUPUS VULGARIS*).

Like Darwin, popular writers on science questioned the classification systems on the grounds of the mutability and intensity of variation within marine organisms. Language itself seemed inadequate to describe such organisms for some writers. The naturalist Agnes Catlow, in her book *Drops of Water* (1851), for instance, argues that it is frequently impossible to classify microscopic water-creatures as either animal or vegetable: 'their existence proves a nonsense of such categories'.[36] The popular science writer G. H. Lewes, in *Sea-Side Studies* (1858), shares this view:

> Much hot, and not wise, discussion has occupied the hours of philosophers in trying to map out the distinct confines of the animal and vegetable kingdoms, when all the while Nature knows of no such demarcating lines. The Animal does not exist; nor does the Vegetable: both are abstractions, general terms, such as Virtue, Goodness, Colour, used to designate certain groups of particulars, but having only a mental existence.[37]

Many historians of science trace this uneasiness about classificatory systems to Darwin's challenge to uniformity within species in *On the Origin of Species* (1859): 'before Darwin, species were seen as invariable, fixed units, much more capable of being pigeonholed'.[38] But numerous books of natural history and particularly marine biology *prior to* Darwin's *Origin* show classificatory systems creaking under the weight of the new forms being discovered in British rock-pools by amateur collectors. However, it was not only the volume of new species which tested the taxonomic systems but the difficulty of putting such creatures *into language*. The newly perceived permeability of the animal–vegetable boundary in the world of marine zoology opened the way for Darwin's world of fluxing and mutating forms. In marine zoology aimed at a more popular audience, systematising was less important than the entertaining pleasures of speculism, and in some of these works marine invertebrates became the site for comic fantasies about socio-sexual and familial behaviour and animal–human kinship which produced a new art of what we might call 'the marine grotesque'.

However, while an uneasiness with classification systems and a tendency to describe these creatures through analogy are common features of most popular marine zoology books of the 1850s, there is a great deal of variation in the scope and nature of the analogies used and the effect produced. In devotional natural history books comedy tends to be limited and the analogies simple – used, for instance, to support arguments about the unity of design in God's creation or the interconnectedness of material and spiritual worlds. (Philip Gosse and Charles Kingsley are interesting exceptions, of course, for their marine zoological writings, though very different, move easily between the lyricism of natural theology and comedy produced by anthropomorphism.) Agnes Catlow, for instance, in *Drops of Water* (1851), likens the simple aquatic organisms under her microscope to domestic 'objects with which we are familiar' – tops, trumpets, pincushions, telescopes, balls, leaves, sticks, threads, bells and hollow spheres – but the function of her analogies is to take away the strangeness of aquatic forms in order to reveal the unity of God's design.[39] Mary Roberts claimed in 1851 that limpets might 'remind the traveller of Anchorites dwelling by the sea-side in solitary tents', but she uses such comparisons not to speculate on human–animal kinship but to provide moral emblems for her natural theology.[40] Narratives of natural theology tend to maintain the singularity of natural forms, for while a limpet might *look like* an anchorite, or a zoophyte a pincushion, the boundaries of the organism itself are preserved. It remains primarily a classical rather than a grotesque body.

Other writers, however, such as Charles Kingsley and G. H. Lewes, tend to use analogy to collapse the body boundaries of the organism they are describing, and the results are often grotesque morphological palimpsests in which the borderlines blur between animal and human, animate and inanimate, domestic and alien. Thus when Charles Kingsley celebrates variety and excess in the natural world, in his popular marine zoology manual, *Glaucus, or the Wonders of the Shore* (1854), his analogies move through numerous metaphorical fields, from razors to scimitars, from spires to squirrels' tails, working not to locate his readers but to disorientate them:

> [W]hat a variety of forms and colours are there, amid the purple and olive wreaths of wrack, and bladder-weed, and tangle, (oar-weed, as they call it in the south) and the delicate green ribbons of the Zostera, (the only English flowering plant that grows beneath the sea) ... What are they all?

> What are the long white razors? What are the delicate green–grey scimi-
> tars? What are the tapering brown spires? What are the tufts of delicate
> yellow plants, like squirrels' tales, and all other finely cut animal and veg-
> etable forms? What are the groups of grey bladders, with something like a
> little bud at the tip? What are the hundreds of little pink-striped pears?
> What those tiny babies' heads, covered with grey prickles instead of hair?[41]

This excess of metaphor and of shifting frames of reference and size
within single sentences is also typical of Kingsley's description of the sub-
marine world of *The Water-Babies* (1863). In this children's fantasy, influenced by Kingsley's reading of the grotesque realism of Rabelais and
Cervantes, Tom, the child chimneysweep assumes the mutating body of a
water-baby in order to undertake his journey to manhood. Produced in
the wake of Darwin's *Origin* and in part inspired by it, Kingsley's narrative uses both apes and marine invertebrates for its evolutionary fantasies,
but whereas the marine invertebrates embody progress and possibility,
the ape-like DoAsYouLikes are used to warn Tom of the dangers of degeneracy, of going backwards. The comedy of the marine invertebrates in this
book, and in *Glaucus*, depends upon an excess of description that resists
classification of any kind and speaks of *process* and *becoming*. Everything
protrudes out of everything else in this aquatic polymorphic fantasy
about Tom's metamorphosis into adult masculinity:

> His whole husk and shell had been washed quite off him, and the pretty
> little real Tom was washed out of the inside of it, and swam away, as a
> caddis does when its case of stone and silk is bored through, and away it
> goes on its back, paddling to the shore, there to split its skin, and fly away
> as a caperer, on four fawn-coloured wings, with long legs and horns.[42]

G. H. Lewes's *Sea-Side Studies*, written as short pieces in the summers of
1856 and 1857 for *Blackwood's Edinburgh Magazine* and published in
book form in 1858, is a remarkable piece of comic and celebratory writing. Lewes is much more interested in the comedy of this world than in
using nature to reveal a divine plan. He uses marine creatures to challenge
and satirise Victorian conventions and social types, particularly the relations between men and women. At a time when George Eliot, who accompanied him on his seaside expeditions and stayed with him in seaside

boarding houses, was writing an essay called 'Silly Novels by Lady Novelists' for the *Westminster Review,* this description of the *Doris Tuberculata* (sea-anemone) is particularly resonant:

> [L]et us admire the various colours of its cloak, and the delicate beauty of its frilled brachiae, for there is nothing in its general demeanour to admire. It has no pretty ways to captivate our hearts – a mere drawing-room beauty, large, lazy, lymphatic and unintellectual.[43]

Lewes does not suggest that the anemone 'is like' the 'drawing room beauty': he simply runs the two into the same sentence, blurring the distinction. The analogy here works not by the juxtaposition of objects as in the work of Catlow and Roberts, which maintains the singularity of each component, but by a superimposition of images as in a stereoscope – an image of one organism laid on top of another to reveal the similarities. As a result the singularity of each component of the analogy is dissolved.

Although Lewes does sometimes liken the marine invertebrates to women, like Darwin and Kingsley he tends usually to concentrate on the comic similarities between the *male* human and the marine invertebrate, blurring the boundaries between the normal and the abnormal: 'Men began to appear like molluscs; and their ways the ways of creatures in a larger rock-pool.'[44] In his later book *Studies in Animal Life* (1862), for instance, in which Lewes speculates on the implications of Darwin's *Origin*, the male barnacle reappears, once again offered as a prototype of the human transition from bachelorhood to life as a husband. Here Lewes offers us the sedentary male barnacle as a comic figure of maturity and responsibility, which is particularly entertaining given his extravagantly unusual domestic arrangements at that time, living with George Eliot while providing financially for his wife and her lover Thornton Hunt:

> Many animals (Polypes, Polyzoa, Barnacles, Mussels, &c.), after passing a vagabond youth, 'settle' once and for ever in a maturer age, and then become as fixed as plants. Nay, human animals not unfrequently exhibit a somewhat similar metempsychosis, and make up for the fitful capriciousness of wandering youth by the steady severity of their application to business, when width of waistcoat and smoothness of cranium suggest a sense of their responsibilities.[45]

There are fewer women writing on marine zoology in this period than there are writing books on conchology and marine botany (particularly seaweed).[46] Mary Roberts's *A Popular History of the Mollusca* (1851) and Anne Pratt's *Chapters on the Common Things of the Seaside* (1850) are both narratives of natural theology, which, as I have argued, tended as a genre to eschew the comic anthropomorphism which Lewes and Kingsley used to dissolve animal–human boundaries. Instead, they tended to maintain the singularity of natural organisms represented as having a unique place within a hierarchical structure or social order. In *The Popular History of the Mollusca* Mary Roberts argued, for instance, that what we learn from studying the molluscs is that we will be happy if, like them, we 'steadily perform our portion of allotted duty' and 'fulfil the purposes for which [we] are designed'.[47] Socio-sexual comedy is not a dominant feature of the few works of marine zoology published by women in the 1850s. There are one or two instances in which women writers describe marine invertebrates in terms of the husband, for instance, but I have found no instances where this is offered as a narrative of loss (like Huxley's comic barnacle life cycle) or a narrative of parasitism (like Darwin's). Mary Roberts offers us another 'settling down' narrative when she uses the oyster to represent the married male's state as one of fulfilment, community and contentment – it has fulfilled its purpose, she claims.

> They possess, when young, the faculty of swimming by means of a simple yet admirable development of their powers; but when arrived at full growth, this faculty or inclination ceases, and while some of their active relatives are darting around them, they remain contently in their places of abode, surrounded by a numerous and continually increasing progeny.[48]

Interestingly, both Anne Pratt and Mary Roberts tend to emphasise the nurturing and reproductive role of the female marine invertebrate represented as the centre-point of a complex community of dependants.

The comic anthropomorphism of Lewes's *Sea-Side Studies*, focusing particularly on the socio-sexual behaviour of the sexes, was used by *Punch* cartoonist John Swain in 1860 to provide comic material (see figure 7.4). Swain takes Leech's famous cartoon of 1857 (figure 7.2) and eroticises it by using a caption taken from Lewes's book. Here the pleasures mentioned in

SEA-SIDE STUDIES!

Impertinent Cousin (reads). "*The rocks along our Coast may be seen studded with these beautiful zoophites. * * * * The skin is soft, and the tentacles are of the finest violet, mingled often with pink, mauve, green, and yellow; indeed the colours vary so much in different individuals, all alike beautiful, that it is impossible to describe them rigidly. * * * * During the ebb of the tide, these creatures may be contemplated on a fine day to great advantage, and few spectacles are calculated to afford more pleasure to a lover of Nature.*" "H'M!—Here are Two Lovely Specimens, Fred! You take One, and I'll take the Other!"

7.4   John Leech, 'Sea-Side Studies!' (1860), *Punch*

Lewes's study hint at seduction and the erotic pleasures promised by the analogy of human and zoophite anatomies. It might also be a sly reference to Lewes's notoriety. This is a marine vision marked by play, slippage and excess, but above all by pleasure in what a later writer might call polymorphous perversity, and a social comedy stimulated by such explorations of the kinship between animal and human, a pleasure to which Lewes testifies in *Sea-Side Studies*.[49]

What happened to the comically anthropomorphised marine invertebrate when the ape came to dominate the cultural fantasies of the later nineteenth century? In the early 1860s, as previously, the two icons of evolutionary speculation existed side by side, as they did in *The Water-Babies*, but the two new talking-points of 1861 were the debates about Huxley's hippocampus minor and du Chaillu's gorillas; and, as Lynn Barber argues, newspapers of the early 1860s 'could never mention apes without mentioning Darwin'.[50] In George Kearley's book of natural history of 1862, *Links in the Chain or Popular Chapters on the Curiosities of Animal Life*, there are twelve chapters in total, six on marine invertebrates, full of comic analogies (such as that between molluscs and members of the Board of Health, for instance),[51] but the culminating chapter is on the gorilla. The final words of the book reassure the young reader that Professor Owen has proved that the gorilla 'is not for a moment to be thought of as having any ancestral connection with the human family'.[52] The Frontispiece shows the barnacle at the centre of Kearley's scheme, but the monkeys dominate the top of the page.

The marine invertebrate shadows the ape throughout the last decades of the nineteenth century, providing an alternative, less threatening, model for evolutionary speculation, but by the late 1860s the coupling of ape and marine invertebrate begins to rob the marine invertebrate of its comic potential. John Ruskin, for instance, writes in 1873 of 'the filthy heraldries which record the relation of humanity to the ascidian and the crocodile';[53] and Gerard Manley Hopkins wrote in 1874 to his mother:

> I do not think, you know, that Darwinism implies necessarily that man is descended from any ape or ascidian or maggot or what not but only that man is descended from the common ancestor of ascidians, the ancestor of maggots, and so on: these common ancestors, if lower animals, need not have been repulsive animals.[54]

By the late 1860s the marine invertebrate was once again at the centre of new theories about the interconnectedness of plant and animal kingdoms – through the notion of protoplasm put forward by Ernst Haeckel and Max Johann Sigismund Schultze in the early 1860s, and popularised by Huxley in a lecture of 1868, published in 1869 in *The Fortnightly Review* as 'On the Physical Basis of Life'.[55] Huxley claimed that protoplasm was the homogeneous ground substance common to all plants and animals, and argued for the basic unity of all living forms. Once again Huxley turned to marine creatures to illustrate human–animal kinship, by arguing that, if he were to eat a lobster, human protoplasm would become lobster protoplasm, and if he were to be eaten by a lobster the process would be reversed.[56]

In 1880 a significant change takes place in the representation of this alternative evolutionary icon with the publication of *Degeneration: A*

Chapter in Darwinism, in which E. Ray Lankester, marine biologist turned moral prophet, uses the barnacle as an icon of degeneracy. For Lankester, work and struggle result in what he calls 'Elaboration' of form, while parasitism and immobility are the guarantors of 'Degeneration' of form. Like the Romans, barnacles had it too easy:

> The habit of parasitism clearly acts upon animal organisation in this way. Let the parasitic life once be secured, and away go legs, jaws, eyes, and ears; the active, highly gifted crab, insect or annelid may become a mere sac, absorbing nourishment and laying eggs.[57]

The barnacle's degeneration, he claims, is 'due to sessile and immobile habit of life'.[58] He claims that these simple sea-creatures, far from being relics of ancestors, are instead descendants of more elaborate and biologically sophisticated ancestors, living warnings of what could happen to the human anatomy if the conditions of life became too easy. Hence these creatures, for Lankester, are not relics of the past but harbingers of the future: 'It is well to remember that we are subject to the general laws of evolution, and are as likely to degenerate as to progress ... Possibly we are all drifting, tending to the condition of intellectual Barnacles or Ascidians.'[59]

In the wake of Lankester's book, Andrew Wilson, a lecturer in zoology at the Edinburgh Medical School, used marine invertebrates of a parasitical nature, such as the barnacle, as evidence of creatures who 'go to the bad' in a series of articles in the *Gentleman's Magazine* in 1881.[60] While he repeats Lankester's conclusion that nature can go backwards as well as forwards, he corrects Lankester's stress on human endeavour as a means to avoid degeneration by insisting that degeneration is a natural and *unavoidable* part of progress.

In 1891 H. G. Wells joined these debates in the *Gentleman's Magazine* about the lessons of marine zoology and degeneration with an essay called 'Zoological Retrogression'. Wells had studied zoology under T. H. Huxley between 1884 and 1885, and he claimed that not only had it been the 'most educational year' of his life but he could have set himself up as a professor of zoology 'upon the basis [he] had secured' during that time.[61] In this essay of 1891 he argued that zoology proves there is no simple 'march of

mind' but instead that nature is characterised by periods of progress followed by periods of extinction or degeneration. Like Lankester and
Wilson before him, he uses the barnacle and ascidian life-cycle as evidence
of this oscillation between progress and retrogression within a single life-
cycle. Furthermore he suggests that in its likeness to the life-cycle of the
middle-class male, particularly when that male settles down, it hints at the
degeneracy of the adult male human. At a time when such comic zoological writing is almost extinct, Wells's comic grotesque marine invertebrate
here seems to surface through the tragic discourse of dethroned man that
characterises so much of his writing, like a ghost of the mid-century
comedy of Lewes and Kingsley:

> And here one may note a curious comparison which can be made between
> this life history and that of many a respectable pinnacle and gargoyle on the
> social fabric. Every respectable citizen of the professional classes passes
> through a period of activity and imagination ... He shocks his aunts.
> Presently, however, he realises the sober aspect of things. He becomes dull;
> he enters a profession; suckers appear on his head; and he studies. Finally,
> by virtue of these he settles down – he marries. His Bohemian tail is dis-
> carded. Henceforth his life is a passive receptivity to what chance and the
> drift of his profession bring along; he lives an almost entirely vegetative
> excrescence on the side of a street, and in the tranquillity of his calling finds
> that colourless contentment that replaces happiness.[62]

However, when he comes to write fiction, Wells gives the marine invertebrate no such comic potential, and he uses it instead as a warning of
the end of humankind and an expression of biological nightmares of
the future. He uses the ape anatomy in the figure of the Morlocks in
The Time Machine, and elsewhere, but it is the marine invertebrate
anatomy that gives him material for nightmare, particularly the anatomy
of the octopus, a 'bearer of leechy menace'.[63] Peter Kemp has pointed
out Wells's horror of man-eating crustacea and malign cephalopods
(octopi) and his obsession with the slime, tentacles and mouths of such
creatures.[64] The barnacle used here in the 1880s and 1890s by Wells,
Wilson and Lankester, has lost its capacity both for comedy and for the
celebratory grotesque. None of these writers is interested in the pleasures of polymorphous perversity, slippage and morphological variation

and excess. At the end of *The Time Machine* the Time Traveller sees a vision of the end of the world. He sees a beach and a shallow sea in which one useless marine invertebrate flops about, inanely, under the last rays of a dying sun.

Of the several branches of natural history, marine zoology has been relatively neglected by modern historians of science. Studies of Victorian natural history writing such as Lynn Barber's *The Heyday of Natural History 1820–1870* and Lynn Merill's *The Romance of Victorian Natural History* tend to treat popular interest in marine zoology as a craze, another Victorian oddity. Harriet Ritvo's book, *The Platypus and the Mermaid and Other Figments of the Classifying Imagination*, despite its title, is largely concerned with the classification of terrestrial, not aquatic, animals. Historians studying the cultural assimilation of the evolutionary sciences have tended to focus on the late nineteenth century, and therefore on the figure of the ape as an icon of degeneracy.

I have tried to show that the Victorian interest in the marine invertebrate was not a passing phase; nor was it brought about solely by the popular craze for marine zoology of the 1850s. The marine invertebrate was at the centre of transformism in specialised science from the beginning of the nineteenth century in Edinburgh and dominated the evolutionary fantasies of the mid-Victorian period as the site for speculation about animal–human kinship. Furthermore, detailed study of the representation of the marine invertebrate in this decade reveals it to have been a period in which evolutionary speculation about animal–human kinship is full of social comedy about human socio-sexual arrangements in general and the condition of the married male in particular. It is part of what Frederick B. Churchill has described as a penchant among naturalists and comparative anatomists in the 1850s for documenting wide varieties of sexual behaviour in the living world.[65] It is important to see this aspect of Darwin's barnacle work in particular as significant in terms of his continuing interest in sexuality, generation and reproduction, an area of Darwin research that has been developed by Adrian Desmond, Jim Moore and M. Richmond. But while the anthropomorphised marine invertebrate tended to be used to raise issues about gender and sexuality it tended not to be used to address questions of class or 'race'. Those were the pressing questions of the late

Victorian period, and such questions would focus upon human–ape kinship in the fiction of H. G. Wells, Robert Louis Stevenson and others. Furthermore, Darwin's barnacles and the marine invertebrates of his contemporaries, characterised by orifices, fragmented body parts and blurred boundaries between human and animal, played an important part in what Krasner has called the post-Darwinian way of seeing, as bodies of morphological liminality or 'the marine grotesque'.

Notes

My thanks to Rick Rylance, Jim Moore, Jim Secord and John Tyler for commenting on previous drafts of this essay.

1 Jean-Baptiste Lamarck, *Philosophie zoologique* (Paris: Dentu, 1809), 2 vols.
2 See M. Richmond, 'Darwin's Study of the Cirripedia', in F. Burkhardt and S. Smith (eds), *The Correspondence of Charles Darwin* (Cambridge: Cambridge University Press, 1988), vol. 4; W. A. Newman, 'Darwin's Cirrepedology', *Crustacean Issues*, 7 (1993); Adrian Desmond, *Archetypes and Ancestors: Paleontology in Victorian London 1850–1875* (London: Blond & Briggs; Chicago, IL: University of Chicago Press, 1984); R. J. Richards *Darwin and the Emergence of Evolutionary Theories of Mind and Behaviour* (Chicago, IL: University of Chicago Press, 1987); M. P. Winsor 'Barnacle Larvae in the Nineteenth Century', *Journal of the History of Medicine*, 24 (1969).
3 Christian Gottfried Ehrenberg, *Die Infusionsthierchen als Vollkommene Organismen* (Leipzig: Leopold Voss, 1838).
4 Christian Gottfried Ehrenberg, 'Über die Akalephen des rothen Meeres und den Organismus der Medusen der Ostsee', *Abh.königl.Akad.Wiss.Berlin* (Jhrg. 1835): 223.
5 Frederick B. Churchill has documented the debates about infusoria anatomy from the 1840s to the 1870s in 'The Guts of the Matter: Infuoria from Ehrenberg to Butschli: 1838–1876', *Journal of the History of Biology*, 22, 2 (1989).
6 Charles Darwin, Preface, *A Monograph on the Sub-Class Cirripedia, with Figures of all the Species*, vol. 1: *The Lepididae; or, Peduculated Cirripedes*, Ray Society Publications no 21 (London: Ray Society, 1851), p. vii.
7 Jean-Baptiste Lamarck, *Histoire naturelle des animaux sans vertèbres* (Paris: 1815–22), 7 vols.
8 Lynn Barber, *The Heyday of Natural History 1820–1870* (London: Jonathan Cape, 1980), p. 121. For further discussion of the microscope, see Isobel Armstrong's chapter, this volume.

9 G. H. Lewes, *Sea-Side Studies at Ifracombe, Tenby, The Scilly Isles and Jersey* (London: William Blackwood & Sons, 1858), p. 115.

10 Letter from Darwin to Huxley, 11 April 1853, in *Charles Darwin's Letters: A Selection*, ed. Frederick Burkhardt (Cambridge: Cambridge University Press, 1996), pp. 127–8.

11 *The Autobiography of Charles Darwin and Selected Letters* [1892], ed. Francis Darwin (New York: Dover Publications, 1958), p. 13.

12 Adrian Desmond and James Moore, *Darwin* (Harmondsworth: Penguin, 1992), p. 39. For further information on Grant, see Adrian Desmond, *The Politics of Evolution: Morphology, Medicine and Reform in Radical London* (Chicago, IL: University of Chicago Press, 1989). See also P. R. Sloan, 'Darwin's Invertebrate Program, 1826–1836: Preconditions for Transformism', in D. Kohn (ed.), *The Darwinian Heritage* (Princeton, NJ: Princeton University Press, 1985).

13 Phillip R. Sloan, 'Darwin's Invertebrate Program', pp. 76–7. See also Phillip R. Sloan, 'Darwin, Vital Matter and the Transformation of Species', *Journal of the History of Biology*, 19 (1986).

14 Sloan, 'Darwin, Vital Matter and the Transformation of Species', p. 78.

15 Robert E. Grant, *An Essay on the Study of the Animal Kingdom: Being an Introductory Lecture Delivered in the University of London on the 23rd of October 1828* (London: Taylor, 1828), p. 20.

16 Phillip Sloan has argued from a careful study of the notebooks that Darwin's interest in invertebrate zoology does not emerge from nowhere in the 1840s but that instead 'his interests were continual, discriminatory, and suggestive of a recurrent set of problems that he was possibly working on'. See Sloan, 'Darwin's Invertebrate Program', p. 92.

17 Letter from Darwin to Joseph Hooker, 25 September 1853, in *Charles Darwin's Letters*, p. 129.

18 Letter from Darwin to Huxley, 11 April 1853, in *ibid.*, p. 128.

19 Letter from Darwin to Huxley, 23 April 1853, cited in Adrian Desmond, *Huxley: From Devil's Disciple to Evolution's High Priest* (Harmondsworth: Penguin, 1997), p. 188.

20 Charles Darwin, *A Monograph on the Sub-Class Cirripedia*, vol. 1: 155.

21 Letter from Darwin to Huxley, 11 April 1853.

22 T. H. Huxley, *Westminster Review*, 61 (1854): 264.

23 Letter from Darwin to Henslow, 1 April 1848, in Francis Darwin (ed.), *Selected Letters*, pp. 99–100. See also Letter from Darwin to Hooker, 10 May 1848, in *ibid.*, p. 102.

24 He used his children for his research for the book, *The Expression of the Emotions in Man and Animals* (London: John Murray, 1872), for instance.

25 F. Burkhardt and S. Smith (eds), *The Correspondence of Charles Darwin*, 7 vols (Cambridge: Cambridge University Press, 1985–91), vol. 4: 29–30.

26 Letter from Darwin to Charles Lyell, 2 September 1849, *Selected Letters*, p. 109.
27 Frederick B. Churchill, 'The Guts of the Matter', pp. 200–1.
28 *Ibid.*, p. 213.
29 Letter from Darwin to W. D. Fox, 29 January 1853, Burkhardt and Smith (eds), *Correspondence*, vol. 5: 113.
30 Letter from Darwin to Albany Hancock (10 February 1853), *ibid.*: 114.
31 Letter from Darwin to Albany Hancock (12 February 1853), *ibid.*: 116–17.
32 Letter from Darwin to Charles Lyell (15 February 1853), *ibid.*: 113–15.
33 Mikhail Bakhtin, *Rabelais and His World* [1965], trans. Helene Iswolsky (Bloomington: Indiana University Press, 1984), pp. 30–2.
34 James Krasner, *The Entangled Eye: Visual Perception and the Representation of Nature in Post-Darwinian Narrative* (New York: Oxford University Press, 1992), p. 6.
35 *Ibid.*, pp. 41–2.
36 Agnes Catlow, *Drops of Water; Their Marvellous and Beautiful Inhabitants Displayed by the Microscope* (London: Reeve & Benham, 1851), p. 47.
37 Lewes, *Sea-Side Studies*, p. 121.
38 Lynn L. Merrill, *The Romance of Victorian Natural History* (Oxford: Oxford University Press), p. 86.
39 Catlow, *Drops of Water*, pp. 23–4.
40 Mary Roberts, *A Popular History of the Mollusca* (London: Reeve & Benham, 1851), p. 12.
41 Charles Kingsley, *Glaucus, Or the Wonders of the Shore* (Cambridge: Macmillan, 1855), pp. 57–8.
42 Charles Kingsley, *The Water-Babies* [1863] (Oxford: World's Classics, 1995), p. 44.
43 Lewes, *Sea-Side Studies*, p. 242.
44 *Ibid.*, p. 179.
45 G. H. Lewes, *Studies in Animal Life* (London: Smith, Elder & Co., 1862), p. 62. This was originally published in serial form in *The Cornhill Magazine*.
46 For more about the role of women in Victorian science, see Barbara Gates, *Kindred Nature: Victorian and Edwardian Women Embrace the Living World* (Chicago, IL: University of Chicago Press, 1999).
47 Roberts, *A Popular History of the Mollusca*, p. 224.
48 *Ibid.*, p. 248.
49 See, for instance, Lewes's famous passage on the consuming joys of the microscope in *Sea-Side Studies*, pp. 35–6, and cf. discussions by Armstrong and White, above, pp. 40–1 and 87–8.
50 Lynn Barber, *The Heyday of Natural History*, p. 275.
51 George Kearley, *Links in the Chain, or Popular Chapters on the Curiosities of Animal Life* (London: James Hogg & Sons, 1862), pp. 133–4.

52 *Ibid.*, p. 288.

53 John Ruskin, *Love's Meinie* (Kent: Keston, 1873), p. 59, cited in Gillian Beer, 'Forging the Missing Link: Interdisciplinary Stories', in Beer, *Open Fields: Science in Cultural Encounter* (Oxford: Clarendon Press, 1996), p. 131.

54 Gerard Manley Hopkins, cited in Beer, 'Forging the Missing Link', p. 131.

55 T. H. Huxley, 'On the Physical Basis of Life', *The Fortnightly Review*, 5 (1869).

56 For an account of the history of protoplasmic theory, see Gerald L. Geison 'The Protoplasmic Theory of Life and the Vitalist–Mechanist Debate', *Isis*, 60, 3 (1969).

57 E. Ray Lankester, *Degeneration: A Chapter in Darwinism* (London: Macmillan, 1880), p. 33.

58 *Ibid.*, pp. 38–9.

59 *Ibid.*, p. 60.

60 Andrew Wilson, 'Degeneration: Some Animal Biographies and Their Lessons', *Gentleman's Magazine*, 250 (April 1881).

61 See H. G. Wells, *Experiment in Autobiography: Discoveries and Conclusions of a Very Ordinary Brain* (London: Victor Gallancz, 1934), vol. 1.

62 H. G. Wells, 'Zoological Retrogression', *Gentleman's Magazine*, 271 (September 1891): 249–50.

63 Peter Kemp, *H. G. Wells and the Culminating Ape: Biological Themes and Obsessions* (Basingstoke: Macmillan, 1982), p. 29.

64 See *ibid.*

65 Churchill, 'The Guts of the Matter', p. 213.

8

Woman's Share in Primitive Culture: science, femininity and anthropological knowledge

↜

LYNNETTE TURNER

In 1895 Macmillan launched its 'Anthropological Series' with the title *Woman's Share in Primitive Culture* by Otis Tufton Mason, then curator of the department of ethnology in the United States' National Museum. The series aimed at a readership in both Europe and America, and was bought by Macmillan (from Appleton & Co.) as a popular supplement to its growing list of specialised anthropological works. The 'Anthropological Series', which never extended beyond this inaugural volume, was conceived with the aim that the 'grandest and newest of all the sciences, Anthropology – the science of man – may become better known to intelligent readers who are not specialists and who do not desire to become such'.[1] *Woman's Share in Primitive Culture* appeared in the Macmillan catalogue from 1895 to 1908. The growth of its anthropology ('including Folk Lore') list during these years established Macmillan as the leading British publisher of anthropological works at the turn of the century. Mason's small volume kept company with the major works of comparative anthropology, such as J. G. Frazer's *The Golden Bough*, Edward Westermarck's *History of Human Marriage*, Francis Galton's *Natural Inheritance*, J. F. McLennan's *Ancient History* and Edward B. Tylor's *Anthropology*. The list contained also many examples of more particularised, systematic, anthropological studies, emerging largely from expert 'first-hand' knowledge, and which grew in number during the 1890s. It also provided notable evidence of a shifting agenda in disciplinary anthropology through the publication of the first example of a wholly new form of anthropological writing: W. Baldwin

Spencer and Francis Gillen's ethnographic monograph *The Native Tribes of Central Australia*.[2] If the Macmillan list testifies to the two major strands of anthropological writing at this time, *Woman's Share in Primitive Culture* represents something of a generic anomaly. None of the other listed works was 'intended to be of general interest' or was so clearly aimed at a non-specialist audience.[3] Significantly, the book also bears the dedication: 'To all good women, living and dead, who with their brains or by their toil have aided the progress of the world'.

To launch an anthropological series with a volume focusing on, and dedicated to, women is in many ways historically curious. Despite the wave of intellectual interest in the natural history of women occasioned by the publication of Hermann Ploss's *Das Weib* in 1885,[4] the status of women as core subjects of *anthropological* inquiry was diminishing at this time. Ploss's book, a significant presence in the 'extraordinary effloresence of writing' about sexuality in the last two decades of the nineteenth century, was instrumental in advancing discussion of the characteristics and distinctiveness of the female sex.[5] Alongside the writings of Richard von Krafft-Ebing and Havelock Ellis, *Das Weib* greatly assisted the displacement of women from the 'science of man' into the science of sex. But pressures against the analysis of women *qua* women were clearly detectable within the anthropological discipline itself. *Woman's Share in Primitive Culture* was published in England in a climate of energetic attempts to both professionalise anthropological research and standardise disciplinary knowledge. The new generation of academically trained fieldworkers which emerged during that decade was committed to the accuracy of information gained through sustained and involved observation. This new 'participatory' mode led, systematically and conclusively, to a significant recasting of knowledge of cultural difference through its carving out of a central place for same-sex (male) knowledge.

Within this climate of shifting disciplinary interests and property, the decision to promote an anthropological book about women and aimed largely at women readers brings into focus a number of critical discursive and ideological encounters within anthropology at the turn of the century. This chapter is concerned, therefore, with 'woman's share' of anthropology at a watershed moment in disciplinary history. The year

1895 witnessed a number of material milestones, not least of them the appointment of Alfred Cort Haddon – whose 1888 Melanesian field-work set a precedent for the authority of knowledge gained from the intimacy of closed conversations between men[6] – to the first lectureship in anthropology at a British university.[7] So it comes as little surprise that *Woman's Share in Primitive Culture* begins with the question 'What shall we say of women?'[8] But that question is not, of course, merely rhetori-cal. By examining the tensions and preoccupations that inform the book's vision of femininity, my main aim is to assess anthropology's capacity to speak about women, while also exploring the cultural cur-rency and circulation in the 1890s of scientifically informed ideas of the female primitive.

Women in Victorian anthropology

That it was important for anthropology to make some sort of authorita-tive statement on women within the context of claims for women's suf-frage was notably voiced as early as 1868. Luke Owen Pike read a lengthy paper that year to the Anthropological Society (the forerunner of the Anthropological Institute), entitled 'On the Claims of Women to Political Power'. He argued that the 'science' of anthropology 'must deal with prac-tical as well as speculative difficulties', and continued: 'I know of no sub-ject upon which it ought to give a more authoritative decision than upon the claims of women to political power.' In a bald and provocative argu-ment that finds echoes in later eugenically inspired feminism, Pike sug-gested that these claims are associated with 'an attempt to deprive woman of her motherhood'.[9]

As Pike's and Mason's studies indicate, anthropological concern over women's status as social and scientific subjects was voiced intermittently both before and after the political reforms of the 1880s. But anthropology was called on politically during the 1890s because of its apparent scien-tific underpinning of evolutionary models of social progress that sup-ported changes to the legal and social status of women. Ironically, this underpinning was itself manifold, and no single evolutionary model dominated anthropological discussion. As George Stocking points out, 'later-nineteenth-century anthropology in Britain turned out to be an extremely various and multifocal inquiry, for which the term "discipline" seems appropriate only in a rather loose sense'.[10] This diversity no doubt supports Henrika Kuklick's observation that 'anthropology never suffered from being a feminist issue; anthropological evidence could be used by both advocates and opponents of feminism'.[11]

Kuklick's point is vital. The uses to which evolutionary anthropology – and various forms of physical anthropology, such as anthropometrics – could be put pulled in a number of contradictory, conflicting, or politically opposed directions. Despite anthropology's potential for determining thinking on women, the development of more holistic field-research initiatives within British anthropology – alongside the demise of the explanatory force of the promiscuity benchmark in definitions of 'primitiveness'[12] – meant that the enthusiasm expressed outside of the discipline was unlikely to be matched within it. Throughout the 1880s and 1890s, both feminist and anti-feminist interest in evolutionary social theory worked strenuously to provide the impression that the anthropology of women was something of greater concern *to* the discipline than it was in actuality within it.

The fact that Macmillan decided to purchase and promote a book written by an internationally renowned American ethnologist tells us as much about the fraught status of the topic of 'women' in British anthropology as does Mason's singular ability to present authoritative information on the female primitive. Mason was the leading specialist in basketry, a knowledge base that made him, in disciplinary terms, uniquely placed to comment on women's cultures. 'With few exceptions', Mason tells us, 'women, the wide world over, are the basket makers.'[13] His work at the Smithsonian Institution from 1884 until his death in 1908 involved him in cataloguing, arranging and, later, curating 'Aboriginal American' material culture, and his greatest involvement had been with the basketry collection at the United States' National Museum. Mason was the leading comparative ethnologist of his generation in the United States. His knowledge was gained from the museum, not from field research or any direct observation of Native American women's cultures, and his argument reinscribes the kinds of armchair theorisations that were being disturbed and explicitly questioned by the academically trained anthropologists taking to the field during this decade. '[B]ecause of his rank' and the 'weight he can give to his opinions', Mason was the figure whom Franz Boas, the influential early champion of intensive fieldwork, chose to attack in his famous promotion of the inductive method over analogical classificatory ethnology: 'classification is not explanation'.[14] Throughout his career, Mason was far from persuaded by arguments such as William H. Dall's that anthropology should be concerned with the 'culture of each people as an ethnic unit', or Boas's view that the 'object of study is the individual, not abstractions from the individual'. For Boas, the project of anthropology was 'to study each ethnological specimen individually in its history and in its medium'.[15]

Against these calls for methodological innovation and integrity, Mason's study of women is cast in a firm evolutionary comparative mode. It is only partly supported by empirical evidence (based on observations of extant peoples, all of whom were colonised) and largely made up of speculative reconstructions of the cultural practices of the 'savage woman' at clearly marked stages on the evolutionary scale of development. Mason's approach accords with emerging views on the presentation of factual information for mass consumption, articulated with enormous impact in the museum sector by A. H. L. F. Pitt Rivers in his statement that the 'knowledge [the masses] lack is the knowledge of history'.[16] Thus the book offers its readers an authoritative 'narrative of women's earliest history', configured around the simplified journey of a single unnamed protagonist who is followed on her 'upward journey' from lower to upper savagery.[17] Written by an expert in the rudest of female cultural forms, *Woman's Share in Primitive Culture* advances a celebration of the 'occupations of savage women' very similar to the primitivism articulated by radical women writers such as Olive Schreiner and George Egerton.[18] Where Mason's method could not be considered, in disciplinary terms, 'a progress of ethnological researches',[19] his interpretative style offered a transhistorical and transcultural vision of femininity which chimed with a broad-based, commercially profitable, interest in the (re-)articulation of primitive woman.

Anthropological science

For all its aberrant qualities *Woman's Share in Primitive Culture* nonetheless adds an important dimension to our understanding of British anthropology in the 1890s. While far from advancing the frontier of anthropological method and knowledge, the book is significant in focusing knowledge of the 'savage woman' as the producer of material culture, not as the pathologically sexualised or ex-centric being emerging in both sexological and academic anthropological discourse at this time. The homogenous woman who appears in Mason's book is at all moments in history conservative, naturally self-limiting and moderately ingenious, displaying, in equal measure, the 'maternal instinct, the strong back, the deft hand, [and] the aversion to aggressive employment'.[20] The female primitive of contemporary academic fieldwork-based anthropology may well also be all of these things, but her capacity to produce, both culturally and linguistically, is severely restricted. Edward Burnett Tylor's famous 1871 definition of 'culture' as 'that complex whole which includes knowledge, belief, art, morals, law, custom and any other capabilities and habits acquired by man as a member of society' resulted in two major shifts in anthropological thinking.[21] First, as Adam Kuper notes, Tylor's emphasis on the intellectual development of humankind 'increasingly distinguished the history of culture from the history of race'.[22] The second general effect was a considerable modification and refraction of the terms through which 'primitiveness' was understood.

Tylor's cultural categories had existed informally for some time prior to the publication of *Primitive Culture*, and most notably in the handbook, co-authored by Tylor, *Notes and Queries on Anthropology* (1874), a guide designed 'to promote accurate anthropological observation' on the part of travellers and colonial settlers.[23] Yet previous anthropological definitions of the primitive (as the original condition of humankind) tended to fix on the self-explanatory evidence of promiscuity, or apparent communal marriage or incest. John F. McLennan's *Primitive Marriage: An Inquiry into the Origin of Capture in Marriage Ceremonies* (1865), a book described by George Stocking as a 'historical treatise on the "position of women"', was one of the most famous mid-century studies of that kind. For McLennan, 'general promiscuity' defined the most primitive of human relationships, and the sexual practices of women (how many partners they take, who these partners are) were decisive in defining degrees and levels of primitivity.[24] This was similarly the case in H. S. Maine's *Ancient Law* (1861), John Lubbock's *Pre-Historic Times* (1869) and Lewis Henry Morgan's influential *Ancient Society* (1877). Each of these studies confirms Robert J. C. Young's observation that mid-century anthropology was preoccupied with 'marriage-by-capture fantasies', a point Stocking endorses: the 'universal evolutionary significance' of marriage by capture, polyandry, and primitive promiscuity was 'called into question very quickly after their formulation and now seems perhaps to have been ... largely a fantasy of the Victorian male anthropological imagination'.[25]

Precipitating this 'calling into question' was the development within anthropology in the last two decades of the century of fieldwork-based research undertaken by trained academics. The different epistemic regime of fieldwork, based on participant observation and secured through empathic forms of knowledge, meant new objects of interest for anthropology. The new ethnography of the late 1880s and 1890s – exemplars of which are Haddon's paper 'The Ethnography of the Western Tribe of Torres Straits' (1889) and Walter Baldwin Spencer and Francis Gillen's monograph *The Native Tribes of Central Australia* (1899) – shifted the emphasis of the definitional onto what can now be identified as the 'totalising cultural performance'.[26] For Victorian ethnographers, the research period would be brief, and the knowledge of indigenous languages minimal. Spencer and Gillen were among the first to light on large-scale public rituals as providing a highly efficient, symbolically significant cultural performance. Within contemporary cultural anthropology there is broad agreement about the analytical value of definitional ceremonies which function as a collective 'autobiography' by means of which a 'group creates its identity by telling a story about itself'.[27] While it is rarely assumed that cultural ceremonies produce passive consumers and reduce participants to a single subjectivity, such self-reflective performances were nonetheless accepted by Victorian ethnographers as, to use Victor Turner's phrase, 'cultural–aesthetic "mirror[s]"'.[28]

In the 1890s, the ritual in which male ethnographers could observe *as if* participants was the large-scale public event of male initiation, a ceremony which has historically maintained itself as an iconic form, being 'more visible to ethnographic attention' than other cultural or gendered practices.[29] The perceived significance of accounts of group-based male ceremonies regarded as secret – or certainly restricted – established a new method and representational practice in which identification between indigenous male participants and initiate ethnographer (Spencer's 'they [take] no more notice of me than if I were one of themselves which in fact I am now'[30]) becomes the new means through which scientific knowledge is authorised. Not only did large-scale secret rituals appear to dramatise before the ethnographer's very eyes the deep truths of primitive cultures, but the performance of re-iterable rites alluded to the form of validation that underpinned Victorian scientific authority: knowledge gained through repeatable observation and experiment.[31] For Spencer and Gillen, observing the *Engwura* ceremony performed by Arandan men, ritual knowledge simultaneously defined and concentrated both the authority of Arandan culture (as autochthonous) and of the participant–observer who was one of the few Europeans able to communicate these truths, appropriately, to European audiences. Yet as Nancy C. Lutkehaus and Paul B. Roscoe point out, ethnographers then and now have fallen into the 'trap' of 'assuming [that] scale signifies *indigenous* perceptions of significance'.[32] An additional consequence is that the single-sex terms of this dynamic interpersonal exchange means that women's initiate knowledge is largely ignored, a neglect that still perplexes feminist anthropologists.[33]

Although an interest in primitive sexual activity still circulated in the unpublished writings of male anthropologists, the fraternal intimacy of participant-based research practice demands, as James Clifford notes, a 'delicate management of distance and proximity'. Unlike the traditional circuits of knowledge that provided Victorian comparative anthropologists with their data (indigenous informant, through settler spouse, through missionary or colonial official to armchair anthropologist), participant observation could not 'include entanglements in which the ability to maintain perspective might be lost'. Insisting that '[s]exual relations could not be avowed sources of research knowledge', Clifford argues further that the 'disciplinary habitus' of modern ethnography has come to be 'sustained' around 'an ungendered, unraced, sexually inactive subject' who 'interacts intensively' with its interlocutors.[34]

If the disciplining (to use Clifford's term) of ethnography relies on the exclusion of the merest suggestion of cross-sex intimacies, this normative regulation seems equally dependent on the dismissal (both hermeneutical and representational) of active, performative, female bodies, complete with their own differentiated sexualities. While it needs to be noted that this structure of inclusion and exclusion frequently maps directly onto indigenous spatialised gender practices (for Spencer and Gillen, observing rituals among the Aranda community in central Australia, the women were largely unseen during the rituals because their camp was across the river from the men's[35]), modern ethnography privileges a new semiotics of primitivity based on the display of male power and on the performance – and performability – of men's histories.[36] As with other forms of female knowledge among pre-industrial non-European communities (whether operating initiation cults or not), women's initiate knowledge, that knowledge which marks women's *socialised sexuality*, becomes discursively unrealisable in the founding moment of the ethnographic tradition. In presenting women through such selective representational practices as generationally undifferentiated – and with an unsocialised sexuality, ethnography repeats *in obverse* the very same images of femininity that so preoccupy contemporaneous sexology, which eclipses academic anthropology as the major discursive field for the scientific analysis of women.

Popular anthropology and the staging of women

On one important level Mason's vision of the female primitive accords with the epistemic trajectory of disciplinary anthropology through its decision to 'ignore' the type of discussion of woman's 'anatomy and physiology, in health and disease, in savagery and civilisation, from the cradle to the grave' that characterises Ploss's *Das Weib* and Ellis's *Man and Woman*.[37] In bypassing the preoccupations of contemporary sexology, Mason's book resists the pathologising fantasies around women's physiological processes that secured, for sexology, tangible connections between European women and 'primitive' peoples. Havelock Ellis, for example, makes direct comparisons between women and children and draws analogies between modern women and 'savages' in his assessment of the phenomenon of the 'early arrest of the development of girls'.[38] Synthesising and summarising the findings of physical anthropology and psychology, Ellis's examination of the 'constitutional differences between men and women' reproduces the conceptual language of comparative anthropology whose common framework of raced bodies, evolution and hierarchy draws a linear narrative of human development in which the 'lower' races are equated with infancy and the 'higher' with adulthood.[39] Thus where Ellis argues that 'women, taken altogether, present the characters of short men, and to some extent of children', he reproduces the view widespread in anthropometrics that little bodies are a sign of little minds.[40] Arguing throughout that the modern woman remains analogous to children in both stature and intellectual capacity (discussing the 'intellectual impulse', Ellis states that 'women remain children') Ellis produces a vision of woman as physiologically and intellectually delimited, a theory that Karl Pearson described as a 'slur against women'.[41]

Ellis's identification of women as lower beings on the evolutionary scale of development ('We have found over and over again that when women differ from men, it is the latter who have diverged, leaving women closer to the child type') is nowhere more clearly advanced than in his hierarchised topography of the human body in which the 'thoracic organs' predominate in men 'and the abdominal in women'.[42] Driven and governed by the visceral organs, the key differentiator of woman as a physical and psychic organism is rooted less in the 'outward manifestations' of difference than in the tendency of the 'more primitive nervous centres to be stronger than the more recent centres, and to rise up in revolt against them'.[43] Ellis's insistent equation of the primitive with the 'unperceived' aspects of femininity produces investigative principles remarkably similar to those of fieldwork-based anthropology.[44] As with the anthropology of primitive cultures, scientific truth is located in elements concealed or veiled, and what constitutes the deep truths of femininity are those 'hidden' physiological processes, such as menstruation, which, despite concealment, are nonetheless there for the 'skilled observer' to 'detect'.[45] Ellis's codification of the feminine primitive as irrepressible and unregenerate, is shared with anthropology and sociology, and with the psychophysiological models dominating psychiatry in which mental disturbances are linked to a failure to control primitive bodily processes and functions.[46] Ellis's conviction that 'menstruation produces abnormal and diseased conditions', such as 'irritability or depression [which] may be so pronounced as to amount to insanity',[47] firmly locates *Men and Women* within a pervasive network of ideas about female sexuality in which the male imaginary registers very real anxieties about, or emphatically demonises, the active, performative, female body.

If Ellis's account of women's inherent inferiority and developmental stasis speaks loudly of contemporary anxieties over the social status of women, it does so from both a position of scientific authority and the testimony of commercial success.[48] The standing Ellis gained from his position as editor of the Contemporary Science series was reinforced in 1894 by his appointment, by the Italian criminologist Cesare Lombroso, as secretary of the psychiatry section of the International Medical Congress. *Man and Woman* itself went into six editions and in 1894 represented, according to Cynthia Eagle Russett, the 'consensus of medical and scientific opinion of the day'.[49] Yet the seemingly consensual and commercially viable model of *fin de siècle* femininity found in *Man and Woman* differs sharply from the version of womanhood produced in *Woman's Share in Primitive Culture*.

Despite its lack of commercial success, Mason's book conceptualises femininity through the canons of representation appropriate to the (popular) education of the masses: that is, precisely the same constituency (women and the 'lower' classes) that scientific exegesis deemed of 'greater impressionability' and 'greater suggestibility' than higher class men. There are no depth models in Mason's book; there is no hiddenness, no irrationality, no spatialising of the evolutionary paradigm, no female bodies performing anything other than good work.[50] The benevolent paternalism of Mason's style is matched by an organisational method befitting the museum curator's take on popular scientific knowledge. *Woman's Share in Primitive Culture* 'set[s] forth woman's share in the culture of the world

by her works', and her 'honourable achievements' were laid out in meaningful taxonomic units: woman as food bringer, weaver, skin dresser,
potter, beast of burden, jack-of-all-trades, artist, linguist and, finally, as
the founder of society and patron of religion.[51] In contrast to ethno-
graphically based anthropology – actively dismantling the 'hypothesis
that a connection of some kind exists between ethnological phenomena
of people widely apart' – Mason's schema erases cultural and social differences through its perpetuation of the idea of a single human history.[52]
The ideological neatness of the book's organisation exists in its illustra-
tion of evolutionary progression through specific material artefacts. Not
only does this method exemplify the premiss that the past can be found
in the present ('it is most interesting to ... see what a large proportion of
the working women in our cities are still following the paths trodden long
ago by dusky savages of their own sex') but, through tangible exposition,
the narrative emphasises the durability and inevitability of existing social
and cultural formations.[53]

The implied importance of slow and gradual progression is explicitly
realised in the book's conclusion. Echoing Pitt Rivers' view that 'drastic
changes' lack 'the sanction of experience'[54] Mason urges women not 'to
turn aside from the old highways to wander in unbeaten tracks' before
'looking backwards' at '[a]ll this ... stored capital, accumulated experience and energy'.[55] His concluding chapter depicts the narrative preced-
ing it as analogous to a tour through a museum displaying the 'splendid
results' of women's social evolution. In considering the 'great awakening
among women to their own attributes and functions and capabilities',
Mason asks: 'could any study lead them to truer success than the careful
review of those activities and occupations through which they contributed so much to the general mass of happiness?'[56] Through discursive
analogy – persistently secured through a dual emphasis on the visual
dimensions of personal education alongside the self-evident truths of
material culture – Mason deftly merges the growing recognition of the
museum as a national educational resource with an image of women as
the guardians of the nation's wealth, health, and happiness.

Mason's awareness of the role and function of knowledge means
that the book avoids mention of the type of emotionally provocative

material to which women readers were considered peculiarly susceptible. *Woman's Share in Primitive Culture* stabilises the connection between
the knowledge women gain through reading and their social behaviour
by restricting comment on women's sexuality to marriage, morality and
motherhood. Mason's chapter on woman as the 'Founder of Society' discusses women's sexual maturity as the cornerstone of social cohesion.
The book's distilled story of the female subject passing from childhood,
through maidenhood, to motherhood insists that the 'little girl of savagery' is educated by her mother and sisters between the years of 3 and
13. '[S]avage pedagogies' focus on 'her physical education, her mental
training, her morals', but Mason emphasises that her education was
largely 'of the most practical character'. The 'great museums', he suggests,
provide 'innumerable examples of tiny pieces of basketry, pottery, bread,
or weaving, labelled "children's work"'.[57] So keen is the narrative to unite
morality and sexual maturity with diligence and social duty that Mason's
brief mention of the '"bringing out" ordeal' of female initiation enu-
merates only the most modest of the re-enactments of the female life-
cycle that occurs in the ritual sequence: 'She had to walk ever-increasing
distances with a jar on her head and to carry burdens made heavier every
day. In fact, she was drilled in endurance and skill and every wifely
exercise.'[58]

   With no mention of the female body, despite its lengthy inventory of
the systems of primitive marriage first outlined by Morgan in his *Ancient
Society*, Mason removes the sexual from his analysis of the social education of women. Mason does not deny that (primitive) women are the elab-
orators of their culture's worldview; but, as disseminators of its moral
tone, they have repeatedly provided the 'ground work and the reason for
that high moral purpose and purity which mark her in the family life of
cultured society'.[59] Unsurprisingly, Mason's account of women's preparation for, and involvement in marriage, reifies a dyadic model of sexual
identity that limits and prescribes normative behaviour. It also insists that
woman's 'has been a wonderful evolution, resulting in comfort, taste, and
morality'.[60] In keeping with its priority to educate women, Mason's uni-
linear and gradually progressive narrative of women's history is not complicated by the observations of women's precocity being advanced by the

leading sexologists. Mason's women are constrained by the 'inevitable law of survival and conservatism': they carry on the 'same commerce that has been familiar to women during many thousands of years'; they foster the 'industrial and humanizing element in savage culture' and were 'undoubtedly' the 'first *modistes*'.[61] In advancing the primitivist assertion of the savage woman's 'personal courage and noble sentiments',[62] Mason's assessment of the female primitive commutes the *fin de siècle* semantics of savagery into assertions of social redemption firmly located in women's continued involvement in dignified pre-industrial forms of labour:

> [In] transitions from savagery to civilization, and in the vicissitudes of life, women go on housekeeping, spinning, demanding if no longer making pottery, using the same vocabulary, conning the same propositions, reproducing the same forms of ornaments, believing as of old, only making use of modified and bettered appliances.[63]

Uninterested in innovation and showing remarkable resilience in the face of technological and economic change, Mason's women are compelled to repeat the ways and words of their mothers: 'Nearly all women, whether in savagery or in civilization, are doing what their mothers and grandmothers did, and their opinions are therefore born in them or into them'.[64] Suggesting the importance of heredity and/or socialisation, Mason's conviction that women are the driving force behind gradual elevation and steady social progress combines romantic motifs (conservation and tradition, the natural and the organic[65]) with underdeveloped strands of eugenic thinking that hint at both inheritance and the custodial function of maternal femininity while overtly emphasising the propriety of women's involvement in material forms of cultural meaning and transmission.[66] As the guardians and conservators of cultural purity, Mason's pre-industrial female communities are seen as providing women with appropriate education and proper, meaningful, work. His method, with its focus on observable and comparable phenomena, reads femininity through women's 'works' and produces a version of femaleness which is as stable (both psychically and physically) and transparent as are the cultural artefacts that demonstrate women's commitment to the preservation and maintenance of the social community.

Activity, femininity, science and feminism

The proper subject of Mason's volume is the female primitive. Its objective, however, is to educate its Western women readers about their own vital and continuous past. In rendering marginal to its enterprise the examples and illustrations of positive social femininity taken from then-extant pre-industrial cultures, Mason's book ultimately affirms the oversights of disciplinary anthropology at the time: in and of itself, the notion of the female primitive has little scientific value. Yet the versions of primitive femininity offered in the book work against the highly sexualised late nineteenth-century medical models of the primitive. As Sander Gilman argues, when the late Victorians were confronted with the 'female black' they saw her in terms of sexuality, genitalia and degeneracy. Medical myths provided abundant evidence that '[b]lack females do not merely represent the sexualised female, they also represent the female as the source of corruption and disease'.[67] In avoiding commonplace associations of female primitivity with amorality, with unbridled and uncontrollable sexuality, and with degeneracy, Mason's female primitive has an ambiguous presence in the contemporary world: she serves as an indicator of the continuity obtaining between contemporary Western women's cultures and the 'past', but is yet bound up in a conceptual and temporal matrix regulated by repetition, monotony and anachrony.

Mason's focus on women as producers of material culture avoids mention of those contentious aspects of femininity that form the substance of *fin-de-siècle* anxieties and misogynies surrounding the active female body. His production of the woman of primitive culture as subjugated by the desire to make a 'servant of herself, and willingly, before there was any slavery',[68] nonetheless invokes – precisely through this denial of any (insurgent) agential dimension to women's social experience – concerns and preoccupations very similar to those driving scientific analyses. Ironically, but not unsurprisingly, Mason's comparative assessments agree with feminist articulations of the 'shared common experiences' that create 'universal' feminine values, espoused most notably by Olive Schreiner.[69] Yet these 'universal' feminine values are shaped by a problematical colonial imperative, namely, that the 'subjectivity of the European woman is dependent upon non-European space'.[70]

Mobilising Mason's educational project is a version of female primitivity that concurs with the image of black African women found in Olive Schreiner's 'The Woman Question' (1899), not only in their 'self-conscious acceptance' of the 'grim conditions of life', as Carolyn Burdett notes, but in their 'self-imposed' position outside the (modern) temporality of emancipation and self-determination.[71] Mason's book shares the vocabulary and ideological containment of Schreiner's (African) model of racial otherness where the 'primitive' equates with 'maternal instinct', 'gentle pride' and 'devotion to the compact tribe'.[72] And it concurs with Schreiner's view that 'European women of this age ... stand to-day where again and again, in the history of the past, women of other races have stood'.[73] For both writers, primitivity is dependent on placing the ethnically different woman into what Anne McClintock calls 'anachronistic space': 'colonised people do not occupy history proper but exist in a permanently anterior time within the geographic space of the modern empire'.[74] Yet at the point in time when fieldwork-based anthropology was being forced to confront the contemporaneity of primitive cultures and to recast its understanding of racial–cultural difference, *Woman's Share in Primitive Culture* – alongside both feminist and anti-feminist discourses – censors the possibility of truly analysing the female 'ethnological specimen individually in its history and in its medium'.[75] Mason's book may have been more benign in its representations, but it was no less malignant than scientific analysis determined the discourse of female primitivity to have been.

Notes

My thanks to Jonathan Andrews and Roger Luckhurst for comments on earlier drafts of this essay.

1 Otis Tufton Mason, *Woman's Share in Primitive Culture* (London and New York: Macmillan, 1895), p. vii.

2 My thanks to Robert Machesney, archivist at Macmillan, for providing copies of the relevant pages of these catalogues and for information on the anthropology list.

3 The exception was Mary Kingsley's *Travels in West Africa*, quite rightly classified in the catalogue as an anthropological work. Kingsley's book sold
   extremely well, as did much travel writing on Africa at that time, though her
   remit (as directed by George Macmillan) was not primarily to produce a work
   of popular anthropology. Her more anthropological volume, *West African
   Studies*, never went into a second edition. Interestingly, the abridged volume of
   Kingsley's *Travels* sold for 7 shillings and 6 pence in 1899, Mason's *Woman's
   Share in Primitive Culture* for 6 shillings. Volumes in the Contemporary
   Science series, edited by Havelock Ellis for the Walter Scott Company, were
   some 300–400 pages in length (the same length and dimensions as *Woman's
   Share in Primitive Culture*) and sold for 1 shilling. Intended 'principally for the
   intelligent layman', the series was priced for the popular market. Nearly fifty
   titles were produced in this series, including Ellis's *Man and Woman*. See Phyllis
   Grosskurth, *Havelock Ellis: A Biography* (New York: SUNY Press, 1985), p. 114.
4 Hermann Heinrich Ploss, *Das Weib in der Natur und Völkerkunde* was first
   published in Leipzig in 1885. The second edition was published in 1887,
   edited by Max Bartels, and by 1908 nine editions had been published, each
   under the supervision of Max Bartels. The first English translation appeared
   in 1935: Hermann Heinrich Ploss, Max Bartels, and Paul Bartels, *Women: An
   Historical and Gynæcological and Anthropological Compendium* (London:
   Heinemann Medical Books, 1935), 3 vols.
5 Jeffrey Weeks, *Sexuality and its Discontents: Meanings, Myth, and Modern
   Sexualities* (London: Routledge & Kegan Paul, 1985), p. 63.
6 A. C. Haddon describes his Torres Straits' visit to study marine biology thus:
   'In the summer of 1888 I went to Torres Straits to investigate the structure and
   fauna of the coral reefs of that district. Very soon after my arrival in the Straits
   I found that the natives of the islands had of late years been greatly reduced
   in number, and that, with the exception of but one or two individuals, none
   of the white residents knew anything about the customs of the natives, and
   not a single person cared about them personally. When I began to question
   the natives I discovered that the young men had a very imperfect acquain-
   tance with the old habits and beliefs, and that only from the older men was
   reliable information to be obtained. So it was made clear to me that if I neglected to avail myself of the present opportunity of collecting information on
   the ethnography of the islanders, it was extremely probable that the knowledge would never be gleaned.' (Alfred C. Haddon, 'The Ethnography of the
   Western Tribe of the Torres Straits', *Journal of the Anthropological Institute*, 19
   (1890): 297–8.) This erosion of the islanders' history and culture was brought
   on by accelerated formal contact with Europeans from 1863 when the island
   communities were subjected to Anglo-Australian rule. Missionary attention
   followed in 1871, and by the time of Haddon's first visit, many islanders had

converted to Christianity. Haddon 'induced the old men to come in the evenings and talk about old times and tell me their folk tales. In this way, without any previous experience or knowledge, I worked single-handed among the Western islanders and amassed a fair amount of information.' See Alfred Cort Haddon, Introduction, *Reports of the Cambridge Anthropological Expedition to Torres Straits* (Cambridge: Cambridge University Press, 1935), vol. 1: xi. For commentary, see Henrika Kuklick, *The Savage Within: The Social History of British Anthropology, 1885–1945* (Cambridge: Cambridge University Press, 1993), p. 134.

7 Haddon was appointed to lecture in physical anthropology at Cambridge University, an event that enabled anthropology to gain 'what was to become a permanent place in the teaching curriculum'. Arthur Thomson, lecturer in human anatomy at Oxford University, first lectured on physical anthropology in Oxford in the same year (1895). See George Stocking, *Victorian Anthropology* (New York: Free Press, 1987), p. 265.

8 Mason, *Woman's Share of Primitive Culture*, p. 5.

9 Luke Owen Pike, 'On the Claims of Women to Political Power', *Journal of the Anthropological Society* (1869): xlvii and xlviii.

10 Stocking, *Victorian Anthropology*, pp. 268–9.

11 Kuklick, *The Savage Within*, p. 53.

12 The relation of primitiveness to promiscuity is discussed on pp. 187–8. The principal studies that propose this connection are John F. McLennan, *Primitive Marriage: An Inquiry into the Origins of Capture in Marriage Ceremonies* (Edinburgh: Adam and Charles Black, 1865) and H. S. Maine, *Ancient Law* (London: John Murray, 1861).

13 Mason, *Woman's Share of Primitive Culture*, p. 42.

14 First citation, Franz Boas, response to Otis Tufton Mason's 'Museums of Ethnology and Their Classification', *Science*, 9 (17 June 1887): 588. Second citation, Franz Boas, 'The Occurrence of Similar Inventions in Areas Widely Apart', *Science*, 9 (20 May 1887): 485.

15 William H. Dall, response to Otis Tufton Mason's 'Museums of Ethnology and Their Classification', *Science*, 9 (17 June, 1887): 588; and Boas, 'The Occurrence of Similar Inventions': 485.

16 Lieutenant-General Pitt Rivers, 'Typological Museums as Exemplified by the Pitt Rivers Museum at Oxford, and His Provincial Museum at Farnham, Dorset', *Journal of the Society of Arts*, 40 (1891): 116.

17 Mason, *Woman's Share in Primitive Culture*, pp. 12 and 62.

18 *Ibid.*, pp. 42 and 280. I discuss Schreiner in my concluding remarks, but of particular relevance here are Olive Schreiner's *Woman and Labour* and George Egerton's short story 'A Cross Line' in her notorious 1894 collection *Keynotes*, which explores female desire in 'primitivist' terms.

19 Boas, 'The Occurrence of Similar Inventions', p. 485.

20 Mason, *Woman's Share in Primitive Culture*, p. 4.

21 This is the opening sentence of E. B. Tylor's *Primitive Culture: Researches into the Development of Mythology, Philosophy, Religion, Language, Art, and Custom* (London: John Murray, 1871), 2 vols.

22 Adam Kuper, *The Invention of Primitive Society: Transformations of an Illusion* (London: Routledge, 1991), p. 81.

23 British Association for the Advancement of Science, *Notes and Queries on Anthropology: For the Use of Travellers and Residents in Uncivilized Lands* (London: Edward Stanford, 1874), p. iv.

24 McLennan, *Primitive Marriage*, pp. 170–1.

25 Robert J. C. Young, *Colonial Desire: Hybridity in Theory, Culture and Race* (London: Routledge, 1995), p. 181 and George Stocking, *Victorian Anthropology*, p. 316.

26 George Stocking, 'The Ethnographer's Magic: Fieldwork in British Anthropology from Tylor to Malinowski', in George Stocking (ed.), *Observers Observed: Essays on Ethnographic Fieldwork* (Wisconsin: University of Wisconsin Press, 1985), p. 79.

27 Barbara Myerhoff, *Number Our Days* (1978), cited in Victor Turner, 'Are There Universals of Performance in Myth, Ritual, and Drama?', in Richard Schechner and Willa Appel (eds), *By Means of Performance: Intercultural Studies of Theatre and Ritual* (Cambridge: Cambridge University Press, 1990), p. 9.

28 Turner, 'Are there Universals of Performance', p. 8.

29 Frank Gillen described his participation as the 'pretence of sympathetic credulity' in a letter to Walter Baldwin Spencer, 18 June 1897, Spencer Papers [Gillen 28], Archives, Pitt Rivers Museum, Oxford University. Citation of Nancy C. Lutkehaus and Paul B. Roscoe's Preface, in Lutkehaus and Roscoe (eds), *Gender Rituals: Female Inititiation in Melanesia* (London: Routledge, 1995), p. xiv.

30 Walter Baldwin Spencer, letter to Lorimer Fison, Alice Springs, 21 November 1896, Spencer Papers [Fison 1], Archives, Pitt Rivers Museum, University of Oxford.

31 'Rites of initiation are among the most common and prominent of ... symbolic productions, occurring in communities of all sizes, subsistence bases, and social types'. Lutkehaus, and Roscoe, *Gender Rituals*, Preface, p. xv.

32 *Ibid.*, p. xiv (original emphasis).

33 *Ibid.*

34 James Clifford, 'Spatial Practices: Fieldwork, Travel, and the Disciplining of Anthropology', in James Clifford, *Routes: Travel, and Translation in the Late Twentieth Century* (Cambridge, MA: Harvard University Press, 1997), p. 72.

35 Walter Baldwin Spencer and Francis Gillen, *The Native Tribes of Central Australia* (London and New York: Macmillan, 1899), p. 274. The topography of the encampments, with a river segregating the men from the women, repeats the familiar mapping device of colonial exploration which Anne McClintock describes as the masculinisation of *terra firma* and the feminisation of *terra incognita*. McClintock does not explore the relations (and possible similarites) between European and indigenous readings of space and place. See Anne McClintock, *Imperial Leather: Race, Gender and Sexuality in the Colonial Contest* (London: Routledge, 1995), p. 24.

36 For Emile Durkheim, in his reading of Spencer and Gillen, women's exclusion from *the* 'ceremonial ground' marks them as 'the profane'. Emile Durkheim, *The Elementary Forms of the Religious Life*, trans. Karen E. Fields (New York: Free Press, 1995), p. 384.

37 Mason, *Woman's Share of Primitive Culture*, p. 1.

38 Ellis, *Man and Woman*, p. 246.

39 *Ibid.*, p. iii.

40 *Ibid.*, p. 387. In a different though analogous context, Henry Maudsley argues: 'It is most certain that there exist great natural differences between different people in respect of the development of their cerebral convolutions. In the lower races of men these are visibly less complex and more symmetrical than in the higher races; the anatomical differences corresponding with differences in intellectual capacity.' Henry Maudsley, *The Physiology and Pathology of Mind* (London: Macmillan, 1867), p. 217.

41 Ellis, p. 185. Karl Pearson, then professor of biometrics at University College, London, attacked Ellis for expressing 'pseudo-scientific superstition'. To underline his attack he also withdrew his *Grammar of Science* from Ellis's Contemporary Science Series. See Grosskurth, *Havelock Ellis*, pp. 170–1.

42 Ellis, *Man and Woman*, pp. 387 and 243.

43 *Ibid.*, pp. 248 and 298.

44 *Ibid.*, p. 256.

45 *Ibid.*, p. 253

46 Henry Maudsley anticipated Ellis in his assessment of women's periodic insanity. Maudsley argued: 'No one goes mad because he or she happens to be a man or a woman', and he went on to document those 'special physiological changes' that 'are apt to run into pathological effects'. He continues: 'The monthly activity of the ovaries which marks the advent of puberty in women has a notable effect upon the mind and body; wherefore it may become an important cause of mental and physical derangement. Most women at the time are susceptible, irritable, and capricious, any cause of vexation affecting them more seriously than usual; and some who have the insane neurosis exhibit a disturbance of mind which amounts almost to disease ... It is a

matter also of common experience in asylums, that exacerbations of insanity often take place at the menstrual periods.' Henry Maudsley, *Body and Mind: An Inquiry into their Connection and Mutual Influence, Specially in Reference to Mental Disorders* (London: Macmillan, 1870), pp. 78 and 87–8.

47 Ellis, *Man and Woman*, p. 254.

48 Ellis cautions (*ibid.*, p. 257) that the 'existence of the monthly cycle is, lastly, a factor which cannot be ignored in considering the fitness of women for any business position ... it is no longer possible to regard the physiological periodicity of women, and the recurring menstrual function, as the purely private concern of the woman whom it affects'.

49 Cynthia Eagle Russett, *Sexual Science: The Victorian Construction of Womanhood* (Cambridge, MA: Harvard University Press, 1989), p. 28.

50 Ellis, *Man and Woman*, p. 253. Pitt Rivers was especially concerned that the fact that the 'masses were ignorant ... lays them open to the designs of demagogues and agitators'. Pitt Rivers, 'Typological Museums', p. 116. My thanks to Roger Luckhurst for pointing out that the discourse on feminine nerves can mark women, paradoxically, as more evolutionarily advanced (through their 'greater' sensitivity) as well as more primitive.

51 Mason, *Woman's Share*, pp. 1 and 286.

52 Boas, 'The Occurrence of Similar Inventions', p. 485.

53 Mason, *Woman's Share*, p. 5.

54 Pitt Rivers, 'Typological Museums', p. 116.

55 Mason, *Woman's Share*, p. 286.

56 *Ibid.*, p. 273.

57 *Ibid.*, p. 208.

58 *Ibid.*, p. 210.

59 *Ibid.*, p. 230.

60 *Ibid.*, p. 235.

61 *Ibid.*, pp. 89–90, 179, 274 and 236.

62 *Ibid.*, p. 238.

63 *Ibid.*, p. 274.

64 *Ibid.*, p. 275.

65 These are precisely the motifs that Carolyn Burdett sees as 'saturating' Olive Schreiner's *Woman and Labour*. See Burdett, *Olive Schreiner and the Progress of Feminism* (Basingstoke: Palgrave, 2001), p. 75.

66 See especially Mason, *Woman's Share of Primitive Culture*, p. 275.

67 Sander Gilman, 'Black Bodies, White Bodies: Toward an Iconography of Female Sexuality in Late Nineteenth-Century Art, Medicine, and Literature', in Henry Louis Gates, ed., *"Race," Writing, and Difference* (Chicago, IL: University of Chicago Press, 1986), p. 250.

68 *Ibid.*, p. 284.

69 Burdett, *Olive Schreiner*, p. 77.
70 Laura Chrisman, 'Empire, "Race" and Feminism at the *Fin de Siècle*: The Work of George Egerton and Olive Schreiner', in Sally Ledger and Scott McCracken (eds), *Cultural Politics at the Fin de Siècle* (Cambridge: Cambridge University Press, 1995), p. 55.
71 Carolyn Burdett, 'Capturing the Ideal: Olive Schreiner's *From Man to Man*', in Angelique Richardson and Chris Willis (eds), *The New Woman in Fiction and Fact: Fin de Siècle Feminisms* (Basingstoke: Palgrave, 2000), p. 168; Mason, *Woman's Share*, p. 284.
72 Mason, *Woman's Share*, p. 284.
73 Olive Schreiner, 'The Woman Question' [1899], reprinted in Carol Barash (ed.), *An Olive Schreiner Reader* (London: Pandora, 1987), p. 100.
74 Anne McClintock, *Imperial Leather*, p. 30.
75 Boas, 'The Occurrence of Similar Inventions', p. 485.

9

From *The New Werther* to numbers and arguments: Karl Pearson's eugenics

~

CAROLYN BURDETT

I am afraid I am a scientific heretic – an outcast from the true orthodox faith – I do not believe in science for its own sake. I believe only in science for man's sake.[1]

By the mid-point of the nineteenth century, as democratic representative government was slowly becoming a reality for Britain's male population, the language heard at the House of Commons began to alter. According to G. M. Young, in his study of Victorian England *Portrait of an Age*, changing styles of political rhetoric saw a decline of declamatory erudition in favour of closely reasoned speeches which relied more and more on a knowledge of facts and figures. Fiscal and currency matters were the topics which packed Parliament's benches.[2] Quantifying the business of the state was to become an increasingly important activity: the statistical department of the Board of Trade was founded in 1832 and the Royal Statistical Society in 1833; the first nationwide census was undertaken in 1851 and, before very long, in warning against lies, damned lies and statistics, Benjamin Disraeli signalled that numerical quantification had become part and parcel of national political life.[3]

In this chapter, I examine one significant figure in the making of a distinctively mathematical and quantifying mode of understanding and managing society. This is Karl Pearson, widely acknowledged as the founder of a modern mathematical statistics which, as one critic puts it, 'was eventually to change the character of almost all social science'.[4] For

Pearson, scientists (and especially social scientists) formed a new elite, with special, and fully political, responsibilities. The central goal to which Pearson eventually harnessed his considerable mathematical skill – and what the *Dictionary of National Biography* called his 'demonic energy' – was the 'science of improving stock', which Francis Galton named *eugenics*. As I explain below, Galton's enthusiasm for classification and quantification, fuelled by his Malthusian pessimism, provided the ground rules for a theoretical and political enterprise in which the scientist occupies the highest place: as the new high priest, the seer – but also the doer – of the modern era.

The growing authority of quantitative expertise in public decision making in the nineteenth century and after is widely acknowledged. The historian of science Theodore Porter suggests, however, that the history of its development has not always been well told. This is largely a consequence of the sterility of rival views which see quantification as either representative of the progressive development of a more properly scientific, and therefore truer, method of knowing about human beings, on the one hand; and, on the other, as a particularly powerful and pernicious ideological tool for domination.[5] There are surely few better-placed contenders for confirming the latter view than eugenics, a repulsive product of the will-to-order which motivated a good deal of the reforming zeal of all political colours in the latter part of the nineteenth century. Foucault famously designates eugenic programmes as one of the 'two great innovations' (the other is the medicine of perversions) in the drive to 'administer' sex and fertility that is characteristic of modern power.[6] In this chapter I describe and illustrate the development of this troublingly potent mixture of Darwinism and mathematics which, in the form of eugenics, comes to seem so redolent of the dangers inherent in Enlightenment modernity's over-regulating and ever-calculating tendencies.[7]

However, while Pearson quickly developed a reputation for bellicose promotion of scientific rigour, and came increasingly to ignore or castigate all forms of knowledge which failed to conform to scientific standards (for example, he held the popularising Eugenics Education Society in contempt for that reason), there is another, and complicating, impulse in his contribution to eugenic, scientific and social thinking which I

intend to highlight. For motivating Pearson's work are powerfully idealist and sometimes romantic notions of scientific knowledge, of the
modern nation state and of the role of the scientist. Pearson's encounter
with the ideas of German humanism, socialism and idealist philosophy,
which occurred during a year spent as a young man studying in Germany,
survived beyond his youthful attempt at romance in a Goethe-inspired
novel called *The New Werther*, into his mature work on the development
of a national eugenics. It is the sometimes peculiar, and almost always
buried, effects of this idealism and romanticism – the latter of which is
commonly associated with *resistance* to the idea of 'calculable' man –
which form my focus here. Pearson's attraction to such ideas is not an
early phase, abandoned in favour of mature and unemotional objectivity,
but is rather integral to his eugenic ideas. That history will, I hope, contribute to the unearthing of a more nuanced account of quantification for
which Theodore Porter has called.

The chances of death

Karl Pearson was born in 1857. His father, who moved from Yorkshire to
London to practise as a barrister and QC, impressed on the family habits
of strict self-discipline and industriousness. Later in his life, in refusing a
career leg-up from a friend, Pearson ascribed his need to be 'a fighter' to
the 'long line of Quaker yeomen behind me'.[8] In 1875, he gained a scholarship to King's College, Cambridge, where his aptitude for mathematics
resulted in a fellowship in 1880. He spent a year in Germany (1879–80),
before making a rather desultory attempt at following his father into law.
In 1884 he made a definitive career move when he accepted the post of
professor of applied mathematics and mechanics at University College,
London, where, in the early 1890s, he began to collaborate with the
recently appointed Jodrell Professor of Zoology Walter F. R. Weldon.
Through Weldon he met Francis Galton, who helped him to consolidate
his various political and social interests, together with his enthusiasm for
mathematical quantification, into the advocacy of eugenics.

More than twenty-five years earlier, Galton had begun counting,
recording and correlating numbers in order to illuminate the origins of

natural ability in human beings. His initial findings, published in *Macmillan's Magazine*, were subsequently developed into his enormously influential *Hereditary Genius*.[9] Beginning with the conviction that the concentration of eminence in a relatively small number of families proved that mental ability was inherited rather than learned (a conviction aided by the recent publication of his cousin Charles's *On the Origin of Species*), Galton came to formulate what he claimed to be a new science of eugenics, the 'science of improving stock'.[10] Born into a commercially successful and intellectually renowned family (his mother was the daughter of Erasmus Darwin), Galton was adamant that progress and improvement lay not with a decaying landed gentry, nor with a vulgar and self-interested entrepreneuralism, but with the aristocracy of intellect found in the professional classes. Inheritance, in the modern world, meant the passing on of a healthy physique and a good brain, rather than property and land.

Galton's own mathematical ability, and his liking for counting and measuring, meant that he readily imbibed the enthusiasm for statistics that was developing by the mid-point of the nineteenth century. His pleasure in counting and the conviction that quantities furnish truths are nowhere better illustrated than in a paper in which he claimed objectively to prove that prayer has no 'influence on temporal success'. The 'proofs' lay in a statistical demonstration of the similarity of life expectancy between clergymen and lawyers, and other such bizarrely literal examples.[11] Once convinced that society was properly understood as made up of the measurable hereditary stuff (defined in terms of 'natural ability' and 'civic worth'[12]) of the individuals composing it, Galton set about refining the tools for making such measurements. Most notably, he adapted the 'law of error' – so-called normal or Gaussian distribution – in order to analyse variation from the mean in human populations.[13]

It was this numerical skill which prompted Weldon's initial approach to Galton. Seeking to make his own evolutionary biology more rigorous, Weldon believed that mathematics could resolve the problems he had encountered in using morphological methods.[14] In Pearson he had a University College colleague with the mathematical skills needed to pursue seriously the development of statistical methods for studying biological life. In Weldon, Pearson found a commitment to dealing only with

observable quantities (which, as will be seen, fitted well with his philosophy of science); and in Weldon's ambition to give measurable operational
meaning to evolution he discovered a mathematically oriented field in
which his long-held political interests, as well as his attraction to social
Darwinism, could be realised. Thus, in his mid-thirties Pearson began
biological work.

Through their collaborations in the following decade, Pearson and
Weldon created the new discipline of 'biometry', which was based on the
conviction that biological life could be studied quantitatively. They were
embarked, Pearson believed, on taking 'the first step to making biology a
mathematical science', biometrics providing the necessary new 'sharp-
edged tool'.[15] They were also keen to provide for their work an institutional infrastructure capable of meeting both research and pedagogic
needs, and which would act as a source of data available for translation
into social policy. In the mid-1890s, Pearson set up the Biometric
Laboratory, and in 1901 he and Weldon founded the journal *Biometrika*,
in which much of Pearson's statistical writing, and that of his fellow-
researchers, would be published. In 1906, Galton himself financed the
establishment of another laboratory – the Galton Laboratory for National
Eugenics – and, on his death in 1911, he endowed a chair at University
College, instructing that it be offered to Pearson. The latter, accordingly,
became the first Galton Professor of Eugenics and, from that position, was
able to amalgamate the two laboratories into the first ever Department of
Applied Statistics. There is no doubt about Pearson's aptitude as an institutional operator. By 1911, he had established an extensive research infrastructure, with a strong pedagogic element, manifested in the training and
supervision of students. From that institutional base, Pearson and his co-
workers put out an extensive range of publications based on their statistical research.

The bibliography of Pearson's published work, brought out some
three years after his death, bears witness to an unusually prolific academic
career. Besides his numerous 'Contributions to the Mathematical Theory
of Evolution', which were published throughout the 1890s in the mathematical volumes of the *Philosophical Transactions* of the Royal Society,
Pearson was actively involved in authoring, co-authoring and editing the

material put out by the research laboratories. Among the most important were a series of eugenic studies, a biometric series, interventions in political and social issues called 'Questions of the Day and of the Fray', as well as the 'Studies in National Deterioration' issued by the Biometric Laboratory. There is clear evidence of Pearson's dedication to the collegiality of scientific endeavour: a great deal of the work listed is co-authored, mostly with workers from the laboratories to which Pearson was connected, some of which is signed 'By the Staff of the Biometric Laboratory'.[16] The Foreword to the bibliography points out that Pearson wrote and rewrote much of the material collected by others. While he was renowned among his team for his guidance and commitment to students' maximising the fruits of their labour, he also jealously guarded the style and content of the writings that issued from the laboratories.[17] Pearson was forming a 'school', and one with a clear social mission.

Writing the Royal Society's obituary notice on Pearson's death, George Udny Yule, a statistician with whom Pearson had collaborated until the two fell out, describes the walls of the laboratory where Pearson worked as covered with quotations from philosophers, mathematicians and scientists, including this contribution from Plato: 'But the best part of the Soul is that which trusts to measure and calculation? Certainly.'[18] Pearson wanted to rid public life of the messiness that was, for him, characteristic of the individualism of both John Stuart Mill *and* Herbert Spencer. Even before meeting Weldon and Galton he had learned that order and meaningfulness are conferred by large numbers. Thus he chose, as indicated by the title and lead chapter of his 1897 collection *The Chances of Death and Other Studies in Evolution*, to demonstrate the predictability of death. From the medieval period onwards, he argued, chance has been associated with the throw of the dice. Chance is chaotic, and those who take chances are gamblers. The biggest human gamble is with death, 'the lawless one'. Referring to the age-old idea of death's hand striking with no respect for human rhyme or reason, Pearson reconstructs a statistically informed modern model of the medieval 'Bridge of Life' in order to argue: 'Artistically, we no longer think of Death as striking chaotically; we regard his aim as perfectly regular in the mass, if unpredictable in the individual instance.'[19] Pearson's conviction that statistics provide access to 'perfect regularity' in the mass wards off the contingent, the messy, the *un*predictable, even in death.

When Theodore Porter asks, in his Preface to *Trust in Numbers: The Pursuit of Objectivity in Science and Public Life*, what is special about the language of quantity, his 'summary answer' is that 'quantification is a language of distance'.[20] While the implications of the increasing dominance of this 'language of distance', as it developed alongside the establishment of a democratic political structure, have been much explored, its psychical resonances are also too compelling to pass without comment. Psychoanalysis, for instance, understands distancing strategies as motivated by anxiety against which the subject seeks to defend itself by putting it at arm's length. One of my arguments here is that Karl Pearson, who became renowned for his bullying and self-righteous condemnation of 'unscientific' thinking, and his contempt for muddle-headed metaphysics, was in fact deeply affected with a (romantic) sense of a lost religious past. Mathematics, as Porter argues, 'minimizes the need for intimate knowledge and personal trust', precisely those things, I argue, that Pearson saw to be characteristic of the 'socialist' medieval past and which – paradoxically, perhaps – informed his vision of a very different socialist future, one dominated by 'impersonal' science.[21]

History first

Weldon was never an enthusiast for eugenics; but nor, despite their common commitment to eugenics, did Galton and Pearson share a politics. In *The Groundwork of Eugenics*, and in perfect accord with Galton's own thinking, Pearson described his eugenics' work as the 'discovery of a new calculus' by which differentiated groups of humans could be measured 'to ascertain which of these differentiated groups is, according to its characteristics, the most effective for this or that purpose, to determine not only its rate of increase, but the extent to which its qualities are transmitted to its offspring and modified by environment'.[22] His view was that, on its own, environment did little to modify the hereditary material. Paper after paper in his series on eugenics saw Pearson attacking environmental reform and educational provision as the products of misguided philanthropy and muddle-headed, unscientific politics: 'we have placed our money on Environment, when Heredity wins in a canter'.[23] He and Galton also shared the conviction that mental and moral characteristics are inherited in the same way as physical traits:

> We are forced, I think literally forced, to the general conclusion that the physical and psychical characters in man are inherited within broad lines in the same manner, and with the same intensity … We inherit our parents' temper, our parents' conscientiousness, shyness and ability, even as we inherit their stature, forearm and span.[24]

The apparent sympathy between the two men in relation to issues of heredity and statistical methodology tends, however, to mute their evident political differences – and, therefore, the very distinct vision of the nature and purpose of eugenics which Pearson brought to the project. In Newcastle, in November 1900, about a year after Britain had gone to war in South Africa, Pearson delivered an address entitled 'National Life from the Standpoint of Science'. National life, as Pearson pointed out, was in turmoil: despite the military control being exerted on the South African veld by the imperial heroes Lord Roberts of Kandahar and Lord Kitchener of Khartoum, the first months of the Boer War had served to give, in Kipling's words, 'no end of a lesson' to Britain. A series of military defeats at the hands of the supposedly 'backward' Dutch-descended farmers produced a media furore about the pitiful lack of military preparedness of the world's leading imperial power. Subsequently, the 1899–1902 war in South Africa has been seen as perhaps the most important catalyst popularising eugenic thinking. This was the context in which Pearson spoke on 'National Life', an address that proved to be among his most rhetorical and hectoring arguments for a national eugenics.

Pearson argued that aggressive international conflict is an inevitable aspect of evolutionary advance:

> You will see that my view – and I think it may be called the scientific view of a nation – is that of an organized whole, kept up to a high pitch of internal efficiency by ensuring that its numbers are substantially recruited from the better stocks, and kept up to a high degree of external efficiency by contest, chiefly by way of war with inferior races, and with equal races

by the struggle for trade-routes and for the sources of raw material and of food supply.[25]

The *Manchester Guardian*, at the media forefront of liberal opposition to the war (it commissioned J. A. Hobson, soon to become famous as a leading critic of capitalist-driven imperialism, to cover the rising tension in South Africa), condemned the 'National Life' address as the disastrous dabbling of yet another biologist-turned-social-commentator. Pearson's reply, long and wounded, differs from his usual bellicose antagonism towards those who disagreed with him, in that it carries the unmistakable ring of personal truth. Did the reviewer consider, he asks,

> that I may not have spent more years of my life in historical work than in the study of heredity; that I may not possibly have laboured more carefully at history than at biology; that more of my published work may not deal with the former rather than the latter; nay that even my endeavour to understand something of inheritance and of racial struggle may not have arisen from my attempts to read history aright? ... I ask what reason you have for supposing my history an outgrowth of 'biological consciousness' rather than that my interest in heredity has arisen from my conviction of its bearing on historical studies.[26]

The bibliography of Pearson's work bears out his claim. From the end of the 1870s until around the mid-point of the 1890s Pearson wrote copiously on German history and folklore, on 'freethought' and religion, on the Reformation and about socialism and the position of women. Even more strikingly, the Pearson Archive at University College, which gathers together much of Pearson's unpublished writing, including letters to family and friends, also shows how prolific was his thinking and writing and lecturing on German history and religion, philosophy, and socialist and sexual politics.[27]

Biometry thus offered Pearson a methodology appropriate to his philosophy of science, and able to serve his vision of modern society – the latter, in other words, came first and not as a consequence of Pearson's biometrics' work. Among the key elements silently informing Pearson's biometric eugenics are a romantic enthusiasm for the *communität* of medieval German society; a reworking of German idealist philosophy which allowed him to fashion a universal scientific method and, as a corollary, a profoundly important role for the scientist; and a strong attraction to German socialist and social democratic politics. Pearson's ultimate goal is a eugenically organised national socialist state, in which the guiding leaders must emulate the medieval Teutonic knights in being – as Heinrich Himmler was to put it not much later on in the twentieth century – 'merciless and moral'. For Pearson, the 'scientific' view of the nation state, rendered in the neutral formulae of mathematics, is precisely distinguished in its capacity to be 'merciless and moral':

> The struggle [with other nations] means suffering, intense suffering, while it is in progress ... You may hope for a time when the sword shall be turned into the ploughshare, when American and German and English traders shall no longer compete in the markets of the world for their raw materials and for their food supply, when the white man and the dark shall share the soil between them and each till it as he lists. But, believe me, when that day comes, mankind will no longer progress ... Man will stagnate; and unless he ceases to multiply, the catastrophe will come again.[28]

Pearson is a convert to biometry – as he implies in the letter to the *Guardian* – because of a set of philosophical and political ideas largely formed during his period in Germany, and which are elaborated in his Goethe-derived novel *The New Werther*; the essays and lectures collected in *The Ethic of Freethought* and, later, in *The Chances of Death*; in his immensely popular and influential *The Grammar of Science*; as well as numerous lectures and essays and talks given at the South Place Institute, the Sunday Lecture Society and elsewhere, throughout the 1880s. The 'catastrophe' he refers to is the failure of sociality which, for the modern era, means evolutionary stagnation or degeneration but which is prefigured in the loss of community and human vitality that Pearson (in common with the German Romantics) locates in pre-Reformation German life.

Mind, matter and power intellectual

Besides attending formal lectures in Heidelberg and Berlin – including Kuno Fischer's on metaphysics, Mommsen's on history and Du Bois

Reymond's on Darwinism – Pearson read widely and voraciously. He was particularly attracted to the German humanists, and to Spinoza; he also read Kant and Fichte, and began to acquaint himself with medieval history, religion and folklore. Just as importantly, he met a young man called Raphael Wertheimer who introduced him to the ideas of German social democracy, and who was to figure, in fictionalised form, in *The New Werther*.[29] Shortly after returning to England in 1880, he published a piece in the *Cambridge Review* entitled 'Pollock's Spinoza', in which he argues that Spinoza is 'the philosopher of men of science', but that the Spinozan system needed modification: 'We require in fact a kind of *inverted* Spinoza, a Spinoza modified by Fichte.'[30] Through much of his writing of the next decade, and culminating in his enormously influential *The Grammar of Science*, Pearson set out a philosophy of science deeply informed by Johann Gottlieb Fichte's reworking of Kantian idealism.[31]

With his *cogito*, Descartes had severed thought from the external world and had made the *ego* – the thinking I, or consciousness – the certain ground from which all subsequent knowledge of material, sensuous life occurs. The subject is turned inwards to its own mind and confronts the external world – including its own body – as alien to it. One of the things that the idealist philosophers tried to do was to suture this gap – to bring together self and world – in an overarching unity: 'the gap between … subject and object … is bridged by the idea'.[32] Their project has similarities, of course, with the famous romantic impulse to achieve unity from diversity, in nature or in the art-work of genius.

In *The New Werther*, the tragic (and clearly autobiographical) hero Arthur writes to his beloved Ethel of a new philosophical system he has discovered (he is in Germany, submitting to the rigorous self-renunciation of separation, so that he can be sure of the purity of his love for Ethel). Although he is never mentioned by name, it is Fichte whom Arthur describes – or, more precisely, Fichte's attempt to resolve the problems left by Kantian *a priorism*. For Fichte, the 'I' is the absolute ground from which the intelligibility of the world ensues. The outer world, as it is conceived, is entirely the production of the conceiving *ego*. Consciousness – which is the *ego*'s awareness of its own quality – is accompanied by the perception of what it is not (in this, Fichte is close to Hegel's better-known account of the 'struggle for recognition' in the *Phenomenology of Spirit*).[33] What Pearson took from Fichte's system is suggested in the epigraph to his collection *The Ethic of Freethought*: 'The order of Mind is one with the order of Matter; hence that Mind alone is free which finds itself in Nature, and Nature in itself.'[34]

Science, he argues, has not materialised the world, but rather idealised it by showing it to be intelligible.[35] The world can be described but not explained in terms of 'matter' as the latter is useful only as a mental construct. Arthur, in *The New Werther*, makes the wider argument via a gendered and romantic metaphor:

> [L]et us show that the two great schools of materialism and idealism, which have divided the world against itself, are really at one; that the inexorable laws under which science asserts that the universe must ever roll on, are not empiric, but deducible from the pure reason; and that, though the sway of the intellect shall thus be extended from the logical to the empirical, yet that the intellectual, the manly, shall itself be so bound up with feeling, the womanly, that the two shall be united in one being, and in one life, as we have been.[36]

This is what, elsewhere, Pearson calls 'the true meaning of the problem of life, the relation of the finite to the infinite'.[37] As Porter argues, alongside this 'death of the object' in which all 'so-called natural laws are but steps in the "logic of pure thought,"' there is a corresponding fading of the subject.[38] The scientist who properly grasps the nature of knowledge becomes only a disinterested observer and recorder of that knowledge.

In these early efforts to delineate a theory of knowledge, Pearson is really attempting to fill the space left by his rejection of 'dogmatic' religion. A substantial portion of *The Ethic of Freethought* deals with this problem, for which the 'new religion of freethought' provides an answer. For Pearson, 'freethought' takes up the role abandoned by Christianity as a result of Lutheran Protestantism. The medieval Catholic Church, he argues, was a unifying institution, concerned with the widest social and intellectual matters, and drawing all social groups into its system. Without the terrible consequences of Protestant fanaticism – most notably dogmaticism and individualism – the Catholic Church may have developed to become 'the universal instrument of moral progress and mental culture', able to embrace all forms of thought and scientific advance.[39] It is surely striking that Pearson, who did as much as anyone to promote the view of a rigidly – even dogmatically – 'neutral' and non-metaphysical science, originally shaped his views under the influence of idealist philosophy and a thoroughly romantic version of medieval German culture.

In the wake of Protestant fanaticism and the moral collapse of the Roman Church, Pearson argues, freethought must offer a new vision of unity, discoverable in the methods of science. The assertion that mind makes the world forms the core of Pearson's argument in his extraordinarily popular and influential *The Grammar of Science*, first published in 1892. In it, he lays out his philosophy of science-as-universal-method. Sense-impressions, he argues, form 'permanent impresses' in the brain, which join and become more complex, leading to 'constructs' which are then projected 'outside ourselves'. These projections, now thought of as phenomena, *are* the real world: 'These are the facts of science, and its field is essentially the contents of the mind'.[40] It is science that can properly apprehend and work with this 'mind-made' external world, meaning that its scope is *universal*:

> Now this is the peculiarity of scientific method, that when once it has become a habit of mind, that mind converts *all* facts whatsoever into science. The field of science is unlimited; its solid contents are endless, every group of natural phenomena, every phase of social life, every stage of past or present development is material for science. *The unity of all science consists alone in its method, not its material.*[41]

This universalising scientific method – the goal of which is accurately to describe and order perceptions – enables a colonisation of all areas of life: there is no 'legitimate field' for science, as 'the whole range of phenomena, mental as well as physical – the entire universe – is its field', including, of course, the 'private lives' of human sex and procreation.[42]

For science understood in this way, statistics provides the exemplary methodological tools. As Porter argues, statistics are mental constructs which can be mapped onto the world, providing correlations which claim to be not deep truths but, rather, convenient ways of summarising experience.[43] The world is not there to be discovered by science, only to be described (this in part explains Pearson's hostility to the rediscovery of Mendel at the turn of the century: genes were just too realist for his liking). For Pearson, scientific method provides a unity, a oneness which, as I go on to explain, finds its corollary in the unified nation. The scientist – who, in his turn, is the exemplary freethinker – should lead the way in demonstrating that there must be 'no interested motive, no working to support a party, an individual or a theory'.[44] Only through relinquishing subjectivity, and ridding oneself of personal prejudice and ambition, can knowledge really come about; and only the scientist is trained in such disinterested observant impersonality.[45]

The image of the disinterested scientist is extended and developed through Pearson's increasingly antagonistic critique of individualism. This critique is central to his socialist politics, and can be traced through his extensive comments on the public role of the scientist and scholar, the blueprint for which Pearson discovered in the German *Katheder-sozialisten*, or 'socialism of the professors'. He was particularly influenced by the 'historical school' of Gustav von Schmoller, which helped to formulate Bismarck's social policy and was distinguished by its commitment to scholarly historiography, respect for historical fact and its assertion of the supreme importance of the state.[46] The role of the scholar in relation to the state is also central to Fichte's popular 'Some Lectures Concerning the Scholar's Vocation', published in 1794. Fichte describes the state as that in which the best of man – which he defines in terms of rational autonomy and self-identity, or complete harmony and oneness with self – can be realised, and he sees the scholar as 'especially destined for society'. The scholar's knowledge is *for* society: it is the scholar, and the scholar alone, who 'sees the direction in which the human race must now proceed if it is to continue on the path toward its final goal'. The state is thus led by the scholar as the educator of mankind, propelled by a drive to sociality. This, for Fichte, is a necessary aspect of being a rational human subject. The scholar must have both a complete knowledge of the needs of man and a 'knowledge of the *means for satisfying them*': in other words, the scholar must have both the philosophical and the historical knowledge to be used for the perfectibility of man.[47] In his *Addresses to the German Nation* he writes: 'The scholar with his conception must always be in advance of the present age, must understand the future, and be able to implant it in the present for its future development.'[48]

In a lecture given at the South Place Institute in 1885, Pearson similarly argues that the real source of social value lies with the man of the study, the scholar. Only the scholar, trained in the pursuit of truth, can understand, and therefore mobilise for the social good, the forces of history. Only with knowledge can there be morality: *the ignorant cannot be moral* because morality, according to Pearson, is synonymous with a social impulse which can properly be felt only by the educated. The ignorant are propelled by blind feeling, the educated by reason. The enthusiasm of the marketplace is always destructive and irrational, and only study can lead to knowledge of the social law and thus to beneficent social change.[49]

In Fichte, as well as in the ideas of German social democracy, Pearson gained a model of social transformation which emphasised *gradual* and managed change. In *The New Werther*, Arthur's Jewish intellectual friend, based on Raphael Wertheimer, castigates the English for failing to tell the difference between a French communist, a Russian nihilist or a German social democrat. It is only the latter who understands the real nature of gradual (Pearson will come to say evolutionary) transformation.[50] In a piece published in the *Cambridge Review* and called, provocatively, 'Anarchy', Pearson imagines a Carlylean nightmare vision of the immis-erated mob grown uncontrollable. The only means to stay its threat is through *managed* change, according to the historically discernable process of evolution. The latter has always determined the great shifts in the structuring of social rank: from brute strength, through chivalry, to nobility of birth, and thence to (bourgeois) wealth. The next stage is where 'power material shall be divided as equally as may be between the various classes, [but] power intellectual shall form a scale on which the necessary graduation of society may take place. Power intellectual shall determine whether the life-calling of a man is to scavenge the streets, or to guide the nation.'[51]

Hierarchy will thus still exist in Pearson's socialist utopia, but social rank will derive from intellect and education. This is *rational* hierarchy in contrast to what has gone before, and it is based upon an equality of labour, together with an *inequality* of intellect. (This latter is – as I will shortly describe – not exactly a natural inequality. It is rather the product of heredity, which must, via eugenic laws and administration, be subjected to rational control.) The fundamental axiom of socialism is that '*Society must be organized on the basis of labour,* and therefore political power, the power of organizing, must be in the hands of labour.' What is crucial, though, for Pearson, is that labour is of *two kinds*:

> There is labour of the hand, which provides necessaries for all society; there is labour of the head, which produces all that we term *progress*, and enables any individual society to maintain its position in the battle of life – the labour which educates and organizes.[52]

Social organisation should thus be the province of the social scientists who offer counsel 'not in the guise of wise, interested elites but as mere mouthpieces for a disembodied science'.[53] The scientist and the free-thinker are able to transcend both individual *and* class interests. Their example (if not their expertise and power) must then be disseminated through the population at large by way of a scientific education. Science is thus synonymous with moral instruction; its 'frame of mind … an essential of good citizenship'.[54]

Pearson was bitterly opposed to those who preached the *rights* of the working class: the labourer must learn to relinquish self-interest and 'be taught to look upon society as a *whole*'.[55] During the latter half of the 1880s, Pearson's peculiar political interests extended to the position of women, and he formed a group, called The Men and Women's Club, to discuss relations between the sexes from a scientific viewpoint.[56] It is in his comments about middle-class women that Pearson's most ascerbic attacks on individual self-interest occur. In 'Woman and Labour', published in 1894 in the *Fortnightly Review*, he explains that both (middle-class) women and the (male) working class fail to 'grasp the essential value of their functions in the machine as a whole': 'What advocate of "woman's rights" has once and for all thrown John Stuart Mill's *Subjection of Women* overboard, and measured woman's as well as man's "rights" by the touch-stone of general social efficiency?'[57] It is the 'exceptional' women leading the suffrage movement who are 'out-and-out individualists', however; the labour movement has at least recognised the importance of the social value of labour, and the notion that 'social stability depends on the legal protection of labour, on state provision for its efficiency and public regard for its physique, is now a commonplace'.[58] Labour's interests are class-based, and thus its move to disinterested investment in the social body at large constitutes a smaller task than the woman's.[59]

Morality as sociality

Pearson's work is steeped in an ethic of renunciation – workers must be educated to that ethic, and women made to submit to it and to understand that they bear children primarily for the state.[60] A number of the best commentators on Pearson, including Donald MacKenzie and Bernard Norton, emphasise Pearson's own self-interested espousal of the power and influence of the professional classes. While Pearson was clearly a ferociously ambitious man, however, he was not simply or narrowly set on personal preferment: it is worth noting, for example, that he refused to accept either the Order of the British Empire, offered to him in 1920, or a knighthood, offered in 1935. I agree, therefore, with Porter's sense that things were more complicated. Porter examines the 'ethic of puritanical self-denial that pervades [Pearson's] writing' as part of a philosophy of science in which human subjects are turned into objects, to be formed according to social need and judged by strict and quantifiable standards.[61] I would also emphasise again Pearson's intense emotional and intellectual identification with German ideas, especially German Romanticism, the fertile influence of which is evidenced in Pearson's writing on medieval German social and religious life.

   The Schlegels's celebration of a union between the sentiments of Christianity and the rough, honest heroism of the northern conquerors as forming the seedbed of the modern romantic spirit is echoed, as I have already mentioned, in Pearson's insistence that medieval German culture manifests the real spirit of community and social cohesion. In the most typical of all romantic gestures, he chastises the 'Hellenist' for valuing classical Greek culture over the 'colour and incident of the folk-life 500 years ago'.[62] With that community irretrievably lost, the modern state must legislate and administer appropriate social value: 'with the modern as distinguished from the medieval socialistic movement the protection of labour has ceased in the first place to be a moral duty impressed by the Catholic Church more or less efficiently on the individual conscience; it has become a legislative principle based on social expediency'.[63]

In the place absented by this medieval and Christian conscience (for which Pearson's punishing prose evinces only the merest tinge of nostalgia) is a modern form of education, especially scientific education. There is also, however, and increasingly, the conviction that the development of appropriate social sentiment, and thus social morality, can be *managed* through eugenic programmes of selective breeding. Both are presented as a moral duty. For understanding Pearson's view of the function of education, so different from John Stuart Mill's, Fichte is once again an important reference. His famous *Addresses to the German Nation* were a series of popular lectures given in 1807–8 which called for resistance against Napoleon, and which gave shape to an emerging German nationalism. In them, Fichte argues that the old doctrine of free-will no longer holds. The new education, he states, 'must consist essentially in this, that it completely destroys freedom of will in the soil which it undertakes to cultivate, and produces on the contrary strict necessity in the decisions of the will, the opposite being impossible'. Freedom is thus replaced by necessity for the child (and the adult) citizen of the forging nation: 'If you want to influence him at all, you must do more than merely talk to him; you must fashion him, and fashion him in such a way that he simply cannot will otherwise than what you wish him to will.'[64] Compulsion is a necessary part of this process on the way to the perfected state, of children and of nations. Thus, for Fichte, the voluntary obedience of children, their doing without compulsion what their parents command, is not obedience but *insight*.[65] This is what, for Hegel, unalienated freedom means: not individual rights asserted against the state, but a conscious accepting participation in it.[66]

National eugenics

The *voluntary* submission to the needs of the state, albeit derived from an initial compulsion in Fichte's system, is precisely what Pearson wants to

replace the individualism associated with liberalism and political economy. But the state must always properly be understood in its *national*
dimension. In his 1800 work *The Closed Commercial State*, Fichte con-
ceives of a forthcoming 'reign of virtue' characterised by a sealed-off state
which, in closing itself off to worldly competition, will dispel all conflict
and exist in peace and happiness. What each citizen has and can expect to
have is determined by need; economics functions by 'an absolute balance
of value' of resources which is overseen by the state, rather than by a drive
to profit; and the stability of the whole is guaranteed by the state which
unifies all its disparate elements (including the individuals who make it
up) by 'a great deal of business and many calculations and inspections in
order to keep a stable equilibrium'. This closed state, according to Fichte,
will also produce a robust national feeling: in it 'a high degree of national
honour and a sharply distinguished national character are bound to arise
very quickly'.[67] As Robert Nisbet argues, Fichte extends the idea of the
nation state from that of a legal–political entity to one in which all human
needs, including moral and spiritual ones, can be met: 'He is the true
author of national socialism.'[68]

   Like Fichte, Pearson envisaged the socialist state as a national entity:
'Socialism ... teaches us that the first duty of man is to no general concept
of humanity, but to the group of humans to which he belongs, and that
man's veneration is due to the State which personifies that social group'.[69]
But for Pearson, achieving that state will depend on more than education.
In the place of the 'deliberate art' of Fichte's educator, will be the deliberate science of the eugenics administrator. Biology, rather than education,
will be destiny. The 'fashioned will' in Fichte's educational system is
replaced by the hard-wired genetic inheritance of 'good stock'. Where the
borders of commerce are sealed for Fichte's socialistic state, for Pearson
they are thrown open to both aggressive trade and war with 'weaker' peoples, but the nation state is *biologically* sealed in the fantasy of a 'pure'
racial people, breeding from its 'best stocks'. As a young man in Germany,
Pearson briefly espoused a romantic anti-colonialism, but on his return
to England he was quickly affected by the dominance of Darwinian ideas
and began to convert his socialist vision according to social evolutionary
doctrine.

At the heart of that doctrine is the contention that struggle is the condition of progress. In modern societies, however, and particularly under the influence of Herbert Spencer's individualism, the nature of the struggle, Pearson argues, has been fundamentally misrecognised. The older evolutionists emphasised only the individual struggle: 'They forgot that the herd exists owing to its social instincts, and that human sympathy and racial and national feelings are strong natural forces controlling individual conduct.'[70] In other words, they misunderstood the *gregarious* nature of man.[71] The strong socialist nation, however, is one in which social instinct has been developed as synonymous with national sentiment: 'You must not have class differences and wealth differences and education differences so great within the community that you lose the sense of common interest.'[72] The proper location of the struggle is between, and not within, nations. In 'Socialism and Natural Selection' Pearson put it this way: 'No thoughtful socialist, so far as I am aware, would object to cultivate Uganda *at the expense of its present occupiers* if Lancashire were starving.'[73] *Natural* selection – the killing off of the weakest – takes place within, and in relation to, 'inferior' races.

Any attempt to wrest *that* aspect of the 'struggle for survival' from the literalism of brutish physical conflict is condemned by Pearson: there is no space for 'rational' selection in Africa, for example. A thousand times better, he insists, that the white man should never go to claim 'unutilized' lands 'than that he should settle down and live alongside the inferior race. The only healthy alternative is that he should go, and completely drive out the inferior race'.[74] Within the 'superior' white nation, however (and Pearson always presumes that national and racial identity are self-evidently synonymous), *rational* selection replaces natural selection in the guise of eugenic breeding. Selection is handed over to the experts, who disinterestedly work for the good of the nation. Hence the fact that, as Pearson argues in *The Academic Aspect of the Science of National Eugenics*, 'the words "*National* Eugenics" have been rightly used. Every nation has in a certain sense its own study of eugenics, and what is true of one nation is not necessarily true of a second.'[75]

In his Huxley lecture of 1903, however, Pearson warns that: 'We stand … at the commencement of an epoch, which will be marked by a great dearth of ability'; the 'mentally better stock' in the nation reproduce fewer offspring; while the 'less able' remain fertile. The 'remedy lies beyond the reach of revised educational systems … the psychical characters, which are, in the modern struggle of nations, the backbone of the state, are not manufactured by home and school and college; they are bred in the bone'. Britain, Pearson concludes, has ceased 'to give us in due proportion the men we want to carry on the ever-growing work of our empire, to battle to the fore-rank of the ever-intensified struggle of nations'.[76] Elsewhere, Pearson argues: 'Before the second half of the nineteenth century a true theory of the state was impossible', because it needed Darwin and the doctrine of evolution by natural selection, and thus, for Pearson, heredity, to develop. Instead of the Hegelian dialectic, Pearson institutes biology: 'The theory of the state became biological.'[77]

For Fichte, the invincible German nation has to be imagined and fashioned via the linguistic purity of the German tongue. Pearson's romantic nostalgia, his yearning for the lost community of medieval Teutons, is transplanted into a Darwinian world of struggle in which the nation no longer needs to be imagined, only planned and *managed* by its experts and administrators. These, its true priests of freethought, with their disinterested, distancing numbers will remake social (and therefore moral) value. They work to ensure that the nation, 'open' commercially, and prepared for the struggle for existence, remains 'closed' in its hereditary material from all 'inferior' and contaminating difference.

That, at least, was Pearson's goal. From around the end of the 1890s, he devoted himself almost exclusively to statistical work. Amid all the detail of his endless statistical experiments on correlations between hair and eye colour in humans, on the inheritance of coat colour in greyhounds, on partial leucosis in hens, on red blood corpuscles of the common tadpole, on the variability in poppies from Pretoria, and much, much more, Pearson's vision of a eugenically managed nation state remains the central motivating ideal. Writing Pearson's obituary notice for the Royal Society, George Udny Yule commented: 'After the quite early years there seem to have been no more poems nor songs, contributed to the Socialist Song Book or otherwise: after, say, *The Chances of Death* (1897), no more miscellaneous studies, but only the overwhelming mass of scientific work. Had controversy become the sole outlet for emotion?'[78]

Much of the controversy in which Pearson engaged stemmed from his refusal to countenance any rival to biometry in the field of human heredity. This included the theory of genetics that developed after the rediscovery of Mendel. The result, as J. B. S. Haldane, the first occupant of the Weldon Chair of Biometry, pointed out during speeches at University College celebrating the centenary of Pearson's birth, was that, on almost all the fundamentals of heredity, Pearson had got things very wrong.[79] Biometric method was so embedded in Pearson's understanding of the relation of mind, matter, method and politics, and it served so well his vision of a eugenic state, that it simply could not be relinquished, or even moderated, whatever subsequent research might show. Pearson's was a fully *ideological* commitment to numbers.

A further source of controversy surrounding Pearson's work was the violence much of it implied. Such controversy probably was an emotional outlet. Freud argues that the mechanism regulating moral feeling and conduct, which he called the 'super-ego', could act with extraordinary ferocity. A child who is severely regulated and disciplined may internalise a similarly severe and inexorable mental overseer. The result may be self-punishment, but it may also be a near-sadistic attitude towards the conduct of others which, in turn, can act to re-route mental aggression away from the self. Certainly the rigour with which Pearson set himself to work was only matched by the passion with which he preached renunciation for others. A fantasy of order and control of that magnitude, motivated by displaced moralism, inevitably leads to cruelty and violence. Transformed into the neutral and 'distancing' language of numbers, these passions come back as a 'rational' justification for genocide in Africa.

In *The New Werther*, one of Arthur's interminable and turgid letters to his beloved (and soon to be proven perfidious) Ethel, reads as follows:

> I leave numbers and arguments to the statists and blue-bookers. Let them vainly imagine they can judge and rule mankind from them! When the registrar-general complacently publishes that there have been 1000 deaths, 1000 births this week in the metropolis, he cares little whether

a Goethe has died or a Napoleon been born; yet the *one*, who may completely alter the life-course of the other 999, remains for that calculating official only a unit!

Weldon, and especially Galton, provided Pearson with a means of colonising and transforming these 'numbers and arguments' such that whoever is born, if not those who die, is no longer open to chance – or, rather, the relentlessly destructive effects of 'improvident' or 'feebleminded' fertility – for these things were no matters of chance to the statistician. If eugenics could not quite guarantee a Goethe or a Napoleon, it could, Pearson believed, mercifully and morally rid the nation of weakness and want, of difference, in short, and foster instead the racially pure 'good citizen' of a modern imperial nation.

In April 1934, a year after his retirement, University College hosted a dinner for Pearson. Responding to the speeches honouring him, Pearson reflected on a long career dedicated to bettering the human world through science. In particular, he paid homage to the work begun by Galton, which 'culminated in Galton's preaching of Eugenics, and his foundation of the Eugenics Professorship':

> Did I say 'culmination'? No, that lies rather in the future, perhaps with Reichskanzler Hitler and his proposals to regenerate the German people. In Germany a vast experiment is in hand, and some of you may live to see its results. If it fails it will not be for want of enthusiasm, but rather because the Germans are only just starting the study of mathematical statistics in the modern sense![80]

Some of those present did live to see the results, only a little more than a decade later. Pearson was not among them. He died in 1936, before he could witness the devastation wrought by Nazism's 'vast experiment'. Certainly, though, especially under the auspices of the SS *Ahnenerbe*, Nazi Germany turned to some of its most prestigious scholars and scientists, its archaeologists and anthropologists, to investigate the ancestral heritage of a pure Aryan race.[81] The *Ahnenerbe*'s methodology would presumably have pleased Pearson in its dedication to the diligent *observation*, the measuring and classification of those deemed 'inferior' in the scale of civilisation.

Karl Pearson's prodigious labours might seem dedicated to small-scale things, as he counted and correlated tadpoles and hens and poppies in his laboratories, but Pearson was out for a very much grander prize. His goal was nothing less than Britain's status as an aggressively successful imperial power, fitted for the struggle of life no less than the Teutonic knights of Romantic Germany's past. Small wonder he had begun to be seduced by Hitler, who really knew how to put power intellectual at the service of the nation state's aggressive aims. It is, of course, specious to argue that romanticism inevitably leads to national socialism, just as it is folly simply to reject the ordering impulses of a mathematically minded modernity. Nevertheless, Pearson is a chilling example of how the complex histories of Enlightenment modernity can fuse in terrifying ways. Adorno and Horkheimer, with hearts heavy from witnessing the 'vast experiment' of the Nazi state, claim at the beginning of their *Dialectic of Enlightenment*: 'The task to be accomplished is not the conservation of the past, but the redemption of the hopes of the past.'[82]

In relation at least to Europe's history, that remains the risky but nonetheless necessary task.

Notes

1 Karl Pearson, *The Science of Man: Its Needs and its Prospects* (Cambridge: Cambridge University Press, 1920), p. 2.

2 G. M. Young, *Portrait of an Age: Victorian England* (Oxford: Oxford University Press, 1936), p. 305.

3 Theodore M. Porter comments on the difference of a 'world without suicide rates, unemployment figures, and intelligence quotients. To be sure, this prenumerate age was not entirely deprived of statistical tables, but the great explosion of numbers that made the term statistics indispensable occurred during the 1820s and 1830s. The demands it placed on people to classify things so that they could be counted and placed in an appropriate box on some official table, and more generally its impact on the character of the information people need to possess before they feel they understand something, are of the greatest interest and importance.' T. M. Porter, *The Rise of Statistical Thinking 1820–1900* (Princeton, NJ: Princeton University Press, 1986), p. 11.

4   Victor L. Hilts, 'Statistics and Social Science', in Ronald N. Giere and Richard S. Westfall (eds), *Foundations of the Scientific Method: The Nineteenth Century* (Bloomington and London: Indiana University Press, 1973), p. 207.

5   Theodore M. Porter, *Trust in Numbers: The Pursuit of Objectivity in Science and Public Life* (Princeton, NJ: Princeton University Press, 1995), p. 6.

6   Michel Foucault, *The History of Sexuality: An Introduction*, trans. Robert Hurley (Harmondsworth: Penguin, 1981), p. 118.

7   See Theodor Adorno and Max Horkheimer, *Dialectic of Enlightenment* [1944] (London: Verso, 1979), pp. 5–8, for the idea that in Enlightenment thinking 'whatever does not conform to the rule of computation and utility is suspect'.

8   Cited in Porter, *Statistical Thinking*, p. 303.

9   Francis Galton, 'Hereditary Talent and Character', *Macmillan's Magazine*, 12 (June and August 1865); and *Hereditary Genius: An Inquiry into its Laws and Consequence* [1869] (London: Watts, 1892).

10 Francis Galton, *Inquiries into Human Faculty and its Development* (London: Macmillan, 1883), p. 25.

11 See Porter, *Statistical Thinking*, p. 137.

12 See Donald A. MacKenzie, *Statistics in Britain 1865–1930: The Social Construction of Scientific Knowledge* (Edinburgh: Edinburgh University Press, 1981), p. 16.

13 On Galton's statistical methodology, see Porter, *Statistical Thinking*, pp. 128–46.

14 See Daniel Kevles, *In the Name of Eugenics: Genetics and the Uses of Human Heredity* (Cambridge, MA: Harvard University Press, 1985), pp. 27–31; and MacKenzie, *Statistics in Britain*, pp. 88–9.

15 Karl Pearson, 'On the Inheritance of the Mental and Moral Characters in Man, and its Comparison with the Inheritance of the Physical Characters', *Journal of the Anthropological Institute of Great Britain and Ireland*, 33 (1903): 201; Pearson cited in Kevles, *Name of Eugenics*, p. 308, note 39.

16 See G. M. Morant with B. L. Welch (eds), *A Bibliography of the Statistical and Other Writings of Karl Pearson* (Cambridge: Cambridge University Press, 1939).

17 Foreword, *ibid.*.

18 G. Udny Yule, 'Karl Pearson 1857–1936', *Obituary Notices of the Fellows of the Royal Society*, 3 (London: 1936-8): 103.

19 Karl Pearson, 'The Chances of Death', in *The Chances of Death and Other Studies in Evolution* (London: Edward Arnold, 1897), vol. 1: 39.

20 Porter, *Trust in Numbers*, p. ix.

21 *Ibid.*

22 Karl Pearson, *The Groundwork of Eugenics* (London: Dulau, 1909), pp. 9–10.

23 Karl Pearson, *The Problem of Practical Eugenics* (London: Dulau, 1912), p. 36.

24 Pearson, 'Mental and Moral Characters', p. 204.

25 Karl Pearson, *National Life from the Standpoint of Science* (London: Adam & Charles Black, 1901), pp. 43–4.

26 Karl Pearson, letter to the *Manchester Guardian*, 15 February 1901, cited in Bernard Norton, 'Karl Pearson and Statistics: The Social Origins of Scientific Innovation', *Social Studies of Science*, 8 (1978): 20–1.

27 Morant with Welch, *Bibliography*; the Karl Pearson Papers are housed in the Archives at University College, London; see also Norton, 'Karl Pearson'.

28 Pearson, *National Life*, pp. 24–5.

29 For Pearson's biography, see E. S. Pearson, *Karl Pearson: An Appreciation of Some Aspects of His Life and Work* (Cambridge: Cambridge University Press, 1938); Churchill Eisenhart's entry on Pearson in the *Dictionary of Scientific Biography* (New York: Charles Scribner's Sons, 1974), vol. 10.

30 Karl Pearson, 'Pollock's Spinoza', *The Cambridge Review*, 2, 32 (1880): 94.

31 It is worth noting, in the context of my overall argument about Pearson's romanticism, that one of the most famous German Romantics, Friedrich Schlegel, deemed Fichte's *ego* psychology one of the three greatest influences of the romantic age. The other two were the French Revolution and *Wilhelm Meister*. See George Armstrong Kelly's Introduction to Johann Gottlieb Fichte, *Addresses to the German Nation* (New York: Harper Torchbooks, 1968), p. xii.

32 Introduction to Rudiger Bubner (ed.), *German Idealist Philosophy* (Harmondsworth: Penguin, 1997), p. xvi.

33 See Kelly's Introduction to Fichte, *Addresses*, p. xviii; Andrew Bowie, *From Romanticism to Critical Theory: The Philosophy of German Literary Theory* (London: Routledge, 1997), pp. 41–52.

34 Pearson, *The Ethic of Freethought* (London: T. Fisher Unwin, 1888).

35 Pearson, 'Matter and Soul', in *Ethic of Freethought*, p. 56.

36 'Loki' (Karl Pearson), *The New Werther* (London: C. Kegan Paul & Co., 1880), p. 11.

37 Pearson, 'The Ethic of Freethought', in *Ethic of Freethought*, p. 31.

38 See Theodore M. Porter, 'The Death of the Object: *Fin de siècle* Philosophy of Physics', in Dorothy Ross (ed.), *Modernist Impulses in the Human Sciences 1870–1930* (Baltimore, MD, and London: Johns Hopkins University Press, 1994). The citation is from Pearson, 'The Ethic of Freethought', p. 30.

39 Pearson, 'Martin Luther', in *Ethic of Freethought*, pp. 213 and 216.

40 Pearson, *The Grammar of Science* (London: Walter Scott, 1892), pp. 90–1.

41 *Ibid.*, p. 15.

42 *Ibid.*, p. 29.

43 Porter, *Trust in Numbers*, p. 21.

44 Pearson, 'The Ethic of Freethought', pp. 19–20.

45 See Porter, 'The Death of the Object', pp. 143–51.

46 See Joseph A. Schumpeter, *History of Economic Analysis* [1954] (London: Allen & Unwin, 1982), pp. 802–20.

47 Johann Gottlieb Fichte, 'Some Lectures Concerning the Scholar's Vocation' [1794], in Ernst Behler (ed), *Philosophy of German Idealism: Fichte, Jacobi, and Schelling* (New York: Continuum, 1987), pp. 34, 36 and 31.

48 Fichte, *Addresses*, p. 158.

49 Karl Pearson, 'The Enthusiasm of the Market-Place and of the Study', *Ethic of Freethought*, pp. 115–34.

50 'Loki', *New Werther*, pp. 33–4.

51 Pearson, 'Anarchy', *Cambridge Review*, 2, 43 (March 30 1881): 270.

52 Pearson, 'Socialism: In Theory and Practice', *Ethic of Freethought*, p. 355.

53 Porter, 'Death of the Object', p. 148.

54 Pearson, *Grammar*, p. 8.

55 Pearson, 'Socialism: In Theory and Practice', p. 366.

56 For discussion of the Club, see Lucy Bland, *Banishing the Beast: English Feminism and Sexual Morality 1885–1914* (Harmondsworth: Penguin, 1995); and Carolyn Burdett, *Olive Schreiner and the Progress of Feminism: Evolution, Gender, Empire* (London: Palgrave, 2001).

57 Pearson, 'Woman and Labour', *Fortnightly Review*, 55 (1894): 564.

58 Pearson, 'Woman and Labour', p. 565.

59 For a full discussion of Pearson and feminism in the 1880s, see Burdett, *Olive Schreiner*.

60 Pearson, 'Woman and Labour', pp. 576–7.

61 Porter, *Trust in Numbers*, p. 75.

62 For the Schlegels's romanticism see, for example, August Wilhelm Schlegel, *Lectures on Dramatic Literature* (1809–11). The citation is from Pearson, 'The German Passion-Play', in *Chances of Death*, vol. 2: 398.

63 Pearson, 'Woman and Labour', p. 565.

64 Fichte, *Addresses*, pp. 17 and 18.

65 See Morton Schatzman, *Soul Murder: Persecution in the Family* (Harmondsworth: Penguin, 1976), pp. 145–6, which is an account of Daniel Paul Schreber, about whose condition Freud wrote his famous account of psychosis. Schreber's father was a leading German physicist and pedagogue, much influenced by Fichte's educational ideas, who believed that the child's human will could be fashioned only through a rigorous control of her or his body.

66 Robert Nisbet, *History and the Idea of Progress* (London: Heinemann, 1980), p. 281.

67 Johann Gottlieb Fichte, *The Closed Commercial State* [1800], in I. H. Fichte (ed.), *Sämmelte Werke* (Berlin: 1845–46). The quoted passage derives from 'History of Ideas: Nineteenth-Century Studies Dossier', Hatfield Polytechnic.

68 Nisbet, *Idea of Progress*, p. 272.
69 Pearson, 'The Moral Basis of Socialism', *Ethic of Freethought*, p. 319.
70 Pearson, *National Life*, p. 53.
71 Pearson is drawing from the influential critique of the early social Darwinist emphasis on struggle and competition which stressed instead sociability and the 'mutual aid' characteristic of both natural and human life. See Greta Jones, *Social Darwinism and English Thought: The Interaction between Biological and Social Theory* (Sussex: Harvester, 1980).
72 Pearson, *National Life*, p. 48.
73 Pearson, 'Socialism and Natural Selection', in *Chances of Death*, vol. 1: 111.
74 Pearson, *National Life*, p. 21.
75 Karl Pearson, *The Academic Aspect of the Science of National Eugenics* (London: Dulau, 1911), p. 4.
76 Pearson, 'Mental and Moral Characters', p. 207.
77 Karl Pearson, *The Function of Science in the Modern State*, 2nd edn (Cambridge: Cambridge University Press, 1919), 1: 2.
78 Udny Yule, 'Karl Pearson', p. 101.
79 *Karl Pearson 1857–1957: The Centenary Celebration at University College, London 13 May 1957* (Cambridge: Biometrika Trustees and Cambridge University Press, 1958), pp. 4–7.
80 Karl Pearson, Reply to *Speeches Delivered at a Dinner Held in University College, London in Honour of Karl Pearson, 23 April 1934* (Cambridge: Cambridge University Press, 1934), p. 23.
81 The *Ahnenerbe* emerged from Himmler's decision to set up, in 1935, a foundation dedicated to the study of the Germanic ancestral heritage. The research branch consisted of eminent academic archaeologists and anthropologists who travelled to Tibet, South America, Greece and Rome in order to trace Aryan civilisation.
82 Adorno and Horkheimer, *Dialectic of Enlightenment*, p. xv.

Index